Nine Essays on Homer

Greek Studies: Interdisciplinary Approaches
Series Editor: Gregory Nagy, Harvard University
Assistant Editor: Timothy Power, Harvard University

On the front cover: A calendar frieze representing the Athenian months, reused in the Byzantine Church of the Little Metropolis in Athens. The cross is superimposed, obliterating Taurus of the Zodiac. The choice of this frieze for books in *Greek Studies: Interdisciplinary Approaches* reflects this series' emphasis on the blending of the diverse heritages—Near Eastern, Classical, and Christian—in the Greek tradition. Drawing by Laurie Kain Hart, based on a photograph. Recent titles in the series are:

Aglaia: The Poetry of Alcman, Sappho, Pindar, Bacchylides, and Corinna
     by Charles Segal
Eurykleia and Her Successors. Female Figures of Authority in Greek Poetics,
     by Helen Pournara Karydas
Immortal Armor: The Concept of Alke in Archaic Greek Poetry
     by Derek Collins
Homeric Stitchings: The Homeric Centos of the Empress Eudocia
     by M. D. Usher
Recapturing Sophocles' Antigone
     by William Blake Tyrrell and Larry J. Bennett
Nothing Is As It Seems. The Tragedy of the Implicit in Euripides' Hippolytus
     by Hanna M. Roisman
Lyric Quotation in Plato
     by Marian Demos
Exile and the Poetics of Loss in Greek Tradition
     by Nancy Sultan
The Classical Moment: Views from Seven Literatures
     Edited by Gail Holst-Warhaft and David R. McCann
Nine Essays on Homer
     Edited by Miriam Carlisle and Olga Levaniouk
Dionysism and Comedy
     by Xavier Riu
Allegory and the Tragic Chorus in Sophocles' Oedipus at Colonus
     by Roger Travis

Nine Essays on Homer

EDITED BY
MIRIAM CARLISLE AND OLGA LEVANIOUK

ROWMAN & LITTLEFIELD PUBLISHERS, INC.
Lanham • Boulder • New York • Oxford

ROWMAN & LITTLEFIELD PUBLISHERS, INC.

Published in the United States of America
by Rowman & Littlefield Publishers, Inc.
4720 Boston Way, Lanham, Maryland 20706

12 Hid's Copse Road
Cumnor Hill, Oxford OX2 9JJ, England

British Library Cataloguing in Publication Information Available

Library of Congress Cataloging-in-Publication Data

Carlisle, Miriam
    Nine essays on Homer / edited by Miriam Carlisle and Olga Levaniouk.
      p. cm. — (Greek studies)
    Includes bibliographical references and indexes.
    ISBN 0-8476-9423-2 (cloth : alk. paper). — ISBN 0-8476-9424-0
(paper : alk. paper)
      1. Homer—Criticism and interpretation. 2. Epic poetry, Greek—History
and criticism. 3. Odysseus (Greek mythology) in literature. 4. Greece—in
literature. I. Levaniouk, Olga. II. Title. III. Series.
    PA 4037.C277 1999
    883'.01—dc21   99-11159
                                                                          CIP

Printed in the United States of America

Contents

PART III: VISUAL HOMER

PART IV: TEXTUAL HOMER

Foreword

Building on the foundations of scholarship within the disciplines of philology, philosophy, history, and archaeology, this series spans the continuum of Greek traditions extending from the second millennium BCE to the present, not just the Archaic and Classical periods. The aim is to enhance perspectives by applying various disciplines to problems that have in the past been treated as the exclusive concern of a single given discipline. Besides the crossing-over of the older disciplines, as in the case of historical and literary studies, the series encourages the application of such newer ones as linguistics, sociology, anthropology, and comparative literature. It also encourages encounters with current trends in methodology, especially in the realm of literary theory.

Nine Essays on Homer, edited by Miriam Carlisle and Olga Levaniouk, is a volume that evolved out of a 1996 Homer Seminar in Harvard University's Classics Department. That year, the seminar was conducted jointly by Emily Townsend Vermeule and myself, and it was attended regularly by Charles Segal (traces of whose helpful advice are evident on many a page). Eight of the original seminarians, plus an *enatos* coopted by them, have put together a set of essays that achieve a unity of purpose in their systematic applications of methods originally perfected at Harvard by Milman Parry and Albert Lord in the course of their pioneering research on living oral poetic traditions.

The methodological expertise of the nine contributors is matched by their sharp appreciation of the mechanics and esthetics of Homeric poetry. All nine treat Homer *as literature*, and they do so in rigorously historical terms, keeping foremost in mind the literary reception of Homer in the Classical era and beyond.

This book's scholarly ambidexterity in literature on the one hand and in history, archaeology, and art history on the other reflects the intellectual legacy of Emily Vermeule at Harvard. Her own cumulative work as a Classicist has been a model of interdisciplinarity for this book—and may it shine as an ideal for the entire "Greek Studies" series.

Gregory Nagy, *Series Editor*

Acknowledgments

The essays in this volume were conceived in an interdisciplinary seminar on Homer offered at Harvard University by Gregory Nagy and Emily T. Vermeule and regularly attended by Charles Segal. Although we hope that no blame will attach to them for the imperfections of our work, we owe them immeasurable gratitude for the unique experience of that seminar and for their encouragement in this project. We have produced this book in the hope that it will provide some encouragement to other students who are faced with the seemingly impossible task of finding something "new" in Homeric poetry and we are confident that this poetry will never cease to yield new gifts, new surprises. We thank the Department of the Classics at Harvard for its support of our project and we thank each other for the generous-minded collegiality that has characterized our collaboration. Most of all, we thank Gregory Nagy who has inspired us with his scholarship, enriched us with his friendship, and made this project possible. To him we dedicate this book with gratitude and unwilting affection.

Introduction

The essays assembled in this volume differ in focus and method, but they all share something fundamental in their approach to Homeric poetry. To use a parallel from antiquity, this common ground may be described as an attempt to emulate Herodotus, who sees Homer as an organizer of a cultural system.[1] Herodotus credits Homer and Hesiod with nothing less than giving the Greeks their theogony, or, to put it in modern terms, with organizing their universe. Such a perception was far from unique in antiquity. To understand how great a distance lies between the Greeks' perception of Homeric poetry and our modern notions of literature, it is enough to consider how frequently ancient philosophers cite Homeric verses either to clinch or to challenge an argument. Even the eventual decline of the oral tradition did not threaten Homer's authority and influence. In the second century BCE, when Crates of Mallus used his text of Homer as a basis for speculation about the spherical shape of the earth,[2] his world was still in the era of intellectual history when the prestige of all higher learning centered on the study of Homer, as Gregory Nagy argues in a recent study.[3]

Why do the ancient sources see Homer as so exceptionally important? One answer may be found in Calvert Watkins' formulation that, for them, Homeric poetry is "the verbal expression of culture."[4] The contributors to this collection explore Homeric poetry with precisely this understanding in mind, viewing the Homeric tradition as a poetic system that expresses and preserves what is culturally significant. This system is understood not as an abstraction but as a historical reality, developing in time and with different chronological levels discernible even in the final form of the text that we have inherited from antiquity.

The texts of the *Iliad* and the *Odyssey* constitute a window through which modern readers can glimpse the cultural system of Homeric poetry. These

---

1. Herodotus 2.53; Nagy 1990a:216-217.
2. Fragments 23-33 Mette. See Nagy 1998a:221n125.
3. Nagy 1998a:221n126.
4. Watkins 1995:28.

texts are instances of the Homeric tradition, instances that allow inferences and conclusions about the tradition as a whole, but that do not equal the tradition itself. To clarify this approach, a linguistic analogy may be helpful. In his celebrated *Course in General Linguistics*, Ferdinand de Saussure draws a distinction between *parole* (a particular manifestation of language, a speech or a text) and *langue* (a linguistic structure shared to a certain extent by all the speakers of a given language, but not possessed in its entirety by any one speaker).[5] The essays in this collection recognize a parallel distinction between tradition as a system (a *langue* of the tradition) and its particular manifestations (*parole* of the tradition, in this case the *Iliad* and the *Odyssey*). The texts of the *Iliad* and the *Odyssey* constitute the primary evidence for all the contributors, and each has scrutinized this evidence in an attempt to understand some part of the system, of the *langue* of the tradition. Only when such an understanding has been reached can one return to the *parole*, to specific instances, reexamining them in light of conclusions reached about the system.

A distinguished example of the systemic approach applied to poetic diction is Elroy Bundy's *Studia Pindarica*, which demonstrates the consequences of failure to appreciate the "conventional aspects of choral communication."[6] A disregard for the conventional aspects, Bundy shows, can lead to basic misunderstandings. For instance, in praise poetry the poet often confidently proclaims that no one will be able to criticize his composition. By convention such a proclamation is meant to reflect the worth of the person praised, the implication being that his achievement is so great that no eulogy could be excessive. Yet if the conventional nature of these words is not recognized, they are likely to be taken as a sign of the poet's boastful nature.[7] To give another example, the poet may use a grammatical future such as κελαδήσω 'I will sing'. Readers unfamiliar with the conventions of choral poetry have tended to assume that the poet refers to something he plans to compose in the future; some have even looked for the promised song among his preserved works. However, Bundy shows that this future actually refers to the very poem within which it occurs, for it is a

---

5. Saussure 1916:27-32.
6. Bundy 1962:2.
7. Bundy 1962:14-17; 3n11.

convention of choral lyric to speak of the present song as if it were going to happen in the future.[8] On each of these occasions, the immediate context is of little help. On the other hand, by comparing all instances of the future "I will sing" in choral poetry, it is possible to determine what it means in the *langue* of the convention and thus arrive at a better interpretation of a particular future in a particular poem. That this is as true for Homer as it is for Pindar is a theme that runs through most of the essays in this volume.

In their attempts to look at Homeric poetry in a systemic way, the contributors to this volume aim simultaneously at learning more about Homeric poetry and at testing their methods: what kinds of things can we expect to learn by studying the *Iliad* and the *Odyssey* as the *parole* of a tradition whose *langue*, inaccessible in some respects, can be reconstructed only in parts?

In order to recover the *langue* of Homeric tradition, the object of study must be viewed, as much as possible, on its own terms. Claude Lévi-Strauss compares a person analyzing cultures other than his or her own to a person in a train seeing other trains out of the window. Some of the trains will seem to be fast and short because they go in the opposite direction; others will seem slow and long because they go in the same direction as the train on which the viewer rides; still others may go by too quickly even to be identifiable as trains.[9] Of course, one cannot "jump trains," thereby adopting completely the perspective of another culture, nor would this necessarily be desirable. Still, the contributors to this volume have made an effort to let Homeric poetry itself set the terms of the discussion while at the same time recognizing that Homer should not and cannot be considered in isolation. Thus we return to the systemic approach: it is necessary to go beyond an immediate context in order to develop an understanding even of what constitutes appropriate terms of discussion.

"Going beyond an immediate context" often means going beyond epic. Anthropological studies and studies of Modern Greek traditions can conform and enhance what can be gleaned from Homeric epic. The rhetoric of modern Cretan laments, as studied by Michael Herzfeld,[10] is surprisingly similar to

---

8. Bundy 1962:21-22.
9. Lévi-Strauss 1976:341.
10. Herzfeld 1993.

the rhetoric of Helen's Iliadic lament for Hektor, and the social realities that underlie lament-rhetoric in modern Crete are helpful in understanding the social context of women's laments in the *Iliad*. Even something as seemingly literary as a simile can be better interpreted by turning to the tradition beyond its immediate context. An Odyssean simile comparing Nausikaa and Artemis can be read in the light of the tradition of *eikasia*, the comparison of a bride to a goddess or a heroine, which has been shown by Rebecca Hague to be a typical motif in Greek wedding songs.[11] Two essays in this collection examine similes, and, in both, similes are viewed as compact encapsulations of culture, or, in Leonard Muellner's words, as "a transformation of traditional lore that has, over time, developed into a coherent, generative, poetic system with formal aspects that are typical of folklore genres."[12]

The concept of Homeric poetry as a "verbal expression of culture" implies that it develops and changes over time together with the culture itself. Consequently, in studying Homer, both synchronic and diachronic perspectives must be used, each functioning as a check and control for the other. The way in which a particular word is used in a particular passage (synchronically) can confirm or disprove the meaning of the word established on the basis of its development and its previous and subsequent uses (diachronically). The reverse is also true: an interpretation of a word (or a scene, or a simile) arrived at by a diachronic method can shed light on its meaning in a particular synchronic context. The contributors aspire to use these two methods in conjunction, while giving preference to neither, so that the results of diachronic explorations are deemed relevant to the study of Homeric poetry only when confirmed synchronically. For example, Brian Breed, in Chapter 10, examines the name that Odysseus invents for himself when he meets his father for the first time after his long absence. Several etymologies have been proposed for the name, but linguistic parameters alone are insufficient to decide which one is the most appropriate. Any decision must depend on the synchronic analysis of the name's function in its immediate context and its thematic relevance to the *Odyssey*.

Studies involving etymologies form perhaps the best illustration of what the contributors to this collection understand by a combination of synchronic

---

11. Hague 1983.
12. Muellner 1990:73.

and diachronic approaches. In the past, dealing with etymologies has been considered controversial, often because of misunderstandings about the claims of such an approach. Etymologies can be abused by being applied arbitrarily, but they can also become relevant when they have demonstrably poetic associations and cohere with other elements of the narrative. Since two essays in this book focus on the etymologies of names, it is worth mentioning that both authors believe that the understanding of an ancient audience is the most important aspect of name interpretation and that this ancient understanding may not necessarily be in agreement with modern linguistic knowledge. The associations evoked by names and formalized in antiquity as so-called folk etymologies can reveal as much about Homeric poetry as those associations that happen to coincide with modern etymologies. But here is the complication: the understanding, the associations of what audience? Homeric poetry had multiple and different audiences, each with different associations. That is why both ancient and modern etymologies can become meaningful for the study of Homeric poetry when they are viewed diachronically. A name may be opaque at a later stage in a tradition, but it may have been transparent at an earlier stage. Even if the meaning of a name eventually changes and its etymological meaning is forgotten, it is sometimes possible to establish that this etymological meaning was once known and important, because the name is consistently used in contexts and associated with themes that correspond to the etymology. When such a connection can be made between the etymology of a word and its Homeric usage, then we have evidence for the continuity of the tradition from the time when the name was still transparent.

The diachronic approach to the study of Homeric poetry is enhanced by comparative evidence from living oral traditions outside Greece. Such evidence, for example, may be adduced in support of those contributors who investigate how ideological changes in epic may occur. In the form known to us, Homeric poetry is beyond occasionality and the change associated with it. Still, the study of the ways in which poets in living oral traditions react to the occasion of each performance can help in understanding the Greek oral epic tradition as it once used to be. No single parallel can be completely reliable, but multiple comparisons can suggest possible mechanisms of change and development that shaped the Homeric epic.

Of the countless examples of relevant comparative evidence, two will suffice to illustrate this point. In an essay on the folk songs of Telugu women, Velcheru Narayana Rao explores the transformation that the *Ramayana* tradition undergoes in women's performance.[13] Although the version of the *Ramayana* that has become most prestigious concentrates on the virtues and glory of Rama, some songs of Telugu women cast doubt on his virtues by emphasizing the theme of his wife's suffering, or pay little attention to events of military glory, elaborating instead on "female" themes such as weddings, woman's life among in-laws, pregnancy, and childbirth.

Kathleen Erndl, also writing about the *Ramayana*, demonstrates how an incident that is seen as morally ambiguous by the poem's multiple audiences generates a plethora of variants, each with a different perspective, so that if all the branches of the *Ramayana* tradition were to be seen cumulatively, the tradition itself would appear to be testing, and in fact debating, an ambiguous episode.[14]

It is against the background of such comparative evidence that the reader is invited to view Mary Ebbott's observations on how the *Iliad* as we know it can incorporate voices that question the worth of the war celebrated by the epic as a whole. Miriam Carlisle suggests in her essay that there is even a way for the Homeric tradition to mark by certain verbal tags the variants that it incorporates but does not privilege, a phenomenon that, according to her, indicates a conscious and critical handling of variants within the epic tradition.[15] Andrea Kouklanakis addresses the incorporation of "alternative ideologies" and examines how an element of dissonance, rather than being excluded, is instead allowed but curtailed by the Iliadic tradition.

Comparative evidence also forms a useful background for the essays that deal with questions of performance and of poet-audience interaction in Homeric poetry. Corinne Pache shows that Homeric tradition can still visualize itself, in an idealized form, as responding to the tastes of an audience and satisfying particular individuals. Even though such fluidity may no longer correspond to the actuality of Homeric performance at a given

---

13. Narayana Rao 1991:114-136.
14. Erndl 1991:67-88.
15. For a discussion of the critical awareness of the variants of myth in a myth-making tradition, see Nagy 1990a:57.

historical point, the idealized self-representation of Homeric tradition is in fact quite similar to the attested reality of living oral traditions. Pache's and Carlisle's discussions of the relationship between poet and patron in the context of an "ideal performance" in the *Odyssey* are not purely speculative, since they are supported by ancient as well as modern comparative evidence spanning the distance from Ireland to the Indian subcontinent. On a different level, Kouklanakis, Pache, and Carlisle explore how Homeric poetry sets the tone for the reaction of its external audience by depicting the reaction of an internal audience, so that depictions of performances function as built-in devices for refreshing the contact of Homeric poetry with its audience.

Appreciation of the traditional nature of Homeric poetry affects not only the interpretation of the *Iliad* and the *Odyssey* but also any method that is applied to the text of the poems. If Homeric poetry as a whole does not belong to any one time and place, it follows that a variant cannot be dismissed as spurious on the grounds that it is chronologically later than another one or is of different provenance. The concept of interpolation becomes inapplicable to Homeric poetry, since neither being "late" nor being "inserted" detracts from the authenticity of a variant. This is not to say that determination of the relative date or of the provenance of a verse or an episode is not worthwhile. When possible, such a determination sheds light on ways of innovation and integration of new material within the tradition, subjects that figure prominently in this volume. Even when it is impossible to discriminate between variants on the basis of either time or locale, the variants themselves can shed light on mechanisms of the formulaic style and, in particular, on the extent and quality of its flexibility. The "inserted" episodes that are sometimes written off as interpolations can be used as case studies to show the way in which such "inserted" elements expand the epic not only in size, but also in thematic reference and poetic richness. In fact, such expansions have been shown by Milman Parry and Albert Lord to be a powerful instrument of poetic skill in the arsenal of the oral traditional poet. In this spirit, Thomas Jenkins' essay focuses on "rehabilitating" a supposed interpolation by showing how it enriches the fabric of the epic.

Each of the four parts of this volume represents a different area of Homeric studies, and each essay takes a different direction within its area. In view of the diversity of this collection, a brief outline of the parts of this volume and a synopsis of the essays are in order.

Part I of this book, "Multigeneric Homer," explores ways in which the epic tradition incorporates poetic material from various non-epic genres and how this material, by virtue of becoming an organic component of epic, transforms the poetic dynamic of epic itself. Each of the essays in this part addresses in its own way the role of performance context in the composition of oral traditional poetry.

Mary Ebbott examines elements of Helen's funeral lament in the overall context of lament traditions, both ancient and modern. She singles out conventions of lament whereby a mourner may articulate actual or potential attitudes of others toward herself, thus expressing awareness of her own social position. Ebbott argues that this social aspect of lament allows it to function as a vehicle of nemesis in the *Iliad*. Using a model that posits the development of the story of the Trojan War into the story of the wrath of Achilles, she suggests a pathway for the entrance of nemesis-related conventions into the Iliadic tradition.[16] She focuses, however, on showing how these conventions of lament, once having entered the *Iliad*, change the way in which Helen is represented both formally and thematically. Elements specific to lament tradition penetrate Helen's speeches, becoming part of her overall character in the *Iliad*, and this conceptualization of Helen's character affects the ideological balance of the *Iliad* as a whole.

Corinne Pache focuses on an instance where catalogue poetry enters into Homeric poetry: Odysseus tells the Phaeacians about his visit to the underworld and includes two catalogues, one of the women he met there and another of the heroes who died at Troy. Pache keeps in mind the relationship between audience and performer, and her approach helps uncover the structure and logic of the scene. At the moment when Odysseus tells of his trip to the underworld he is a performer and, as such, he adapts his tale to the tastes of his audience by performing two different catalogues for his two main listeners, Alkinoos and Arete.

Andrea Kouklanakis looks at yet another "genre" within the Iliadic tradition, blame poetry. She focuses on the confrontation between Thersites and Odysseus, especially on Thersites' speech, which she analyzes on two levels, that of narrative and that of mise-en-scène. Kouklanakis goes beyond Richard Martin and Edward Vodoklys' evaluations of Thersites' speech by

---

16. For a detailed discussion of the model, see Lang 1995:149-162.

elaborating on the social dimension.[17] She explores the social status of Thersites as reflected both in his speech and in the reaction of the internal audience of the scene. By analyzing the content and the structure of the speech and the mise-en-scène, she concludes that the implications of Thersites' insubordination are more serious than commonly thought, and that Thersites himself is more deeply involved in the epic tradition.[18]

Miriam Carlisle investigates the meaning of words containing the root *pseud-* as they are used in Homer. These words are generally translated as 'lie, lying', but Carlisle shows that this rendition is misleading. She argues that most Homeric instances of *pseud-*root words have generic implications, designating not only narrative but also a particular type of storytelling that approaches what we call fiction. However convincing the delivery, however welcome the content, however transported the audience, these narratives impart information not corroborated by the larger text. They are fictions, though, rather than lies: folktales, type-tales, already "olden" at the time of their telling and not centered on the customary material of Greek epic poetry—the heroic accomplishments in war of characters living in the epic world of the poem.

The second part of this volume, "Diachronic Homer," comprises two essays that focus on names as elements in the evolving system of conventions of Homeric poetry. If Homeric poetry is viewed only as a text, names appear trivial—but not if the text is recognized as derivative from oral poetic tradition. Names come to life if approached as part the system that underlies the textual traditions of the *Iliad* and the *Odyssey*. This approach works because etymology and context are in conjunction and validate each other. Etymology is not assumed to be pertinent to the poetry simply on the basis of linguistic evidence, but is tested in the laboratory of context. Should context and etymology lack correspondence, the etymology has to be abandoned, not as linguistically incorrect, but as poetically irrelevant. But if an etymology is "confirmed" by the context, it becomes a powerful tool for uncovering a diachronic depth of associations that enrich our understanding of Homeric poetry.

---

17. See Martin 1989; Vodoklys 1992.
18. See Thalmann 1984.

Olga Levaniouk's essay "Penelope and the *Pênelops*" is an attempt to perform just such a test. The etymology of Penelope's name is clear, but is it relevant? Penelope took her name from the *pênelops,* a bird that never appears in Homer. The name seems therefore accidental when analyzed strictly within the limits of the *Iliad* and the *Odyssey.* But consideration of the *pênelops* in other genres of traditional poetry, such as lyric, reveals that this bird is consistently associated with certain themes. Levaniouk forms the hypothesis that this connection belongs to the poetic tradition as a whole. To test this hypothesis, she looks back at the *Odyssey,* and discovers that the themes elsewhere associated with the *pênelops* are not merely present but crucial in the Homeric depiction of Penelope. In particular, the etymology of her name connects Penelope both with mythical themes long commented on in relation to Odysseus and with the traditions of lament, which are preeminent both in the *Iliad* and in the *Odyssey,* as has been demonstrated in recent scholarship.[19]

Brian Breed combines the study of names with the study of another element in the system of tradition, the type scene. Breed addresses the perplexing scene of Odysseus' reunion with Laertes. Why does Odysseus lie to his father? Why does Laertes burst into tears at merely hearing the name of a supposed stranger? If the scene of reunion is not a product of arbitrary artistic choice but part of a system, then there should be elements within the scene that follow discernible traditional patterns. Names, Breed suggests, are just such an element. Taking his cue from Laertes' remarkable reaction to Odysseus' invented names, he uses name interpretation as a tool for elucidating the thematic resonance of the scene. As a result of his investigation, he connects the scene with concern for proper burial and its importance not only for the dead but also for the mourners, major themes in the *Odyssey.*

In the third part of the volume, "Visual Homer," the focus shifts from names to similes, but the fundamental approach remains constant: similes are seen in terms of system, not arbitrary artistic choice. Much has been written about similes. The contributors to this volume add a new dimension by asking what the world of similes has to do with the world of visual art. These

---

19. See in particular Alexiou 1974; Loraux 1998; Nagy 1979:94-117.

essays explore the communication between visual and verbal texts and the similarities between visual and verbal conventions.

John Watrous examines the multiple functions of the lion simile in the encounter between Odysseus and Nausikaa. By establishing a pattern in the deployment of lion similes in the *Iliad* and comparing this Odyssean instance with a variety of very different lion similes in the *Odyssey*, Watrous shows how awareness of what constitutes an unmarked lion simile is exploited in the thematically significant deviations of the *Odyssey*. Such variation illustrates how the tradition itself presupposes creativity: the prominence of traditional associations prepares the ground for the exotic. Relying on I. A. Richards' method of analyzing similes in terms of *tenor* and *vehicle*,[20] Watrous observes in detail the poetic possibilities of shifts and even barrier-breakdowns on three levels: inside the simile, between the simile and the narrative, and between two similes in responsion with one another. Watrous draws not only on literary but also on visual evidence, in particular the figure of *potnia thêrôn* 'mistress of wild beasts' as she appears in Greek vase painting to recover the subtleties of the scene that are overlooked when it is discussed solely in terms of the immediate context.

Although Watrous looks at similes in a systemic way, his focus remains on the Nausikaa scene. Fred Naiden is more interested in the system itself and the variation that it allows. Naiden discusses Iliadic leopard similes by establishing their place among other animal similes. He argues that leopard similes in Homer are bold and unusual, exotic like the animal itself. As the only animal to face the lion without itself becoming prey, the leopard adds an element of unpredictability to similes, and, through them, to the narrative itself. With the leopard as an example, Naiden illustrates the validity of Muellner's comment that "not only is it fruitful to assume that no detail of a given simile is irrelevant, but it is plain that a narrative sequence at least as long as a book can be ruled by a consistent set of metaphors and figures."[21] Thus the spotted hide of a leopard worn by a hero functions in the same way as a simile: it interacts with the narrative as if it were, in effect, a simile materialized. The 'variegated' (ποικίλος) leopard is shown to be an ideal expression of 'variation' (ποικιλία) within the system, a means of creating

---

20. Richards 1936:96.
21. Muellner 1990:98.

suspense. By examining what changes occur if a leopard appears in a simile instead of a lion, Naiden tests the possibilities, consequences, and limits of such variation. Finally, he compares the Homeric leopard with the leopard of visual art, arguing that its role is structurally similar in each medium.

This collection concludes with Thomas Jenkins' essay "*Homêros ekainopoiêse*," which considers the implications of a systemic approach for textual criticism. In connection with a passage that is frequently criticized as an interpolation (*Il.* 3.144-48), Jenkins examines and questions the notions of interpolation and authenticity as applied to Homeric poetry. Rejecting the theory of interpolation, he suggests that the lines in question are a genuine variation within the tradition and analyzes its effects on the immediate context as well as on the *Iliad* as a whole. Although the themes evoked by these verses are never explicitly developed in our *Iliad*, they affect the ideological balance and artistic effect of the scene in which they appear by calling to mind traditional narratives other than the *Iliad*. For an audience listening to the *Iliad* with these stories in mind, seemingly unconnected elements fall into a pattern and seemingly accidental features emerge as characteristic.

I
Multigeneric Homer

1

The Wrath of Helen:
Self-Blame and Nemesis in the *Iliad*

Mary Ebbott

When Aphrodite tells Helen to go to Paris' bed after he has lost his duel with Menelaos, Helen refuses (*Il.* 3.410-412):

> κεῖσε δ' ἐγὼν οὐκ εἶμι—νεμεσσητὸν δέ κεν εἴη—
> κείνου πορσανέουσα λέχος· Τρῳαὶ δέ μ' ὀπίσσω
> πᾶσαι μωμήσονται· ἔχω δ' ἄχε' ἄκριτα θυμῷ.

> I am not going to him—it would arouse nemesis—
> to share his bed. The Trojan women hereafter would
> all reproach me, and I have endless sorrows in my heart.

Here, after the renewal of the original conflict between Menelaos and Paris, Helen says what the Greeks and Trojans probably wish she had said in the first place—that she will not go to Paris' bed, for it would inspire nemesis, and if she did, all the Trojan women would reproach her. In this mix of past and present, Helen expresses not only that it would be blameworthy of her to go to Paris' bed after his loss to Menelaos, but she also portrays her marriage to Paris as itself blameworthy and worthy of reproach by all the Trojan women.[1]

---

1. Suzuki 1989:37 argues that the past Helen and her motivations are omitted from the *Iliad*: "The poet portrays the present Helen and leaves her past self a mystery. He represents Helen as an almost disembodied consciousness passively living out the effects of her fatal act. Despite the uncertainty and ambiguity of her identity and nature, Helen, paradoxically, is overdetermined by that one act in her

3

4 Part I: Multigeneric Homer

A refusal to go with Paris and to comply with Aphrodite's order is not, however, characteristic of the shameless Helen who had wantonly deserted husband, hearth, and child in order to go with the handsome Trojan. Instead, Helen in the *Iliad* is intensely aware of shame, nemesis, and the blame produced by her past actions [2] She is, in fact, the only character to censure her past deeds, and does so in radical contrast to her status as a prize worthy of this war that is voiced by other characters.[3] In each of Helen's appearances in the *Iliad*, she mentions her marriage(s) and the shame involved in the marriage to Paris and regrets her past action. That is, she relates her shameful deed and expresses a reaction to it. Helen's self-awareness and self-blame are key parts of her character, but it may have been through a standard, formulaic discourse—the funeral lament—that this subversive, otherwise suppressed blame of Helen is introduced into her character and into the *Iliad*.

The funeral lament contains elements of regret but also of self-awareness and the perceptions of others. These elements are integral to Helen's speeches throughout the *Iliad* and are also the basis for shame, for, "The basic experience connected with shame is that of being seen, inappropriately, by the wrong people in the wrong condition."[4] The particular discourse of the funeral lament, then, could have introduced the shame that is such a prominent part of Helen's character in the *Iliad*. In addition, however, speaking about the perceptions of others could also lead to the introduction of nemesis, that is, the reactions of others to shameful deeds, into Helen's speeches. I am suggesting in what follows that Helen's funeral lament

---

life." We see the "ashamed" Helen in her speeches as opposed to the presumably "shameless" past Helen, as I discuss below.

2. I confine my examination of Helen's character here only to her character in the *Iliad*.

3. The only mortal character who speaks ill of Helen directly is Achilles, when he calls her ῥιγεδανή at *Il.* 19.325. His choice of adjective, 'to be shuddered at' is, however, very similar to how Helen describes herself at *Il.* 6.344 and *Il.* 24.775. Suzuki 1989:20 notes that it is through focusing on Achilles that the authority of the war and its rationale are questioned. The "shuddering" that they both describe may thus be connected to the questioning of such a war over such a woman, and so it is entirely appropriate for Achilles to speak an adjective that combines dread and awe.

4. Williams 1993:78. He later notes (82) that the "gaze of another" involved in shame can certainly be "the imagined gaze of an imagined other." The "others" that a mourner sings about are real and, in Helen's case, specified, but the internalization of shame is still an important concept for Helen's characterization.

contains the seeds of her characterization and self-blame in the *Iliad* and that her character is defined by both shame and nemesis. My emphasis in this essay is on that aspect of the funeral lament that is concerned with the articulation of others' perceptions of the mourner, since this is the direct connection to the shame and nemesis that characterizes Helen in the *Iliad*.

In a funeral lament a woman might sing not only about the deceased person but also about how his death affects the mourner's position in society, how she is perceived by others, and how she wishes that things were different. Michael Herzfeld, describing a modern Cretan funeral, gives this background:

> Each mourner performs in the face of ever-ready gossip by neighbors and distant kin. If she succeeds in moving them to sympathetic understanding and above all to identification with her personal pain, she may also eventually succeed in raising her social status . . . It is common for a mourner to accuse her recently deceased parent or brother, for example, of having left her. . . This pattern of confusion turned to anger . . . gives lamenting women a medium in which to anticipate what might be said of them—or even done to them—once their source of moral support in an androcentric world has been stripped away.[5]

Helen's funeral lament for Hektor expresses similar sentiments. Helen begins by describing how she is related to Hektor, the very relationship that makes her the object of scorn, and she expresses a wish that she had died before she went with Paris.[6] After reminding everyone that she had left her home in Greece to come to Troy with Paris, Helen then mourns the loss of her protector from the reproach and abuse of "distant" kin, Paris' brothers and their wives, his sisters and mother. Hektor, she says, was her only friend in Troy, besides Priam, for everyone else shudders when they see her:

---

5. Herzfeld 1993:244.
6. Alexiou 1974:178 points out that this wish of the mourners for their own death before that of the dead person's or for never having been born is a common one, and cites Andromache's (Andromache voices this desire at *Il* 22.481) and Helen's funeral laments as ancient examples.

τῇσι δ' ἔπειθ' Ἑλένη τριτάτη ἐξῆρχε γόοιο
"'Ἕκτορ, ἐμῷ θυμῷ δαέρων πολὺ φίλτατε πάντων,
ἦ μέν μοι πόσις ἐστίν Ἀλέξανδρος θεοειδής,
ὅς μ' ἄγαγε Τροίηνδ'· ὡς πρὶν ὤφελλον ὀλέσθαι.
ἤδη γὰρ νῦν μοι τόδ' ἐεικοστὸν ἔτος ἐστὶν
ἐξ οὗ κεῖθεν ἔβην καὶ ἐμῆς ἀπελήλυθα πάτρης
ἀλλ' οὔ πω σεῦ ἄκουσα κακὸν ἔπος οὐδ' ἀσύφηλον·
ἀλλ' εἴ τίς με καὶ ἄλλος ἐνὶ μεγάροισιν ἐνίπτοι
δαέρων ἢ γαλόων ἢ εἰνατέρων εὐπέπλων,
ἢ ἑκυρή—ἑκυρὸς δὲ πατὴρ ὡς ἤπιος αἰεί—,
ἀλλὰ σὺ τὸν ἐπέεσσι παραιφάμενος κατέρυκες,
σῇ τ' ἀγανοφροσύνῃ καὶ σοῖς ἀγανοῖς ἐπέεσσι.
τῶ σέ θ' ἅμα κλαίω καὶ ἔμ' ἄμμορον ἀχνυμένη κῆρ
οὐ γάρ τίς μοι ἔτ' ἄλλος ἐνὶ Τροίη εὐρείη
ἤπιος οὐδὲ φίλος, πάντες δέ με πεφρίκασιν."

(*Il.* 24.761-775)

Then Helen, last of the three, took the lead in the lamentation:
"Hektor, dearest by far of all my husband's brothers to my heart,
Yes, my husband is godlike Alexander,
who brought me to Troy. How I wish I had died before that!
For now it is already the twentieth year
since I left there, departing from my homeland.
But not once have I heard a mean or degrading word from you.
But if someone else in the halls would abuse me,
one of my husband's brothers or sisters or one of the well dressed
    wives of his brothers
or his mother—but his father was always as kind as my own
    father—
then you, winning them over with words, held them back
with your gentle manner and your mild words.
Therefore I mourn you and myself at the same time,
    grieving in my ill-fated heart,
there is no one left for me in broad Troy who is a kind friend;
everyone else is repulsed at the sight of me."

Helen's lament, like a modern Cretan one, "accuses" Hektor of leaving her defenseless, for she says she mourns for herself as well as for him. The wish that she had died before going to Troy with Paris is the regret of someone feeling shame.[7] She also examines what her social position will be. Just as Andromache sings in her lament (*Il.* 24.725-745) about what will happen to her and to Astyanax, Helen, too, sings about what will happen to her. Hektor was the one who was restraining the other members of Paris' family from blaming Helen directly, and Helen's lament expresses a strong awareness of what others will be allowed to say openly about her now that her supporter Hektor has been taken from her. This prior restraint implies, however, that such nemesis is already present. Mention of the public scorn that she knows she will receive (and that she reveals has been present all along) in this familiar mode of discourse may have been the starting point for its introduction into Helen's character: the funeral lament served as the door through which the otherwise unspoken nemesis toward Helen enters the story of the *Iliad*.

The funeral lament could have influenced Helen's character throughout the *Iliad* because of the methods of composition of the *Iliad*. Mabel Lang describes how the current form of the *Iliad* may have resulted from a transformation of a straightforward war story into the story of the wrath of Achilles.[8] Arguing from the fact that the *Iliad* covers most of the entire Trojan War and not just this short period in the tenth year and from the incongruities of the *Iliad* as we have it, she posits three major points about the "poetic pre-history" of the *Iliad*: first is that the story of the Trojan War was very familiar to Homer's audience; second, she observes:

> At least one early and highly influential account of the Trojan War began at the beginning and included at the outset of the Achaean expedition a Catalogue of ships. . . . It almost goes without saying that any account of the war that began at the

---

7. Williams 1993:84 describes the reaction of someone who is feeling shame as "not just the desire to hide, to hide my face, but the desire to disappear, not to be there." The wish to die that is common in funeral laments shapes the wish to disappear into a specific way to disappear *here*.

8. Lang 1995.

beginning with the sailing of the expeditionary force would have
gone on in chronicle form and ended with the war's end.

Her third point is that this "chronicle" story of the Trojan War ended with
an Achaean victory.[9] She goes on to argue that the introduction of Achilles'
story into the tale of the Trojan War resulted in a recomposition of the poem.
This recomposition was designed to "enclose the Trojan War in the wrath
story"[10] by framing the older material within the new focus of the story. Lang
conjectures that this reframing method, "which may have been attempted
earlier but certainly culminated in the *Iliad*, was to intermingle the tales by
means of various kinds of reverberation, echo, and reflection."[11] Since the
earlier war story ended with an Achaean triumph, it would have had to
include the death of Hektor, since his death signals the fall of Troy. Helen, as
his kinswoman, could have given a funeral lament in that earlier version as
well.[12] The focus on the wrath of Achilles, however, is precisely what
introduced the question of the value of the war and its object, whether that
object be Helen herself or the κλέος 'glory, renown' she represents for
Achilles.[13] During this transformation Helen's characterization might have
begun to be shaped by the questioning of the war and of the worth of the
prize, that is, of Helen herself. Helen, as I argue further below, is the one who
brings attention to this question of her worth as the prize of this war, since
she is the one to articulate the blame for her own deeds. Through oral
recomposition, however, sentiments voiced in, and properly belonging to, the
funeral lament could reverberate, echo, and be further developed in Helen's

---

9. Lang 149-50.
10. Lang 150.
11. Lang 150-151.
12. Alexiou 1974:12 makes a point that Helen is given kinswoman status in the
funeral lament, but Suzuki 1989:54-55 also applies Alexiou's point about Briseis' role
as a stranger mourning for Patroklos to Helen, noting the similarities in their laments.
The general ambiguity surrounding Helen allows her to be kinswoman and stranger
simultaneously.
13. Clader 1976:12-13 discusses Helen as a symbol of the κλέος for which
Achilles is fighting, since he was not one of her suitors and thus not bound by the
suitors' agreement. Suzuki 1989:20 argues that the Iliad "questions the authority of
the prevailing ethos among the aristocratic warriors on both sides" by focusing on
warriors like Achilles and Hektor who "experience these fissures in the heroic code."

other appearances to define her role as the voice of nemesis over her own deeds.

Andromache's appearances in the *Iliad* are a parallel example of this infusion of sentiments from the funeral lament into other speeches.[14] Andromache gives a formal funeral lament for Hektor at *Il.* 24.725-745 and also delivers a lament for him when she comes to the walls and sees a dead Hektor being dragged by Achilles (*Il.* 22.477-514). Andromache's laments are prefigured in her one other appearance in the *Iliad*, her speech to Hektor at *Il.* 6.407-439. Here, too, she laments what her and Astyanax' circumstances will be once Hektor is gone: ". . . ἐμοὶ δέ κε κέρδιον εἴη / σεῦ ἀφαμαρτούσῃ χθόνα δύμεναι· οὐ γὰρ ἔτ' ἄλλη / ἔσται θαλπωρή. ἐπεὶ ἄν σύ γε πότμον ἐπίσπῃς. / ἀλλ' ἄχε·· οὐδέ μοι ἔστι πατὴρ καὶ πότνια μήτηρ" ([*Il.* 6.410-413] '. . . and it would be better for me, being deprived of you, to plunge into the earth, for there will be no other consolation when you meet your fate, only sorrows, for I do not have my father and honored mother').[15] The wish to die along with the mourned person and the elaboration of the mourner's inconsolable grief and lack of any "protector" are all elements of a ritual lament. Even Andromache's plea that Hektor not leave her (*Il.* 6.431-434) can be seen as part of a ritual lament, for, after Hektor has left, she and her female servants mourn (γόον) him though he is still living (*Il.* 6.500). Andromache's speech here is defined and developed through the form of the lament.

In an article based on an essay that was first delivered at the CorHaLi conference in Lausanne,[16] Richard Martin argues that Helen's character is a paradigm of the expert performer of laments. He concludes from his examination of these speeches in light of traditional Greek funeral laments performed in modern Greece that Helen's speeches contain phrases and strategies of the lament genre and that the audience would thus think of a

---

14. Lang 1995:157 argues that Andromache's role was shaped during this transmutation into an "equivalent but contrasting role" to that of Briseis. This would be a similar instance of the power that the growing prominence of Achilles' story had to reshape other characters in relation to its new emphasis.

15. Note that even in Andromache's "lament" sentiments proper to the lament, such as wishing to "plunge into the earth," sound like the reaction of someone who is ashamed and thus wishes to disappear completely.

16. May 1995.

mourning woman when they heard Helen's earlier speeches in the *Iliad*. Andromache's speech in Book 6, which echoes her funeral lament, would have the same effect—the audience would hear her lamenting Hektor in her speech even before they hear that she mourns for him after he departs.

Martin produces several examples, especially from Book 3 of the *Iliad* and Book 4 of the *Odyssey*, which convincingly demonstrate that Helen's speeches are "tagged" as laments by certain phrases and sentiments without being explicitly introduced as laments. He compares elements in Helen's speeches to elements in other speeches in Homer that are labeled as laments and to modern Greek laments. My emphasis in this essay is on those elements of the funeral lament—blame, shame, and the social perceptions and treatment of the mourner—that I argue have shaped Helen's character in the *Iliad*. Indeed, basic elements of Helen's funeral lament—the description of her present situation as wife of Paris, her wish that she had died before that happened, and the references to the public scorn she receives from the Trojans—are interwoven into her other speeches. Helen mentions her marriage to Paris and/or her former marriage to Menelaos in each of her appearances (*Il.* 3.174-175, 180, 403-404 when she speaks to Aphrodite; 428-429 when she is back with Paris; and to Hektor at *Il.* 6.344-358). She wishes two other times that she had died before coming to Troy (*Il.* 3.173; 6.345-348) and also mentions the rebuke and reproach that is hers (*Il.* 3.242, 410-412). Mention of the Trojan women at *Il.* 3.411 may also reflect the funeral lament as the source of this emphasis on the women's disapproval in particular, since it is at funerals that women have the lead in speaking.

Helen's speech to Hektor in Book 6 is an excellent example of parallels to her funeral lament. She addresses Hektor as her δαήρ *daêr* 'husband's brother', in both places, emphasizing her relationship with him and possibly using the lament formula of addressing relatives by their relationship title rather than by name.[17] She wishes she had died on the day she was born, before she was brought to Troy:

> δᾶερ ἐμεῖο κυνὸς κακομηχάνου ὀκρυοέσσης,
> ὥς μ' ὄφελ' ἤματι τῷ ὅτε με πρῶτον τέκε μήτηρ

---

17. Martin argues that Helen is using this lament convention when she addresses Priam as her φίλε ἑκυρέ (*Il.* 3.172).

οἴχεσθαι προφέρουσα κακὴ ἀνέμοιο θύελλα
εἰς ὄρος ἢ εἰς κῦμα πολυφλοίσβοιο θαλάσσης,
ἔνθα με κῦμ' ἀπόερσε πάρος τάδε ἔργα γενέσθαι.
(*Il.* 6.344-348)

Brother-in-law to me, a bitch who contrives evil and
    causes others to shudder,
how I wish that on that day when my mother first gave
    birth to me
a violent windstorm had come, bearing me away
to the mountains, or into the waves of the crashing sea
where the tide would have swept me away before these
    things had happened.

Beyond incorporating motifs from a funeral lament, however, we see in this example that Helen's speech has become quite elaborate in her wish to die and in her self-insults. Martin points out that Helen's wish for bitter death in *Il.* 3.173 would make the audience think of grieving language. That may also be the case here in Book 6, but this time Helen wishes for a particularly violent death while describing herself in most unflattering terms. The verbal and conceptual similarities between Helen's funeral lament and her other speeches demonstrate a link that could lead to the intense self-blame that is seen in Helen's speeches.[18] Martin argues that lament as a genre includes blame: grief and revenge coexist in the same laments in modern Greece. The form of lament, which has clearly influenced Helen's speeches in the *Iliad*, has used elements that express blame, shame, and nemesis or revenge to turn these forces back onto Helen herself.

---

18. Graver 1995:57 sees Helen's self-blame as part of another poetic tradition about her story. Referring to lines *Il.* 3.355-358 she says: "From the standpoint of performance, Helen's words direct us to a poetic tradition that treated her and Paris quite harshly, as morally degenerate or as responsible for the deaths of Hektor and other heroes. Only in such a tradition could it be considered an evil fate to be made the subject of song." If Helen's self-blame does reflect a separate tradition, I would still see the funeral lament as the way that this self-blame was incorporated into Helen's character in this tradition.

Awareness of her own social position and of others' perceptions and opinions of her is, we have seen, an integral part of Helen's funeral lament. An awareness of one's own position is fundamental for the experience of shame, and the opinions of others are the basis of nemesis. Bernard Williams defines the relationship between shame and nemesis this way:

> The reaction in Homer to someone who has done something that shame should have prevented is nemesis, a reaction that can be understood, according to the context, as ranging from shock, contempt, and malice to righteous rage and indignation. It should not be thought that nemesis and its related words are ambiguous. It is defined as a reaction, and what it psychologically consists of properly depends on what particular violation of *aidôs* it is a reaction to.[19]

Helen, using speech that resembles both the blame and the self-awareness that are integral to lament, expresses both the shame and the nemesis about her own deeds in her own speeches. Since her particular violation of *aidôs* was a severe one, the nemesis that her own speeches articulate is, in turn, harsh. The insults that Helen hurls at herself, such as κυνῶπις 'shameless' (*Il.* 3.180), στυγερή 'loathsome' (*Il.* 3.404), and κυνὸς κακομηχάνου ὀκρυοέσσης 'a bitch who contrives evil and causes others to shudder' (*Il.* 6.344) with the quite violent wish to die that follows, and κυνὸς 'bitch' (*Il.* 6.356) express the nemesis produced by her own shameful deeds, which she also announces in the same speeches.[20]

Thus both shame, the personal reaction to one's own social transgressions, and nemesis, the community's reaction to these misdeeds, are integral parts of Helen's speeches and her character in the *Iliad*. The recognition of this, however, leads to the question of why these elements became so crucial to Helen's characterization and why she is the one and only person to express the nemesis that her actions have produced.

---

19. Williams 1993:80.
20. See Clader 1976 for a discussion of these epithets as relating to Helen as a bearer or symbol of death. See Graver 1995 for a discussion of the "dog"-related insults as indicating Helen's greed, taking more than her share.

In Helen's first appearance in the *Iliad*, we encounter the contrast between what others say about her and what Helen says about herself. When the elders of Troy behold Helen approaching the walls of the city, they say to one another:

> οὐ νέμεσις Τρῶας καὶ ἐϋκνήμιδας Ἀχαιοὺς
> τοιῆδ' ἀμφὶ γυναικὶ πολὺν χρόνον ἄλγεα πάσχειν
> αἰνῶς ἀθανάτῃσι θεῆς εἰς ὦπα ἔοικεν
> ἀλλὰ καὶ ὣς τοίη περ ἐοῦσ' ἐν νηυσὶ νεέσθω,
> μηδ' ἡμῖν τεκέεσσί τ' ὀπίσσω πῆμα λίποιτο.
>
>   (*Il.* 3.156-160)

There is no nemesis for Trojans and well greaved Achaeans
for suffering hardships for a long time for a woman like this one.
Her face is strikingly like that of an immortal goddess.
But, even though she is such, let her go home in the ships
and not be left as a cause of woe to us and our children in
     the future.

We might suppose that this is the Trojans' opinion of Helen and her place among them, since elders are fitting representatives of the community's views.[21] This is followed by Priam's opinion that Helen is not the cause of the war (*Il.* 3.164). Helen's entrance into the action of the poem, then, inspires many contradictory, or at least confused, statements about her. As Suzuki notes, "The difficulty of interpreting Helen . . . becomes more rather than less acute when she actually enters the poem."[22] According to the elders, she is a worthy cause for a protracted war and the suffering of many hardships by both the Trojans and the Greeks, but the Trojans want her to leave them anyway. Priam's statement to Helen after he calls her over is a

---

21. Obviously, the view expressed by the elders has its own contradictions. Collins 1988:43-44 notes that in the elders' speech, "Helen is here both blamed for the war and yet praised by the fact that the war can be fought over her. For, as the old men see it, the war is a tribute to and affirmation of her worth." Suzuki (1989:35) also notes that "the poet conveys a radical ambivalence in the Trojan counselors toward her [Helen]."

22. Suzuki 1989:34.

strong removal of blame, since he specifically says that the gods, not she, are the cause, the *aitia*, of the war ([*Il.* 3.164] οὔ τί μοι αἰτίη ἐσσί, θεοί νύ μοι αἴτιοί εἰσιν 'In my opinion, you are not at all to blame. Now I think the gods are to blame'). Helen's response, however, is to detail exactly how she is to blame by describing how she left Menelaos for Paris and to wish she had died before those very events that precipitated the war had happened:

ὡς ὄφελεν θάνατός μοι ἀδεῖν κακὸς ὁππότε δεῦρο
υἱέι σῷ ἑπόμην, θάλαμον γνωτούς τε λιποῦσα
παῖδά τε τηλυγέτην καὶ ὀμηλικίην ἐρατεινήν.
ἀλλὰ τά γ᾽ οὐκ ἐγένοντο· τὸ καὶ κλαίουσα τέτηκα.

(*Il.* 3.173-176)

How I wish that wicked death had been pleasing to me,
when I followed your son here, leaving behind my marriage
    chamber,
my relatives, my daughter entering womanhood and my delightful
    age mates.
But this did not happen: and now I have pined away, weeping.

The wish to die recalls or echoes the funeral lament, of course, but nemesis or outward blame is equally apparent. For an audience who is familiar with the shameless Helen, it might not be surprising for someone else to blame Helen with similar words (e.g., "How I wish that death had been pleasing to *her* before she followed Paris here"). Helen emphasizes this blame again when she replies that Priam is looking at Agamemnon, for in her description of him she ends with the fact that he was once her brother-in-law, κυνῶπις 'shameless woman' that she is (*Il.* 3.180). The mention of her relationship to Agamemnon, which implicitly refers to her marriage to Menelaos, coupled with an insult and coming right after her delineation of her past actions, focuses her entire first speech on the marriage that she betrayed. When Helen comes to see the duel for which she is the prize, she is the one to announce that she is the casus belli by recounting exactly what she did.

Helen continues to tell Priam who the men he picks out on the field are, informing him about Odysseus and Ajax, but then she wonders why she does not see her brothers, Castor and Pollux (*Il.* 3.347).[23] She supposes that either they did not come from Lacedaemon to fight or that they did, but now they do not wish to go to the battlefield fearing the shameful words and all the reproach that is hers (*Il.* 3.234-242). The two lines that report the earlier death of Castor and Pollux bring the *teikhoskopia* 'view from the wall' to a rather abrupt close, and we are left with the remark that there is great dishonor for Helen among the Greeks. She assumes that her brothers would be ashamed of her and either would not come to Troy at all to fight for her or would, once at Troy, keep themselves back from battle because of the insults that Greeks fighting on her behalf would heap upon Helen.[24] We hear a great deal of what the warriors say on the battlefield; we do not, however, hear them condemning Helen (*Il.* 3.357).[25] Once again, what Helen says about herself is in direct contrast to what we hear others say about her in the *Iliad*. Helen presents an alternate assessment of her behavior and the reaction of others to it. She presumes the shame her brothers would feel before the nemesis, the reaction of the other Greek warriors, which would naturally follow from her own shameful deed. Helen, however, is the one whom we hear reacting with nemesis to the deeds of Helen.

In the *Iliad,* others do not expressly blame Helen, and so Helen divulges the nemesis that others do not and cannot speak. Others speak of Helen as a prize, as the object of the war, but each time Helen speaks, she reminds us that she left her husband Menelaos and married Paris and that she is an object of blame and scorn. That is, she reminds us that she has acted shamefully and that her actions have produced a resulting nemesis. Although we hear Hektor speak similar reproaches to, and about, Paris (e.g., *Il.* 3.39-40; 6.281-282),[26]

---

23. See Jenkins (this volume) for a discussion of these lines as allusion to the myth of Theseus' rape of Helen and her rescue by her brothers.

24. Austin 1994:48 emphasizes that these lines highlight Helen's shame: "Helen assumes the worst: her brothers, kinsmen and dauntless warriors though they are, did not dare show themselves on the battlefield for shame (*Il.* 3.326-342). Her assumption is incorrect, but that is less important than Helen's reminder that the spectacle to which she has been so gracefully invited, by Iris first on the divine plane, and then by Priam on the human plane, is the spectacle of her own shame, or lack of it."

25. And we *do* hear from Hektor that the Trojans who are fighting on his behalf heap scorn on Paris when he leaves the battlefield in *Il.* 6.524-525.

26. Notice also that, in these reproaches, Hektor wishes that Paris had never been born or would die now; the language is very similar to Helen's language about herself,

we hear of Helen's ignominy only from Helen herself.[27] Suzuki sees Helen as a figure of difference because of her conflicting tradition of blame and exoneration and says that she has a heightened perception because of her position: "Through Helen's liminal position in this society, which divides her loyalties but also gives her a perspective that comprehends such divisions, the poet represents her complex inwardness and subjectivity—much as he does in representing Achilles, a warrior withdrawn from combat."[28] Thus Helen is able to express a view of herself and the war fought εἵνεκα Ἑλένης 'because of Helen, for Helen's sake'[29] that is different from everything else we hear from others.[30] She is the one to challenge her own worthiness as the object of the war by presenting her actions in the light of the nemesis that is provoked by them.

Because shame and nemesis are integral to Helen's character, we must note that she is placed only in situations where she will be the only one to carry out this blame of herself, again allowing this alternative view to be voiced only by Helen herself. For Helen expresses the public condemnation of her actions, but she speaks to people who do not feel the same way. In her conversations in the story, Helen speaks only to Priam, to Aphrodite, to Paris, and to Hektor. Obviously, Helen will not have the opportunity to talk with any Greek men who might reproach her, since she is out of their reach, but Helen does not appear with any Trojan women whose censure she knows and

---

and thus we see that these wishes are not only connected to lament language but also to that of blame and nemesis.

27. Collins 1988:45; Graver 1995:41, where she notes that Helen is doubly unique in her self-reproach, for not only does no one else insult Helen but also no one else insults Paris the way Helen does.

28. Suzuki 1989:19.

29. E.g., *Il.* 2.161,177; 9.339, where Helen is the reason for the war or for the deaths of so many Achaeans.

30. Suzuki 1989:56 also sees Helen's funeral lament as an opportunity to present a different viewpoint on the overall heroic theme: "Homer's Helen, in this final expression of remorse and self-hatred, again poses the question of her responsibility—a question that remains unanswered in the *Iliad*. Achilles' reconciliation with Priam, which accomplishes a bridging of important divisions and oppositions in the poem, is momentary and passing; ultimately it gives way to a renewed perception of the tragic disjunction of heroic society that marks its passing. Helen of Argos, the poem's primary figure of difference, embodies and voices this perception by closing the poem with a funeral lament for Hektor, the best of the Trojans."

says is present.[31] Graver, arguing that Homer is integrating a separate poetic tradition about Helen into his portrait, states that the Homeric epics leave blame poetry out of their songs:

> For in Helen, the epic tradition welcomes the figure of scandal into its own subject matter, but welcomes her on the epic poet's own terms. Both *Iliad* and *Odyssey* present a narrative about her—not the narrative of her infamy, but a different narrative—and both do so in a way that studiously avoids direct censure.[32]

Studious avoidance is partly achieved by having Helen speak only to those who are on her side, who are her protectors, but the poem has plenty of direct censure of Helen from Helen herself. The blame that perhaps existed in a contemporary poetic tradition and that surely would have existed in some story of Helen and Paris has been displaced from a community reaction of nemesis to Helen's own self-blame.

This displacement produces a paradox between the Helen we know—the shameless Helen—and the Helen we find in the *Iliad*. In this poem Helen is a woman who knows and respects shame; yet, by her own admission, she is also a shameless woman.[33] Leslie Collins argues that Helen is espousing the views of the community and that her "posture of self-blame" is meant both to

---

31. Austin 1994:8, 41 points out that Helen is alienated especially from women: "Helen is banished too but to her own room, secluded not only from the men but from the grieving wives and widows, to hide her shame."

32. Graver 1995:57.

33. Austin 1994:12 believes that this partly results from Helen's origins as a local goddess in Sparta. Some divine characteristics are still seen in the *Iliad*'s Helen, although she is mortal: "Helen is strangely both a goddess and a human at the same time and therefore occupies both circles, of Meaning and Being. A woman who has no reason to fear either nemesis or death is not a human but a god. Yet this same person is very much a human in her function as an object of contention among men, as other women are, a prisoner to the social order. As a goddess Helen transcends shame, yet, as a woman, she is acutely conscious of her function, to be the icon of shame." See also Clader 1976 for evidence about the divine origins and aspects of Helen. The paradox of Helen is furthered in that, although she does not have to fear nemesis from others, she is the one to articulate the nemesis that exists but is not expressed.

mitigate her transgression of the social code that she is now manifesting and to allow this paradox to go unnoticed:[34]

> The fact that the blame of Helen is expressed primarily by Helen herself—for Helen is made to testify to a public hostility which Homer otherwise does not directly depict—further advances the ideological interests of the poem. In a word, only Helen can blame Helen without exposing the paradox that the poem wishes to remain hidden: that the very act which necessitates a war over her also condemns her from the poem's point of view, and renders her an unworthy object of struggle. The *Iliad*'s portrait of a reformed and contrite Helen is certainly formed in answer to this paradox.

The complexity and ambiguity of Helen results from her mixed identity of shame and shamelessness[35] and from the mix of a personal reaction of shame and the public reaction of nemesis in her speeches. Collins argues that Helen's own identity is denied when she presents this different view of her own behavior:

> Indeed, it is Helen who is made to bear sole witness to the way in which the dominant community views her. And Helen is made to agree with them, to embrace the orthodox values against which she once transgressed; she is thus made to reject the ethics of her patroness and thus of her own identity.[36]

Austin also describes the ambiguity inherent in Helen:

> The old men's response to Helen epitomizes her ambiguity. 'It is no disgrace that the Greeks and the Trojans suffer long evils for such a woman,' they say, using the word *nemesis*, the strongest term in Homer's shame culture for "blame." The Trojan War is no

---

34. Collins 1988:51, 57-58.

35. Austin 1994:29: "Only she [Helen] must, consistently and from the beginning, learn to convert (or subvert) the stuff of her daily life into her function as the glyph for 'shame/shamelessness' in the storybook of the tribe."

36. Collins 1988:45.

cause shame on either side . . . .But the elders of Troy could not
be more mistaken, thinking their war over Helen was free of
nemesis: Helen is nemesis.[37]

Thus Helen, as Nemesis, presents the righteous indignation about her
marriage to Paris and about the war that has resulted from it. Although the
war may provide the opportunity for κλέος 'glory, renown' for those fighting
over Helen, nemesis still attends the war because of and through Helen
herself.

As Collins argues, the Trojan War is concerned with certain social values,
including a regard for shame and nemesis, but the combatants are fighting for
a woman who has, by her actions, disregarded these same values. This
produces the paradox Collins points out.[38] It is true that only Helen can
blame Helen, for if another person, with the exception of the embittered
Achilles who is able to utter one negative yet awesome adjective about
Helen, were to speak about her as a κυνῶπις 'shameless woman'[39] or to wish
she had died before she caused this war, she would be exposed as a prize
unworthy of the deaths of so many men. But does the paradox go unnoticed?
The nemesis toward Helen and her marriage is fully expressed—by Helen
herself.[40] How would the audience react to a Helen who obviously knows
and feels shame? The reason why the shame and nemesis associated with
Helen emerged may have been the same one that focused the poem on the

---

37. Austin 1994:43. He refers to Hesiod fragments 197.8 MW and 204.82 MW and
Callimachus' *Hymn to Artemis* (232) for a mythical tradition that calls Helen the
daughter of Zeus and Nemesis.

38. Collins 1988:45.

39. A word that Helen uses of herself in both the *Iliad* (3.180) and the *Odyssey*
(4.145), that Agamemnon uses of Clytemnestra (*Od.* 11.424), and that Hephaistos
uses of both Hera (*Il.* 18.396) and Aphrodite (*Od.* 8.319 in Demodokos' song).

40. Graver 1995:59 sees the epic poet's desire to keep blame poetry out of epic as
influencing Helen's self-blame: "This hostility to blame as a mode of discourse may
help to explain the reflexivity of Helen's blame. It is a device answering to the special
need of performers to subjectivize the blame of this character that is so central to the
Troy legend. By restricting the reminders of a defamatory tradition to the purview of a
single character, the poet-narrator is able to protect his own threatened objectivity." I
think that the epic is intentionally allowing this other view into the poem so that Helen
is blamed in some way, which may be what Graver means when she talks about the
poet's "objectivity."

focused the poem on the wrath of Achilles. Since Helen is the object of the war, her very value is examined in conjunction with the question concerning the worth of the war. Like the merit of fighting for κλέος 'glory, renown' itself, the value of Helen cannot stand unquestioned within the *Iliad*.[41] And, as Fuqua has pointed out about the *Odyssey*, "it is the characters and not the 'invisible poet' who set the standards that shape the ideals and principles of the epic."[42] Thus, it cannot be the narrator who questions Helen's worth, but one of the characters must address Helen's disgrace. As we have seen, only Helen can do this and so, to allow the alternative viewpoint to emerge, Helen herself must present the negative reaction to her own behavior.

Helen committed an act that shame should have prevented. The "equal and opposite reaction" would be nemesis. The expression of nemesis from others has been necessarily repressed, however, due to her status as a prize, and so is displaced to Helen herself. The funeral lament, with the mourner's articulation of the perceptions of others, opened the door for this nemesis to enter epic, and the negative view of Helen conventionally belonged to Helen's own lament as an accurate reflection of her status after the death of Hektor. As the focus of the story of the Trojan War shifted to the story of the wrath of Achilles, a critical view of Helen gained importance as an accompanying question about the reasons for the war, and so sentiments proper to the funeral lament became features of all of Helen's speeches. Thus, the blame that Helen speaks is not just an internal one—shame—but, more importantly, she gives voice to the external blame, the nemesis, that her deeds provoke but that is otherwise unspoken in the *Iliad*.

---

41. Suzuki 1989:9-30 argues that Homer emphasizes this challenge to her worth and finds her value inadequate by contrasting her abstractness with the more concrete images of the other warriors' wives and children.
42. Fuqua 1991:57.

2

Odysseus and the Phaeacians

Corinne Ondine Pache

Two unique events occur in Book 11 of the *Odyssey* as Odysseus tells the Phaeacians about his visit to Hades: first, Odysseus includes a story known as the "catalogue of women" that seems to have nothing to do with himself and his own adventures or with anybody else in the *Odyssey*; second, there is an interruption, known as the "intermezzo," in Odysseus' story, and a conversation takes place among Odysseus, Arete, and Alkinoos before the narrative is resumed. These two occurrences have much to say about the interaction between Odysseus and the Phaeacians, and also about the interaction between the epic poet and his audience.

Some experts think that the whole or parts of Book 11 are later insertions, and the catalogue of heroines especially is often regarded as a later "interpolation."[1] The very concept of interpolation is not one that is particularly helpful in dealing with a text that is the result of a long oral tradition rather than the original output of a single individual. It seems to me ultimately irrelevant whether the visit to Hades became part of the story later or when the catalogue of heroines was included in Book 11. My concern is with what is there, and how to interpret it. The *Nekyia* not only makes sense in the received text of the *Odyssey*, but it plays a very central and meaningful role in the story and has many ramifications throughout the narrative.

At Alkinoos' court in Scheria, Odysseus recounts his adventures. Before he does so, he spends a day with the Phaeacians, feasting and competing in

---

1. Kirk 1962:239 and Page 1955:21-51 think the entire book is a later "interpolation." Germain 1954:330-332 considers that parts of Book 11, including the catalogue of women, are later "insertions," although he gives to the *Nekyia* itself a central place in the *Odyssey*. Cf. Heubeck and Hoekstra 1989:75-76, 90-91 for a survey of secondary literature on the subject.

athletic games. During the course of this day, Odysseus learns much about the Phaeacians. Before he even arrives at their court, Nausikaa makes it clear to him that her mother plays a central role in Scheria and that it is from her, rather than from Alkinoos, that he should ask for help (*Od.* 6.303-315). Odysseus hears the Phaeacians' singer, Demodokos, three times and is told by Alkinoos exactly what it is that makes the Phaeacians happy (*Od.* 8.246-249):

> οὐ γὰρ πυγμάχοι εἰμὲν ἀμύμονες οὐδὲ παλαισταί,
> ἀλλὰ ποσὶ κραιπνῶς θέομεν καὶ νηυσὶν ἄριστοι,
> αἰεὶ δ' ἡμῖν δαίς τε φίλη κίθαρίς τε χοροί τε
> εἵματά τ' ἐξημοιβὰ λοετρά τε θερμὰ καὶ εὐναί.

> for we are not faultless in our boxing nor as wrestlers,
> but we do run lightly on our feet, and are the best seamen,
> and always the feast is dear to us, and the lyre and dances
> and changes of clothing and hot baths and beds.

The Phaeacians are a gentle people who delight in peaceful distractions and simple pleasures. Alkinoos' list of the Phaeacians' favorite things culminates with the three words εἵματα, λοετρά, εὐναί 'clothing, baths, beds', which all denote romantic love: εἵματα and λοετρά in the *Odyssey* are often the prelude to love, as is shown by Nausikaa's remark to her father that her three bachelor brothers are 'forever wishing to go to the dances in freshly washed clothing' (οἱ δ' αἰεὶ ἐθέλουσι νεόπλυτα εἵματ' ἔχοντες, *Od.* 6.64),[2] while for Nausikaa herself, washing—of both clothing and herself—is clearly part of wedding preparations (*Od.* 6.92-97).[3] Whereas the Phaeacians enjoy all of the things mentioned by Alkinoos, I will argue that love occupies a special place in the list, not only as something that the Phaeacians like in and of itself but also as a favorite subject of storytelling. Alkinoos plainly discloses the Phaeacians' tastes to Odysseus, perhaps

---

2. It is interesting to note that Penelope has trouble recognizing Odysseus because of his κακὰ . . . εἵματα *Od.* 23.94.

3. See Seaford 1994:35-36 for bathing and putting on fine clothes as preparations for a wedding in the *Odyssey.*

thereby hinting at what his subsequent narrative should focus on. Similarly, Odysseus seems to react to Alkinoos' speech by offering the Phaeacians an account of his adventures that they will enjoy. Not that he needs to change the facts to please them but by emphasizing some details here and there he can adapt his story to suit this particular audience. In one case in particular, when he tells the Phaeacians about his encounter with the heroines of the past in Book 11, Odysseus steps out of his role as autobiographer and switches genre to become a genealogical poet to delight his host and, more particularly, his hostess.

Alkinoos tells Odysseus that the Phaeacians like stories, but he is also very clear that they do not care for deceivers and cheats (*Od.* 11.362-369):

τὸν δ' αὖτ' 'Αλκίνοος ἀπαμείβετο φώνησέν τε
"ὦ 'Οδυσεῦ, τὸ μὲν οὔ τί σ' ἐΐσκομεν εἰσορόωντες
ἠπεροπῆά τ' ἔμεν καὶ ἐπίκλοπον, οἷά τε πολλοὺς
βόσκει γαῖα μέλαινα πολυσπερέας ἀνθρώπους
ψεύδεά τ' ἀρτύνοντας, ὅθεν κέ τις οὐδὲ ἴδοιτο·
σοὶ δ' ἔπι μὲν μορφὴ ἐπέων, ἔνι δὲ φρένες ἐσθλαί,
μῦθον δ' ὡς ὅτ' ἀοιδὸς ἐπισταμένως κατέλεξας,
πάντων 'Αργείων σέο τ' αὐτοῦ κήδεα λυγρά."

Then Alkinoos answered him in turn and said to him:
"Odysseus, as we look upon you we do not imagine
that you are a deceptive or thievish man, the kind
that the dark earth breeds in great numbers, people
    who wander widely,
making up stories, in which one could not see anything.
There is a grace upon your words, and there is
    noble sense within you,
and expertly, as a singer would do, you have told the
story of your own dismal sorrows and of all the Argives."

This is a fascinating passage that reveals much about Alkinoos' expectations, and maybe also about those of the audience, both internal and external. Alkinoos starts by establishing that he does not consider Odysseus to be among the liars and tricksters who make up stories[4] from which one could not learn anything. The criteria by which he judges Odysseus' tales, however, have nothing to do with their truth-value. He praises Odysseus for the grace of his words, μορφὴ ἐπέων, and for his noble mind, φρένες ἐσθλαί. Alkinoos is unquestionably more concerned with aesthetics than truth. Similarly, the catalogue of heroines as it is presented by Odysseus seems to be more concerned with satisfying the Phaeacians' desire for beauty rather than with quenching any thirst for perfect accuracy.

At the beginning of Odysseus' story in Book 11, Odysseus kills the sacrificial sheep and all the *psukhai* gather by the pit of freshly drawn blood (*Od.* 11.36-43):

αἱ δ' ἀγέροντο

ψυχαὶ ὑπὲξ Ἐρέβευς νεκύων κατατεθνηώτων·
νύμφαι τ' ἠΐθεοί τε πολύτλητοί τε γέροντες
παρθενικαί τ' ἀταλαὶ νεοπενθέα θυμὸν ἔχουσαι,
πολλοὶ δ' οὐτάμενοι χαλκήρεσιν ἐγχείῃσιν,
ἄνδρες ἀρηΐφατοι, βεβροτωμένα τεύχε' ἔχοντες·
οἳ πολλοὶ περὶ βόθρον ἐφοίτων ἄλλοθεν ἄλλος
θεσπεσίῃ ἰαχῇ· ἐμὲ δὲ χλωρὸν δέος ᾕρει.

and the souls of the perished dead gathered, up out of Erebus,
brides, and young unmarried men, and long-suffering old men,
virgins, tender and with the sorrows of young hearts upon them,
and many fighting men killed in battle, stabbed with brazen spears
still carrying their bloody armor upon them.
These came swarming around the pit from every direction
with inhuman clamor, and green fear took hold of me.

Elpenor then approaches Odysseus, followed by Teiresias and Odysseus' mother, Antikleia. Elpenor comes to Odysseus with a special request, Teiresias gives him information, and Antikleia talks with her son on a variety

---

4. Cf. Carlisle (this volume) for discussion of *pseudea* as a genre and for a different interpretation of this passage.

of subjects. As Odysseus is talking with his dead mother, crowds of heroines suddenly approach him (*Od.* 11.225-234):

νῶϊ μὲν ὣς ἐπέεσσιν ἀμειβόμεθ', αἱ δὲ γυναῖκες
ἤλυθον, ὄτρυνεν γὰρ ἀγαυὴ Περσεφόνεια,
ὅσσαι ἀριστήων ἄλοχοι ἔσαν ἠδὲ θύγατρες.
αἱ δ' ἀμφ' αἷμα κελαινὸν ἀολλέες ἠγερέθοντο,
αὐτὰρ ἐγὼ βούλευον. ὅπως ἐ ἔοιμι ἑκάστην
ἥδε δὲ μοικατὰ θυμὸν ἀρίστη φαίνετο βουλή
σπασάμενος τανύηκες ἄορ παχέος παρὰ μηροῦ
οὐκ εἴων πίνειν ἅμα πάσας αἷμα κελαινόν
αἱ δὲ προμνηστῖναι ἐπήϊσαν, ἠδὲ ἑκάστη
ὃν γόνον ἐξαγόρευεν ἐγὼ δ' ἐρέεινον ἁπάσας.

So we two were conversing back and forth, and the women came to me,
for splendid Persephone urged them on.
These were all who had been the wives and daughters of the best
    men,
and now they gathered in swarms around the dark blood.
I then thought about a way to question them, each by herself,
and as I thought, this was the plan that seemed best to me;
drawing out the long-edged sword from beside my strong thigh,
I would not let them all drink the dark blood at the same time.
So they waited and came to me in order, and each one
told me about her origin, and I questioned all of them.

Odysseus says that the women are urged on by Persephone (ὄτρυνεν γὰρ ἀγαυὴ Περσεφόνεια). Persephone here appears for the first time in European literature. One scholar thinks that it is implied that Persephone has also summoned the other female shades who appeared previously, and none of the males, because there is some kind of segregation between men and women in Hades.[5] It is far from obvious, however, that Persephone plays any role until she appears with the heroines. Moreover, I think that gender segregation is

---

5. Doherty 1991:153.

belied by the passage quoted above (*Od.* 11.36-43). Women and men, young and old, all approach the pit of blood together. The first shades that approach Odysseus either know him or know something about him. Elpenor and Antikleia know Odysseus personally, and Teiresias has important information to impart to him. These three characters have good reasons to talk to Odysseus; the other women do not. There is need of a further justification for the encounter with the heroines, and Persephone's encouragement provides a plausible, though a little puzzling, explanation.

Just before the heroines approach, Antikleia asks Odysseus to remember everything so that he may tell his wife later on (*Od.* 11.223-224):

ἀλλὰ φόωσδε τάχιστα λιλαίεο· ταῦτα δὲ πάντα
ἴσθ', ἵνα καὶ μετόπισθε τεῇ εἴπῃσθα γυναικί.

But you must strive back toward the light again with all speed;
and remember <u>all these things</u> for your wife, so you may tell
    her hereafter.

ταῦτα δὲ πάντα seems to introduce what follows, the catalogue of heroines, rather than what precedes.[6] Antikleia does not tell Odysseus anything that would be of particular interest to Penelope. The only information she gives that Penelope would not already know is the passage about what happens to the ψυχαί (*psukhai*) after death. This ταῦτα δὲ

---

6. There is only one other attested instance of ταῦτα δὲ πάντα in the Homeric corpus, at *Iliad* 9.35. In this case, it seems to refer both to what precedes and to what follows, as Diomedes rebukes Agamemnon (*Il.* 9.34-36):

ἀλκὴν μέν μοι πρῶτον ὀνείδισας ἐν Δαναοῖσιν.
φὰς ἔμεν ἀπτόλεμον καὶ ἀνάλκιδα ταῦτα δὲ πάντα
ἴσασ' Ἀργείων ἠμὲν νέοι ἠδὲ γέροντες

He starts his speech by telling Agamemnon that he should not have treated him in such a way previously and then goes on to describe Agamemnon's faults and weaknesses. I think that the ταῦτα δὲ πάντα that all the Argives are supposed to know include both Agamemnon's first insult and his more general failings as described by Diomedes.

πάντα stands as a marker that whatever follows is of particular interest not only to Odysseus' wife but also to wives in general and to Arete in particular. As a matter of fact, Odysseus does not mention the women when he tells Penelope about his visit to Hades.

As the women crowd around the blood, Odysseus decides he wants to talk to them. He prevents them from drinking the blood all at the same time so that he may question each one separately. From this passage (*Od.* 11.225-234), the scene seems to be very orderly: Odysseus is standing by the blood with his sword, and the heroines come one by one, αἱ δὲ προμνηστῖναι ἐπήϊσαν, to tell their stories. Odysseus also makes clear that he questions all of them, ἐγὼ δ' ἐρέεινον ἀπάσας. After describing fourteen of these women, however, Odysseus stops his narrative and declares that he could not tell of all the heroines before the night would end, and that, besides, it is time for sleep (*Od.* 11.328-332):

> πάσας δ' οὐκ ἂν ἐγὼ μυθήσομαι οὐδ' ὀνομήνω,
> ὅσσας ἡρώων ἀλόχους ἴδον ἠδὲ θύγατρας·
> πρὶν γάρ κεν καὶ νὺξ φθῖτ' ἄμβροτος. ἀλλὰ καὶ ὥρη
> εὕδειν, ἢ ἐπὶ νῆα θοὴν ἐλθόντ' ἐς ἑταίρους
> ἢ αὐτοῦ·

> But I could not tell about all of them nor name all the women
> I saw who were the wives and daughters of heroes,
> for before that the divine night would give out. But it is time now
> for my sleep, either joining my companions on board the fast ship,
> or here.

The catalogue of women is a whole in itself, and, when Odysseus interrupts himself, saying that there is not enough time to tell everything, he has in fact concluded his own catalogue. There is a progression, both chronological and also "ethical," as one goes from Tyro to Eriphyle—from the very ancient past to more recent time and from a heroine who bears Poseidon's children to an unworthy wife who is bribed with a necklace. This progression makes the catalogue a complete entity. Although only fourteen heroines are actually mentioned, one is left with the sense that many generations of women have come to Odysseus. When he breaks off, Odysseus has said all he intends to say about the women.

Odysseus interrupts his account on the pretext of lack of time and sleepiness. Although he may have completed the catalogue of heroines, Odysseus is in fact still in the middle of his own story when he breaks off. This interruption is the only one and stands at the very center of Odysseus' narrative.[7] The catalogue of heroines, then, is Odysseus' gift to Arete, and he interrupts himself to check whether his storytelling is effective and pleasing to her and the Phaeacians.

The catalogue of women is obviously much to Arete's liking. She compliments Odysseus and calls for more gifts to be given to him. She thus seems to accept Odysseus' offering and to reciprocate it with material rewards.[8]

As we know from Alkinoos' speech (*Od.* 8.246-249), the Phaeacians love to listen to stories, and they also especially appreciate love stories, which in fact make up most of the catalogue. It is also very clear that both Arete's and Alkinoos' thirst for stories is not sated and that they want Odysseus to go on and finish the story of his adventures.

After Arete expresses her delight in Odysseus' storytelling, Alkinoos speaks and asks Odysseus to go on and to tell if he saw any of his companions from Troy. And there Odysseus seems to change his story to accommodate Alkinoos. He could simply answer Alkinoos' question and say, "Oh yes, I did see Agamemnon and Achilles and Ajax," but instead he backtracks to the women. Suddenly, Persephone is back, and she scatters the heroines in all directions (*Od.* 11.385-386):

αὐτὰρ ἐπεὶ ψυχὰς μὲν ἀπεσκέδασ᾽ ἄλλυδις ἄλλῃ
ἁγνὴ Περσεφόνεια γυναικῶν θηλυτεράων.

Now after pure Persephone had scattered the female
psukhai of the women, driving them off in every direction.

---

7. Odysseus interrupts himself at verse 328, at which point the account of the *Nekyia* is halfway through the 640 lines of our received text.

8. As Calvert Watkins puts it, "poet and patron exist on a reciprocal gift-giving basis; the poet's gift is his poem." See Watkins 1994:536-543 for discussion of an Irish word for 'poem' and 'gift'.

Then, Agamemnon very conveniently shows up (*Od.* 11.387-389):

ἦλθε δ' ἐπὶ ψυχὴ 'Αγαμέμνονος 'Ατρεΐδαο
ἀχνυμένη· περὶ δ' ἄλλαι ἀγηγέραθ', ὅσσοι ἄμ' αὐτῷ
οἴκῳ ἐν Αἰγίσθοιο θάνον καὶ πότμον ἐπέσπον.

there came the soul of Agamemnon, the son of Atreus,
grieving, and the *psukhai* of the other men, who died with him
and met their doom in the house of Aegisthus, were gathered
around him.

Of course, Odysseus has to pick up his story at a later stage. After the exchange with Alkinoos, there would be no point in telling about the rest of the heroines, since his host has made it clear he wanted to hear about Odysseus' companions. Still, the transition is a surprising one. If Odysseus has indeed questioned each and every woman in turn, wouldn't they have left after telling their stories to him? Why would Persephone need to scatter them all? None of the other ghosts seem to stay around after they have spoken with Odysseus.

By describing the scattering of the heroines by Persephone and by specifying that his encounter with the heroes happened right after the one with the women, Odysseus makes his own narrative somewhat suspect. It seems that he is changing his story to make it more agreeable to Alkinoos, just as the catalogue of women seems to be included to please Arete.

Although the content of the catalogue is meant mainly to please Arete, Odysseus has to incorporate it in his narrative in a realistic manner. Since the heroines have no direct ties to him, there is need for an outside explanation. And here enters Persephone: the women approach Odysseus because Persephone encourages them to do so, and, when Odysseus wants to go on with other adventures, here comes Persephone again, to do exactly what Odysseus needs. Odysseus uses Persephone as a device to introduce a special kind of performance.

By telling these heroines' stories, Odysseus steps outside his role of autobiographer and switches genre to become a genealogical poet.

Catalogues form a genre in themselves and are found both as independent entities and included in other narratives.[9] Although this is the only formal catalogue in the *Odyssey*, there are several such lists in the *Iliad*. The catalogue of ships (*Il.* 2.484-760) is the most famous example. One also finds Zeus' list of his lovers (*Il.* 14.317-328) and the catalogue of Nereids (*Il.* 18.39-49). In the *Theogony*, we are told that the Muses delight Zeus with genealogies (44-52), much in the same way that Odysseus delights Arete.[10]

Odysseus as a poet seems to do precisely what the poet of the *Odyssey* as a whole avoids. Typically, epic avoids references to particular locales or audiences and tends toward as universal an appeal as possible. Odysseus in the *Odyssey* tailors his tale to his audience and introduces elements that are particularly adapted to it in terms both of content and of form.[11] This is particularly noticeable in the stories immediately preceding and following the intermezzo.[12]

There is a wonderful symmetry on both sides of the intermezzo. The catalogue of women is balanced by Odysseus' encounter with the Greek heroes. Stories of wives and husbands are told by heroines and heroes for the delight of Arete and Alkinoos. This symmetry has been noted before and likened to that of geometric vase painting.[13] Odysseus ends his catalogue with Eriphyle and resumes the narrative with Agamemnon telling about Clytemnestra: on each side of the intermezzo stands a bad wife who has killed her husband. The intermezzo is at the center of the *Nekyia*, with its

---

9. See West 1985 on genealogical catalogues and on the Hesiodic catalogue of women.

10. And just as the Muses tell Zeus about his own genealogy, Odysseus starts his narrative with Poseidon, to whom Arete and Alkinoos are both related. As West 1985:9 notes, the relationship between catalogues and audiences is generally implicit rather than explicit.

11. Although Odysseus somewhat subverts epic narrative rules, he is also appropriating the medium in much the same way Achilles does in the *Iliad* by becoming the epic poet, as it were. Martin 1989:222 notes that Achilles' use of language is unique and that "the 'language of Achilles' is none other than that of the monumental composer." Is there a sense in which the hero of an epic poem has to *be* an epic poet?

12. For more on audience conditioning and the dependence of performers on their audiences, see Nagy 1995:171-172.

13. See Myres 1952:1-11 for a comparison between epic and geometric art. See Webster 1954:259-260 for a discussion of the symmetry of the *Nekyia*.

different episodes carefully arranged around it, while the *Nekyia* itself lies at the center of Odysseus' adventures.[14]

Clearly, then, Odysseus takes the Phaeacians' taste into account as he relates his adventures. Not only do his stories reflect the themes Alkinoos praised in his speech (*Od.* 8.246-249), but he also echoes the very words Alkinoos used. By looking closely at the visit to Hades, one starts to see how Odysseus tailors his tale to his audience. Odysseus gives the Phaeacians what they like and what they ask for.

I would argue that the catalogue of women is mostly about love, εὐναί. The catalogue describes the οὐκ ἀποφώλιοι εὐναί of the gods (*Od.* 11.249). Εὐναί is a recurrent theme throughout the *Odyssey* and Greek literature, and an interesting parallel is found in Mimnermus 1:

> τίς δὲ βίος, τί δὲ τερπνὸν ἄτερ χρυσῆς Ἀφροδίτης;
> τεθναίην, ὅτε μοι μηκέτι ταῦτα μέλοι,
> κρυπταδίη φιλότης καὶ μείλιχα δῶρα καὶ εὐνή,
> οἳ' ἥβης ἄνθεα γίγνεται ἁρπαλέα ἀνδράσιν ἠδὲ γυναιξίν

> What life, what delight is there without Golden Aphrodite?
> May I die when I care about such things no more,
> hidden love and honey-sweet gifts and bed,
> such as are the alluring flowers of youth for both men and
> women.

Love is delightful to both men and women, and so are poems about love. We know that the Phaeacians find εἵματα, λοετρά, εὐναί particularly delightful. Such are the things they care for, and about such subjects are the best songs made. And in the *Odyssey*, the Phaeacians delight in the love stories told not only by their guest Odysseus but also in the one told by their own singer, Demodokos.

Shortly after Alkinoos' speech about the Phaeacians' tastes, Demodokos sings his second song, about the illicit love of Aphrodite and Ares (*Od.* 8.266-366). Here again, the song picks up not only the themes dear to the Phaeacians but also the very words Alkinoos just used. Demodokos uses the

---

14. Germain 1954:333.

word "bed" at the beginning of the song, λέχος δ' ἤισχυνε καὶ εὐνήν 'he disgraced his (Hephaistos') marriage and bed' (*Od.* 8.269). The song then goes on to detail the love affair between Ares and Aphrodite and its discovery by Hephaistos. At the end of the song, Demodokos again uses one of the words just uttered by Alkinoos, ἀμφὶ δὲ εἵματα ἕσσαν ἐπήρατα, θαῦμα ἰδέσθαι 'they put delightful clothing about her, a wonder to look upon' (*Od.* 8.366). Although words like εὐνήν and εἵματα are common enough in the *Odyssey*, I think that there is some significance in finding them in a song that follows so closely upon Alkinoos' speech.

The same phenomenon can be detected in Odysseus' narrative. During the intermezzo, Alkinoos asks Odysseus to tell him more about the other Greek heroes and about his own deeds. He ends his request with (*Od.* 11.374)

οὐ δέ μοι λέγε θέσκελα ἔργα

but tell me about wondrous deeds.

θέσκελα is an old epic epithet found mostly in the formula θέσκελα ἔργα in the Homeric corpus.[15] In the *Odyssey*, the formula is used once by Alkinoos in the passage above and once by Odysseus in his answer to Alkinoos. He describes Herakles' sword-belt (*Od.* 11.610):

ἵνα θέσκελα ἔργα τέτυκτο

where wondrous works had been figured on it

It is striking that Odysseus chooses to use these very same words. It seems as though he was adapting not only the content but also the form of his stories to his audience. Alkinoos asks for stories about heroes and θέσκελα ἔργα, and his guest literally answers those wishes: Odysseus tells of the ghosts of

---

15. The adjective occurs twice in the *Iliad* and twice in the *Odyssey*. At *Il.* 3.130, the formula θέσκελα ἔργα is used by Iris to describe the deeds of the Trojans and the Greeks to Helen and, at *Il.* 23.107, the adjective θέσκελον is used by Achilles to describe Patroklos' ghost.

Greek heroes, and, short of describing actual θέσκελα ἔργα, he puts them on Herakles' sword-belt.

Aversion to liars and cheats, such as those described by Alkinoos, reverberates throughout the *Odyssey* and the *Iliad*. Just as Achilles hates a man who speaks one thing while hiding another thing in his heart (*Il.* 9.312-313), Eumaios abhors as the gates of Hades the man who speaks ἀπατήλια 'deceptive things' (*Od.* 14.157). Whether Odysseus is inventing or modifying his adventures is ultimately a moot question, and to try to determine the veracity of his tale is about as productive as trying to retrace his travels on today's Mediterranean. Loathsome as lies are in Homeric epic, their opposite is found not in truth but in beauty, in μορφή ἐπέων and φρένες ἐσθλαί (*Od.* 11.367).

Odysseus' description of his visit to Hades and the intermezzo throw a fascinating light on the art of storytelling and on the relationship between poet and audience. The intermezzo lies at the very center from which Odysseus' adventures radiate symmetrically. Just before the interruption, Odysseus switches genre to include the catalogue of women, which stands out as his gift to his hostess. The intermezzo shows Odysseus' audience reacting to his story, and, similarly, one can observe Odysseus responding to the desires of his audience. In Book 11, one can see Odysseus performing as an epic poet, while he also—as he is wont to do—breaks the very rules of the medium of which he is a creation, by switching to another genre in the middle of his narrative.

3

Thersites, Odysseus, and the Social Order

Andrea Kouklanakis

The *Iliad* contains various exchanges of formulaic speeches of blame and praise between its characters, and, indeed, many of the speeches one encounters in the poem serve one or the other function.[1] In this essay I will examine Thersites' blame speech beginning in *Il.* 2.225 and Odysseus' blame speech in reply in *Il.* 2.246-264. Although the analysis of both Thersites' and Odysseus' speeches undeniably reveals a poetics of blame,[2] the passage in which these speeches appear also discloses certain ambiguities of a moral and social nature.

These ambiguities emerge from the structure of the passage on two distinct levels: the narrative and the speeches. Further, these two levels appear to be in tension with one another. For the purpose of this essay I will be treating both speeches—Thersites' and Odysseus'—as a mise-en-scène within the narrative. On the one hand, I argue that the tension between these two levels may indicate a certain Homeric ambivalence in the representation of the dynamics of power between the two characters and perhaps also in the poem as a whole. On the other hand, I intend to show that these moral ambiguities are critically underscored by the relatively liminal position of both characters.

Since Odysseus appears as an epic hero, he may well be a product of a historical transition in social values, a transition toward a set of values by which his quasi *homo novus* status is beginning to gain importance vis-à-vis an older tradition of the heroic standard based on nobility and physical

---

1. For further analysis of formulaic speeches, particularly praise and blame speeches, see Nagy 1979; Martin 1989; Vodoklys 1992.
2. Ibid.

prowess. As we also shall see, Thersites' character is likewise not altogether fixed as a common fighting man, but, as with Odysseus, his character seems to shift. It is this relative fluidity of both characters that prevents their interaction from being strictly speaking a tension between opposites along the lines of power.

At the beginning of Book 2, Zeus, fulfilling the promise he had earlier made to Thetis, sends a deceitful dream to Agamemnon with the misleading message that the time had come for the Greeks to attack the Trojans and assure victory for themselves (*Il.* 2.26-30):

"νῦν δ' ἐμέθεν ξύνες ὦκα· Διὸς δέ τοι ἄγγελός εἰμι,
ὃς σεῦ ἄνευθεν ἐὼν μέγα κήδεται ἠδ' ἐλεαίρει.
θωρῆξαί σε κέλευσε κάρη κομόωντας Ἀχαιοὺς
πανσυδίῃ· νῦν γάρ κεν ἕλοις πόλιν εὐρυάγυιαν
Τρώων."

"But now heed me, quickly. Because, you see, I am
the messenger of the god who, being afar, cares greatly for you
     and has compassion.
He orders you to arm the longhaired Achaeans
with all haste. For now you might capture the broad-streeted city
of Troy."

Agamemnon summons the Greek host in order to tell them about the dream's message, but first he decides to test the courage of the Greek warriors, by proposing that they leave and sail home:

"ἀλλ' ἄγεθ', ὡς ἂν ἐγὼ εἴπω, πειθώμεθα πάντες·
φεύγωμεν σὺν νηυσὶ φίλην ἐς πατρίδα γαῖαν
οὐ γὰρ ἔτι Τροίην αἱρήσομεν εὐρυάγυιαν."
                                        (*Il.* 2.139-141)

"But carry on as I shall declare. Let us all comply.
Let us flee with our ships to our dear fatherland
since we no longer shall capture broad-streeted Troy."

His test does not turn out according to his anticipation, and the fighting men begin to make a rush to their ships very eagerly indeed, as the following simile indicates (*Il.* 2.147-150):

ὡς δ' ὅτε κινήσῃ Ζέφυρος βαθὺ λήιον ἐλθών,
λάβρος ἐπαιγίζων, ἔπί τ' ἠμύει ἀσταχύεσσιν,
ὣς τῶν πᾶσ' ἀγορὴ κινήθη· τοὶ δ' ἀλαλητῷ
νῆας ἔπ' ἐσσεύοντο, ποδῶν δ' ὑπένερθε κονίη
ἵστατ' ἀειρομένη

And just as when far-reaching Zephyr stirs when it comes to the field,
storming violently, the field bows down with its ears of grain.
In the same way as these, the whole assembly was stirred and with a shouting,
they rushed to the ships and beneath their feet, a rising dust stood.

Odysseus manages to reassemble them in order to give a speech, and once they are seated again, Thersites stands up and tries to appeal to the warriors, that they should in fact abandon the war and desert Agamemnon. Before presenting Thersites' speech, let us consider the narrative introduction to him and to his words. It is strong, colorful, and it predisposes the audience unfavorably against him (*Il.* 2.211-224):

Ἄλλοι μέν ῥ' ἕζοντο, ἐρήτυθεν δὲ καθ' ἕδρας·
Θερσίτης δ' ἔτι μοῦνος ἀμετροεπὴς ἐκολώα,
ὃς ἔπεα φρεσὶ ᾗσιν ἄκοσμά τε πολλά τε ᾔδη,
μάψ, ἀτὰρ οὐ κατὰ κόσμον, ἐριζέμεναι βασιλεῦσιν,
ἀλλ' ὅ τι οἱ εἴσαιτο γελοίιον Ἀργείοισιν
ἔμμεναι· αἴσχιστος δὲ ἀνὴρ ὑπὸ Ἴλιον ἦλθε
φολκὸς ἔην, χωλὸς δ' ἕτερον πόδα· τὼ δέ οἱ ὤμω
κυρτώ, ἐπὶ στῆθος συνοχωκότε· αὐτὰρ ὕπερθε
φοξὸς ἔην κεφαλήν, ψεδνὴ δ' ἐπενήνοθε λάχνη.
ἔχθιστος δ' Ἀχιλῆι μάλιστ' ἦν ἠδ' Ὀδυσῆι·
ὀξέα κεκληγὼν λέγ' ὀνείδεα· τῷ δ' ἄρ' Ἀχαιοὶ

ἐκπάγλως κοτέοντο νεμέσσηθέν τ' ἐνὶ θυμῷ.

αὐτὰρ ὃ μακρὰ βοῶν 'Αγαμέμνονα νείκεε μύθῳ

And the others were sitting, restrained in their seats,
but Thersites alone without measure in his words kept on
  brawling,
he who in his mind knew many disorderly words,
in a reckless way and not according to proper arrangement, in
  order to vie with kings.
Moreover, he knew how to speak whatever seemed to be hilarious
  to the Argives.
But he was the ugliest man who came to Ilium:
bow-legged, lame of one foot, his two contorted shoulders
cramped together upon his chest, while on top,
his head was peaked and sparse hair grew thereon.
He was also the most hateful to Achilles especially, and to
  Odysseus.
For he kept quarreling with both. Then still against bright
  Agamemnon
he was screaming and heaping insults. And the Achaeans
were terribly angry at him and with one common sentiment they
  felt indignant.
But he shouting loudly was rebuking Agamemnon by means of
  his *mûthos.*

His entrance takes on a dramatic form, and he starts his performance
loudly (*Il.* 2.224). The use of μακρά 'far, long' with βιβάς and βιβάντα
'long-striding' is interesting if one takes Thersites as one who carries his
boldness too far. His loud voice and freakish appearance function as markers
for his character, as a kind of allegorical mask. In a few lines we have an
entire description of the character—outer and inner. He is ugly in an
unseemly way (*Il.* 2.216-219), he is inarticulate (*Il.* 2.212-214), mean-spirited
(*Il.* 214-215, 222-224), and most importantly he is hated by both Achilles and
Odysseus (*Il.* 2.220). The narrative introduction to Thersites then prepares the
audience to his speech, in which one might expect all these qualities to
become self-evident, but as we shall see they are not quite so. As a dramatic

scene, such description along with the following speeches could provide at least on one level a sort of relief from the main narrative at a critical point, when there still exists the possibility that the Greek warriors might leave the war at Troy. The introduction of Thersites as a grotesque figure at such a critical moment, his speech, and Odysseus' reply all seem to have facilitated a much needed release from tension. The warriors had been distressed but, by the end of the whole incident, they laugh.

The following is Thersites' verbal performance, his blame speech and what I treat as the first part of the mise-en-scène (*Il.* 2.225-242):

Thersites' Speech:

"'Ατρεΐδη, τέο δὴ αὖτ' ἐπιμέμφεαι ἠδὲ χατίζεις;
πλεῖαί τοι χαλκοῦ κλισίαι. πολλαὶ δὲ γυναῖκες
εἰσὶν ἐνὶ κλισίης ἐξαίρετοι. ἅς τοι Ἀχαιοὶ
πρωτίστῳ δίδομεν. εὖτ' ἄν πτολίεθρον ἕλωμεν.
ἦ ἔτι καὶ χρυσοῦ ἐπιδεύεαι. ὅν κέ τις οἴσει
Τρώων ἱπποδάμων ἐξ Ἰλίου υἷος ἄποινα,
ὅν κεν ἐγὼ δήσας ἀγάγω ἢ ἄλλος Ἀχαιῶν;
ἠὲ γυναῖκα νέην, ἵνα μίσγεαι ἐν φιλότητι.
ἥν τ' αὐτὸς ἀπονόσφι κατίσχεαι; οὐ μὲν ἔοικεν
ἀρχὸν ἐόντα κακῶν ἐπιβασκέμεν υἷας Ἀχαιῶν.
ὦ πέπονες, κάκ' ἐλέγχε', Ἀχαιΐδες, οὐκέτ' Ἀχαιοί,
οἴκαδέ περ σὺν νηυσὶ νεώμεθα, τόνδε δ' ἐῶμεν
αὐτοῦ ἐνὶ Τροίῃ γέρα πεσσέμεν, ὄφρα ἴδηται
ἤ ῥά τί οἱ χἠμεῖς προσαμύνομεν, ἠὲ καὶ οὐκί.
ὃς καὶ νῦν Ἀχιλῆα. ἕο μέγ' ἀμείνονα φῶτα.
ἠτίμησεν ἑλὼν γὰρ ἔχει γέρας. αὐτὸς ἀπούρας.
ἀλλὰ μάλ' οὐκ Ἀχιλῆι χόλος φρεσίν. ἀλλὰ μεθήμων
ἦ γὰρ ἄν, Ἀτρεΐδη, νῦν ὕστατα λωβήσαιο."

"Son of Atreus, with what indeed do you again find fault,
and what else do you need? Your lodges are
full of bronze and many women are in your tents,
the choicest ones, whom we the Achaeans
give to you first whenever we capture a city

What more gold do you still want, which some son of Ilium,
of horse-taming Troy, will bring as a ransom
for someone I, or another of the Achaeans, might capture?
Or do you need a young woman to join with in
    lovemaking
whom you keep away for yourself?[3] But it does not seem fitting
for a leader to bring the sons of the Achaeans into misery.
Oh, you weaklings, evil wretches, you are Achaean women, no
    longer men!
At any rate let us return home with our ships, let us leave him
alone to enjoy his prizes in Troy, so that he may see
whether indeed in some way we are helping him or not,
he who even now has dishonored Achilles, a man much better
    than he is.
For he himself having taken and seized Achilles' prize, still keeps
    it.
Yet there is not much anger in Achilles' heart, but he is remiss.
Isn't this the case, son of Atreus, that now for the last time you
    would commit an outrage?"

In his analysis of Thersites' speech, Edward Vodoklys argues that
Thersites is finally punished by Odysseus because he fails to use blame
speech formula, that his speech *qua* blame poetics was incorrectly
expressed.[4] Although this analysis accounts for the degree to which blame
poetry is formulaic in the *Iliad*, it does not account for other factors such as
Thersites' social position,[5] his challenge of a higher authority, his potentially
rebellious speech, his awareness of the various and true implications of the
war for Agamemnon (the king's pride, greed, lack of sound leadership, and
so on), and his extremely curious physical appearance. In fact, if one were to
bracket off all of these elements, leaving only the stylistic analysis of blame

---

3. I deviate here from Allen, preferring to read lines 229-233 as rhetorical
questions.

4. Vodoklys 1992:42-43.

5. Note that Thersites is given considerable space to speak, but he is the only such
character who lacks a patronymic. Even if he is of noble birth, this lack of patronymic
seems to indicate that, at least during his epic moment, he is someone with no name.

speech alone, and Thersites' violation of its conventions, then one could conceivably come to the conclusion that Thersites deserved ridicule and severe physical punishment in order that the very integrity of the poem *qua* epic formula not be violated.

For Richard Martin, Thersites' speech cannot be validated because, among other factors, he cannot recall his own deeds of war: "again, style for the hero is a total notion, a proportion of words and deeds."[6] Martin also draws our attention to the adjective ἀκριτόμυθε 'without judgment', which Odysseus uses to address Thersites in the beginning of his speech in 246. He makes a differentiation between ἀκριτόμυθε and the other insult words such as ἀμετροεπής 'without measure' in verse 212 above. From the root of the adjective *kri-* 'to judge', and its negation here, *akri-*, Martin suggests that Thersites is in fact unable to judge his own acts, and his acts are unable to be judged by whatever audience, because the audience "cannot perform the critical judgment necessary to validate his *mûthos*. It remains 'indeterminate' or 'undiscriminated'." Martin's conclusion is based on comparison with other passages in which the same root is used to indicate precisely the mental activity required for critical ability.[7] In passages, where one finds the opposite of critical ability, and where *mûthoi* are described as uncritical, "we can see the lack of connection between verbal behavior and martial performance."[8] In addition, Martin argues: "Thersites slurs his words" because his speech has a high ratio of correption and synizesis.[9] Again, the analysis of the passage in terms of style and diction is illuminating, but it does not completely explain how the other factors like Thersites' social

---

6. Martin 1989:111. See also *Il.* 9. 438-443, where Phoenix describes this balance between words and deeds in Achilles.
7. Martin 1989: 111; see *Il* 2.362 for *kri-*; *Il.* 7.337 for *akri-*.
8. For lack of connection between words and deeds, see *Il.* 2.796-797.
9. Martin 1989: 112-113. Note the instances of correption and synizesis in lines 225 (δὴ αὖτ ἐπιμέμφεαι ἠδέ); 227 (ἐξαίρετοι, ἅς τοι ᾽Αχαιοί); 229 (ἐπιδεύεαι, ὅν); 230 (᾽Ιλίου υἱός); 232 (μίσγεαι ἐν); 233 (κατίσχεαι; οὐ); 237 (αὐτοῦ ἐνί); 238 (καὶ οὐκί). Martin brings in Stephen Kelly's work (1974) on rate of correption for verses of plain narration in the *Iliad*, which are respectively 20 percent and 40 percent. From this Martin concludes that Thersites' speech "is quite literally 'without meter' in his performance."

position, his insubordinate speech, and so on, coincide with or differ from this construction of Thersites' character derived from his verbal style.[10]

Perhaps the most significant ambiguity in the passage is the extent to which the narrative level and Thersites' speech are not consonant with each other in their respective constructions of his character. Thersites' speech, however compromised by the narrative introduction to it, is succinct and coherent, and thus it counters the narrative's assertion in 212 and 213 that he is 'unmeasured' (ἀμετροεπής), and that his words are 'disorderly' (ἄκοσμα).[11] Thersites' speech is in fact a fairly elaborate piece of rhetoric divided in two parts. The first is his argument (225-233): that Agamemnon is greedy to the point of risking the warriors' lives. The second part (233-242), which itself has two sections, is his conclusion that the Achaeans should not risk their lives for such a rapacious and careless leader.

In the first part, Thersites substantiates his allegations with concrete examples of Agamemnon's greed, remarking how both the Achaeans and the Trojans are constantly filling his coffers and facilitating his sexual desires (227-233). He develops his arguments with a series of three rhetorical questions (225, 229, 232), to which he provides answers subordinated into his speech (227, 229, 231, 233). In the first section of the second part, Thersites more directly calls on the men to desert and leave Agamemnon (236). He starts by teasing the warriors and calling them women (235), which is doubtless an effective way of stirring them up. However, in the second section (237-238), he indirectly praises the warriors by pointing out that Agamemnon needs them, and here also he is elaborate in his language. Instead of directly telling the warriors that they are important, he uses the opportunity to rebuke Agamemnon further: "he will see whether we are

---

10. Martin 1989:110. To be sure, Martin does point out that there are other factors that contribute to Thersites' "flawed performance," namely his "class, . . . his demagogic tendency to generalize and speak for the entire contingent, while Achilles had spoken for himself alone; and his misrepresentation of the true tradition surrounding Achilles' anger." It seems obvious from Martin's analysis that these other factors only corroborate Thersites' flawed *mûthos*, but we should note that class, demagoguery, arrogance, and deceit are not necessarily related concepts, that they do not, by necessity, cause lack of verbal dexterity, and indeed neither is physical appearance a prerequisite of a good *mûthos*. Cf. *Il.* 3.42-43, where Paris, despite his good looks, elicits blame and laughter

11. See nn 5, 7.

helping him or not" 238).[12] Note moreover his use of irony in πεσσέμεν 'to enjoy' in 237.

Another significant structural feature in both the first and the second part of Thersites' speech is his switch between the use of first person plural and singular, on one hand, when he is clearly including himself among the warriors δίδομεν 'we give' (228), ἕλωμεν 'we seize' (228), νεώμεθα 'let us return' (236), ἐῶμεν 'let us leave him alone' (236), ἡμεῖς προσαμύνομεν 'we defend' (238), ἐγὼ . . . ἀγάγω 'I lead' (231), and the use of second person plural when he is addressing the warriors from the point of view of their self-appointed leader (ὦ πέπονες 'Oh you weaklings'[235]). Finally, in the last four verses, the second section of the second part, Thersites introduces the quarrel between Agamemnon and Achilles (239-240). His praise of Achilles is a crafty way to reinforce his rebuke of Agamemnon, and cannot be sincere, but it has the added function of echoing the theme of *Iliad* 1, and therefore of creating a sense of continuum between Books 1 and 2.[13] The diction in Thersites' passage is fairly uncomplicated, but the complex structure and the quick pace with which he moves from argument to conclusion seem to be neither disorderly nor unmeasured.

Gregory Nagy argues that the reason Thersites' speech is disorderly is because he misrepresents Achilles' pathos, by denying that Achilles is angry (241), and, consequently, he misrepresents the very subject of the *Iliad*. And yet, Thersites' praise of Achilles is underhanded and his intention seems to reinforce his reproach of Agamemnon. Although the narrative does inform us that Thersites was hateful to Achilles and to Odysseus (221-222), and earlier (214), that he was disposed to quarrel with kings,[14] such messages as the narrative provides seem dubious, and their function is not necessarily to tell the truth but to construct Thersites' character in a coherent way so that his speech may be anticipated and expected. Perhaps a more stable reading than

---

12. It is interesting to note the occurrence of indirect praise through the medium of blame. This does not seem surprising, considering the importance of alliances and rivalries in the context of a drawn out war. Nevertheless, Thersites' indirect praise of the fighting men highlights the lack of acknowledgment that the rank and file are a fundamental tool for the war.

13. See Mazon 1967:146-149 for further discussion of problems of transition between Books 1 and 2.

14. Compare the *Aithiopis*, where Achilles finally kills Thersites.

what the narrative offers would take into consideration that it is unlikely for Thersites to be unaware of the possible consequences, at least for himself, of his misrepresentation of Achilles' anger. He has already been shown to be capable of rationally considering what both his and the warriors' best interest might be, and he also seems conscious of the politics of war (225-233). Therefore his motivation for so blatantly misrepresenting Achilles' disposition is precisely that—a motivation, rather than the result of a thoughtless tirade as the narrative tells it.[15]

The fact that behind Thersites' motivation there may be a desire simply to instigate strife among the Greek chiefs does not alter the potentially subversive content of his speech, yet this plausible desire is what Vodoklys calls "non corrective in intent" because "[Thersites'] language is serious but he is intent on arousing τὸ γελοῖΐον 'the hilarious, the laughable thing, the ridiculous'. But again contrary to the narrative's characterization Thersites arouses anger (220, 222-223), not laughter in everyone probably because his *mûthos* cannot be as readily dismissed as the narrative would have us believe. Indeed given that a few verses earlier the warriors were so eager to sail back home, one could expect that at least some of the warriors would agree with Thersites' message, even if they despised the messenger. In fact, it is not until Odysseus confirms the unacceptability of challenging authority by punishing Thersites that the warriors respond by engaging in laughter and jests (272-277).

Thersites' grotesque character might be on one level parallel to a representation of the epic view of the multitude as a thoughtless herd, but considering that the Greek chieftains depended on this same multitude for their very own personal glory—a point raised by Thersites (238)—it is essential from the epic point of view to disassociate Thersites' arguments from the rest of the multitude. Since this disassociation was not neatly done by Thersites' social position alone,[16] it was effected by turning him into a freak and providing him with Odysseus as a kind of a circus animal trainer.

---

15. Kirk 1985:140. I agree with Kirk's assertion that "Thersites *ingeniously* (my italics) drags in the quarrel over Briseis."

16. Although Thersites' social position is an essential component of his role as the poor-man's anti-hero, it does not of course suffice in and of itself to discredit his speech. The very fact that Odysseus minds to engage with him should make this apparent.

Still, despite such portrayal, Thersites is given a well-reasoned speech, albeit one that transgresses stylistic convention. It is the internal clash between the pull to discredit Thersites versus Thersites' own words that makes his speech more poignant, his character more liminal, and the epic stance on the matter equivocal and richer.

The argument that Thersites violates the norms of blame expression and that he does not have a good record of deeds to back his speech are important for my own argument, which is that the character of Thersites represents dissent and rebellion on a social level, and this dissent is magnified into a caricature of both his verbal style[17] and his physical appearance. Nevertheless, as we have seen in Thersites speech, the caricature of his verbal style is not as successful as the caricature of his physique, so that the disparity between the narrative and the mise-en-scène becomes clearer. Ultimately Thersites' violation of formulaic modes of expression and his lack of heroic standard can be seen as a linguistic metaphor for the Homeric construction of rebellion, and whatever inconsistencies in such representation could in turn be seen as a reflection of a possible historical transition in traditional values by the time Thersites makes his way into the epic.

Similarly, the type of blame expression Odysseus uses, culminating in physical punishment, can be read as a representation of the Homeric view on the appropriate manner in which to manage rebellion, but one should also note that Odysseus' speech, just as with his character itself, has some unconventional elements from the point of view of epic poetic tradition, and in this sense Odysseus too can be said to violate accepted norms and conventions of blame speech, though he is not punished. After Thersites' speech Odysseus enters the scene announced by a vivid introduction, and accordingly he assumes a dramatic posture before his speech (*Il.* 2.243-245):

Ὣς φάτο νεικείων Ἀγαμέμνονα ποιμένα λαῶν,
Θερσίτης· τῷ δ' ὦκα παρίστατο δῖος Ὀδυσσεύς,
καί μιν ὑπόδρα ἰδὼν χαλεπῷ ἠνίπαπε μύθῳ·

---

17. Martin 1989:112-113n55. On the stylistic level and still on the matter of correption and synizesis, Martin states that "it may be that such slurring indicates another genre of speech; vowel elision, prefixation, and other linguistic markers can function this way."

Thus Thersites spoke, insulting Agamemnon, the shepherd of the
people.

But again right away stood brilliant Odysseus
and looking at him from under his brow he scolded him with a
harsh *mûthos*

Odysseus' Speech (*Il*. 2.245-263):

"Θερσῖτ' ἀκριτόμυθε, λιγύς περ ἐὼν ἀγορητής,
ἴσχεο, μηδ' ἔθελ' οἶος ἐριζέμεναι βασιλεῦσιν·
οὐ γὰρ ἐγὼ σέο φημὶ χερειότερον βροτὸν ἄλλον
ἔμμεναι, ὅσσοι ἅμ' Ἀτρεΐδῃς ὑπὸ Ἴλιον ἦλθον.
τῶ οὐκ ἂν βασιλῆας ἀνὰ στόμ' ἔχων ἀγορεύοις,
καί σφιν ὀνείδεά τε προφέροις νόστόν τε φυλάσσοις.
οὐδέ τί πω σάφα ἴδμεν ὅπως ἔσται τάδε ἔργα,
ἢ εὖ ἦε κακῶς νοστήσομεν υἷες Ἀχαιῶν.
τῶ νῦν Ἀτρεΐδῃ Ἀγαμέμνονι, ποιμένι λαῶν,
ἦσαι ὀνειδίζων, ὅτι οἱ μάλα πολλὰ διδοῦσιν
ἥρωες Δαναοί; σὺ δὲ κερτομέων ἀγορεύεις;
ἀλλ' ἔκ τοι ἐρέω, τὸ δὲ καὶ τετελεσμένον ἔσται·
εἴ κ' ἔτι σ' ἀφραίνοντα κιχήσομαι ὥς νύ περ ὧδε,
μηκέτ' ἔπειτ' Ὀδυσῆϊ κάρη ὤμοισιν ἐπείη,
μηδ' ἔτι Τηλεμάχοιο πατὴρ κεκλημένος εἴην,
εἰ μὴ ἐγώ σε λαβὼν ἀπὸ μὲν φίλα εἵματα δύσω,
χλαῖνάν τ' ἠδὲ χιτῶνα, τά τ' αἰδῶ ἀμφικαλύπτει
αὐτὸν δὲ κλαίοντα θοὰς ἐπὶ νῆας ἀφήσω
πεπλήγων ἀγορῆθεν ἀεικέσσι πληγῇσιν."

"Thersites, you of indiscriminate speech, though you are a clear-
sounding speaker,
hold back and do not wish to be the sort to fight with kings.
For I say that there is no other worse than you are,
of all that came to Ilium with the son of Atreus.
Therefore you should not hold your mouth up to speak
with kings, you had better not heap insults on them
and watch for a chance to return home.

In no way at all do we clearly know how these deeds will be,
whether well or badly will we sons of the Achaeans journey
home.
Therefore now against Agamemnon, son of Atreus, shepherd of
the people do you
sit there throwing abuses, saying that to him the Danaan heroes
give many things?
And do you keep on tormenting him and speaking?[18]
But I will say to you, and even this thing will be accomplished.
if again I find you playing the fool just as you are even now,
no longer then shall the head of Odysseus be on his shoulders
nor yet will I be called Telemachus' father
if I do not, taking you, strip off your clothing
and your cloak and your chiton which covers your genitals
and you yourself, I will send you off wailing to the swift ships
beaten from the assembly with unseemly blows."

As Kirk has noted, Odysseus' blame speech in response to Thersites "derives its force from its content and elaborate syntax rather than from any apparent urgency in the delivery."[19] Odysseus' speech is filled with apocalyptic threats, and it also becomes an opportunity for him to reassert his position in the social fabric of the epic by invoking his son, and thereby establishing a lineage, which Thersites so obviously lacks. But note that he identifies himself in terms of his descendant and not his ancestral lineage, a fact that perhaps reinforces his status as the man of tomorrow who depends fully on what he is able to accomplish and on his ability as a speaker, rather than simply deriving his strength from a noble origin. Odysseus' words and behavior also shed light on the liminal position he occupies insofar as his status as a hero is concerned. Since Agamemnon is silent in the face of Thersites' invective, Odysseus becomes the king's self-appointed defender—a neat parallel to Thersites as spokesperson for the warriors—and as such not only is the hierarchical gap between Odysseus and Agamemnon

---

18. I deviate here from Allen, preferring to read verses 254-256 as rhetorical questions.

19. Kirk 1985:143.

made clear, but also the difference in character between the two figures, Odysseus being the one with the more appropriate moral disposition to quarrel with the rank and file. Indeed, Odysseus seems to be the perfect middleman, mediating between the multitude and Agamemnon. He is able to speak the language of the multitude: he has, as it were, street-wisdom, and he is beloved for it. In fact, the part of the interaction between the two characters that pleased the warriors the most was Odysseus' physical punishment of Thersites. The addition of some spectacle helped relax the warriors, and it is clear that they will no longer abandon the war (*Il.* 2.265-270):

Ὣς ἄρ' ἔφη, σκήπτρῳ δὲ μετάφρενον ἠδὲ καὶ ὤμω
πλῆξεν ὁ δ' ἰδνώθη, θαλερὸν δέ οἱ ἔκπεσε δάκρυ
σμῶδιξ δ' αἱματόεσσα μεταφρένου ἐξυπανέστη
σκήπτρου ὕπο χρυσέου ὁ δ' ἄρ' ἕζετο τάρβησέν τε,
ἀλγήσας δ' ἀχρεῖον ἰδὼν ἀπομόρξατο δάκρυ.
οἱ δὲ καὶ ἀχνύμενοί περ ἐπ' αὐτῷ ἡδὺ γέλασσαν·

Thus then he spoke and with his scepter he struck his back
and shoulders and he was bent down and a warm tear escaped
him.
And a bloody weal raised from his back
from the golden scepter. And he then sat down and was terrified
and grieving and looking helpless he wiped off his tear.
But the others, though they were distressed laughed heartily at
him.

Odysseus then manages to restore order, but, ironically, this is accomplished with the inadvertent cooperation of Thersites, whose rebellion turns out to function as a catalyst for the renewal of order. Thersites' accidental corroboration toward this renewal of order comes not only from the spectacle of his beating, but from the kind of antagonism he elicits in all. According to my argument this antagonism must be explained not only by what the narrative tells us about him, but, more importantly, by what it does not, namely the way in which Thersites positions himself ambivalently against authority (Odysseus/Agamemnon). He aligns himself with the warriors, but at the same time he elevates himself above them by playing the role of their self-appointed leader. In addition he plays the role of the common man, but, as some commentators have noted, his arguments reflect those of Achilles. His daring to call on desertion could be seen as terribly audacious, if not courageous, yet he quickly becomes meek once Odysseus strikes the scepter against him. Moreover, judging from Odysseus' own acknowledgment of his speech and given the actual space granted for his *mûthos*, one might credit Thersites' desire to compete with heroes in words, since, as Martin has pointed out, he cannot measure up to any in deeds.[20]

It is the combination of Thersites' position as an outsider, but an outsider manqué, and Odysseus' liminal position as a neoteric hero that engenders the quick inversion from chaos (147-159) to order (270-276). To put it differently, there is a momentary inversion of the status quo, when the voice of dissent is given a brief, but substantial, space to be expressed, only to be cast in the most negative light, that is, as the product of a lonely and freakish mind. Thersites is in fact the only one who stood up to speak, and Odysseus' rebuke further isolated him, so that dissent quickly changed from the mass movement of the warriors to an isolated incident. Such a social dimension in this passage does not neatly depict the dichotomy "ruler vs. subordinate" between Thersites and Odysseus, but, more significantly, it reveals the social function and representation of the multitude, of what is popular in the epic, and these elements should be brought to bear on the analysis of blame poetry as used by these two characters, especially when one considers them as two different versions of the same nonaristocratic world. Thersites is the obvious example of this popular role, but, with Odysseus, this other world becomes clearer through his position vis-à-vis Agamemnon and his ability to get down and dirty with the fighting men. Such a social dimension then reveals the unstable position of both characters, a factor that would be harder to discern through stylistic and linguistic analysis alone.

Thersites' main problem is that he does not fit in any way the heroic ideology of the epic world he inhabits. Even his rebellion is at variance with the heroic ideology of dissent (compare the way in which Achilles is also a rebel). His speech also falls outside the proper heroic mode of expression, as does his ancestry, or lack thereof, and, of course, his physical appearance. Thersites is stripped of any credibility before he even speaks, and this is why

---

20. Note Thersites' claim of what he has done in verse 231 of his speech.

it is remarkable that his speech should contain the degree of truth it does in the face of his characterization. By the same token, Odysseus' main problem is to gain credibility at every step of the way, and this is why he must get involved with the kind of man Agamemnon would not, and why he must not only consider the morale of the warriors, but also speak their language and be liked by them. The confluence of such elements drives both characters to perform the inversion from chaos to order, and ultimately to reinforce the status quo, so that both outsider and middleman are incorporated into the social order.[21]

Looking at Aristotle's formulation of blame poetry, Nagy restates it this way: "blame poetry has a potential for the comic element . . . But blame poetry itself is more inclusive and thus cannot be equated with comedy."[22]

---

21. Lincoln 1989:142-143 presents an illuminating study on discourse and society. In Chapter 9, titled "The Dialectics of Symbolic Inversion," he analyzes the phenomenon of symbolic inversion as a tool for the dominant culture to reinforce its own ideology concerning power. One of the examples he uses comes from Livy 2.32.9-11. This is the account of the first secession by the Roman plebs (c. 494 BCE) and the "Apologue of Menenius Agrippa." According to Livy, Menenius Agrippa, a man of plebeian origin, who had risen in rank and thus was the perfect intermediary sort of man, managed to persuade the plebs to abandon their secession by means of a story, which Lincoln goes on to analyze as a successful symbolic inversion for the benefit of the patricians. Menenius Agrippa created an analogy based on the relationship between the patricians and the people, where the people were equated with the parts of the body, and the patricians with the belly. This was his first inversion, since in the traditional discourse the patricians were always identified as the head. Menenius then gained the sympathy of the plebs who thought that the patricians were indeed this insatiable belly for whom the rest of the body had to work. Once this inversion was established, Menenius proceeded once again to invert the symbols, so that now the belly gained prominence over the rest of the body, because, according to his story, the parts of the body that revolted against the belly had in the end wasted away, and therefore it was clear that without the belly, the rest of the body could not live. The relevance of Lincoln's study for this essay is of course the importance of discourse in the manipulation of power, and such discourse might be the most effective if brought out by someone in such an intermediary position as Menenius and likewise Odysseus. See also Lincoln's study of professional wrestling and the importance of symbolic discourse there. Lincoln shows how, among other things, the "heroes" of wrestling invariably must have a manager who is articulate in his speeches.

22. Nagy 1979:256. Furthermore, Nagy observes that this potentially comic aspect of blame poetry does not make the Epos comical, but rather, it ridicules the one engaging in blame expression—in this case, Thersites, and I add Odysseus.

This wider inclusiveness of blame poetry underscores the ambiguity of the passage, so that it is possible to doubt whether the epic's intention is simply to ridicule Thersites. The passage seems to be too self-referential and emphatic for that, especially when one considers that its absence would prove no crucial loss to the plot or to character development. In fact, if Thersites' speech and the following response from Odysseus were to be removed, there would be a rather smooth transition between *Il.* 2.210 and the second half of verse 282, that is, between the chronologically natural order of events from the time when the warriors reassemble to Odysseus' address to them. After all, the *Iliad* is not about Thersites or anti-heroes.[23] Thersites' character is intriguing because, among other things, it is developed in such a brief time frame only to be dropped forever.

Nevertheless, as it has been observed, blame poetry has the potential for the comic element, and, according to Aristotle's formulation of comedy, this mode of expression pertains to the world of the base, because laughter belongs to the universe of baseness, and therefore in blame poetry, the one engaging in blame must also be base.[24] It follows, then, from such a formulation that Odysseus must be base, despite his relatively superior social status, because he engages not only in blame poetry but also in physical violence.[25] Indeed, if Thersites is ridiculed, so must Odysseus be and also the soldiers—Odysseus for engaging in base behavior, and the warriors for

---

23. To be sure, Achilles is a special kind of an anti-hero.

24. Nagy 1979:257. Nagy points out, however, that some passages in the *Iliad* do not conform to this Aristotelian formulation.

25. Ste. Croix 1981:413 writes that "the aristocratic society for which the Homeric poems were composed would have regarded Odysseus' brutal treatment of Thersites as perfectly right and proper, and characteristic of a great man." While I believe that Ste. Croix's class analysis of Thersites and Odysseus is important, it suffers from the lack of a literary and anthropological dimension, from which one could infer that the aristocracy would probably have laughed, just as the warriors did, and that in this the lines may not have been so rigidly discerned as to present a fundamental distinction between what is comical for the noble and for the average man. Recalling Bakhtin, it is important to remember that according to him, the division between the ridiculous and the sublime as correlatives of the "lower" and the "upper" class was not characteristic of the archaic period, nor of the classical period. Rather, it was a product of the Middle Ages. Nevertheless, one must reconcile Aristotle's formulation, that the ridiculous equals the base, and the idea that laughter is the stuff of the world of baseness, and therefore it would seem that the concept itself was not a product of the Middle Ages, but rather it might have been merely formalized during this period.

enjoying the circus. In fact, immediately following Odysseus' punishment of Thersites, the warriors begin to banter with one another, confirming thereby not only that their very recent attempt to desert Agamemnon is forgotten, but, more importantly, they confirm Odysseus' authority (*Il.* 2.271-278):

> ὧδε δέ τις εἴπεσκεν ἰδὼν ἐς πλησίον ἄλλον
> "ὢ πόποι, ἦ δὴ μυρί' Ὀδυσσεὺς ἐσθλὰ ἔοργε
> βουλάς τ' ἐξάρχων ἀγαθὰς πόλεμόν τε κορύσσων
> νῦν δὲ τόδε μέγ' ἄριστον ἐν Ἀργείοισιν ἔρεξεν,
> ὃς τὸν λωβητῆρα ἐπεσβόλον ἔσχ' ἀγοράων.
> οὔ θήν μιν πάλιν αὖτις ἀνήσει θυμὸς ἀγήνωρ
> νεικείειν βασιλῆας ὀνειδείοις ἐπέεσσιν."

And each looking at his neighbor was speaking thus:
Oh my, Odysseus has already accomplished a myriad of noble things,
bringing in good counsels and arming for the war.
But now this is by far the best he has done,
who, speaking in the assembly held back this word-flinging slanderer.
Not indeed again will his manly courage spur him to insult kings with offensive words.

The warriors' talk could thus form a third speech within the narrative, but the function of their side-discussion in the verses above comes closer to a comic chorus voicing their delight in raillery than it does to a speech proper for it to be considered a third part of the mise-en-scène. This is why their role seems more properly defined as the audience for the mise-en-scène, but it is also possible to see them as the substitute audience for the epic poem itself. If one considers the first alternative (the warriors as the audience of the mise-en-scène), their portrayal is clearly negative, and they appear as an easily goaded flock of sheep. This portrayal would justify their need of a leader, and the implication of Thersites asking them to abandon Agamemnon is extremely dangerous. In this case, the Homeric view of the multitude seems to acknowledge that their misperception of reality is both advantageous and dangerous. Ironically, though, by presenting the multitude in this light,

Odysseus' *mûthos* becomes by default less impressive than it might be in its contrast to that of Thersites. In the second alternative (the warriors as the poem's audience), the narrative would seem to be conscious of the real audience's level of engagement in the story being told. The *epos* is presenting the audience with the tension of possible subversion of order (relying on the audience's suspension of disbelief), but in the end order is restored and the audience can laugh, before the real battle begins.

It appears, then, that the ambiguities I have pointed out in this passage would come not only from its structure alone, divided into these two levels (narrative and speeches) in tension with one another, but also from the unmistakably unstable position of the two characters involved. There is no doubt that a dichotomy is being set up between Odysseus and Thersites along the lines of good and evil, hero and non-hero, effective *mûthos* and non-effective *mûthos*, but, as I hope to have shown, the opposition of Thersites and Odysseus is undermined by other factors that destabilize this otherwise neat distinction. Consider for example the narrative description of both Thersites and his verbal skills before we hear his own speech—a description that directs, even instructs, the audience about how to receive Thersites' *mûthos*. Consider as well the inconsistency between the narrative description of his speech-making ability and his actual speech—the most flagrant being the fact that he provokes anger rather than laughter. Note Odysseus' liminal position—above the warriors as their leader, but below kings. Note also Thersites and Odysseus as two different roles of the same performance and, ultimately, but almost by default, advancing the same cause. Think of the restoration of order and of the status quo through chaos, and especially consider the possible historical transition in heroic ideology whereby an important space is created for someone like Odysseus, whom one could call a hustler. Finally, although outside the scope of this essay proper, it is interesting to remember that Book 2 opens with a dream carrying a deceitful message, the purpose of which was to cause much destruction to the Greek host, so that the withdrawal of Achilles—the other sort of rebel—might be deeply felt, and Agamemnon might regret his insult against the epic hero. Although order was achieved through the momentary chaos engendered by Thersites and Odysseus, chaos once again is to come to the Greek host in battle.

4

Homeric Fictions: *Pseudo*-Words in Homer

Miriam Carlisle

Homeric vocabulary includes a variety of words that indicate deception: ἀπατάω *apataó*, ἠπεροπεύω *êperopeuó*, and ψεύδομαι *pseudomai* are a few examples. Such words are translated into English as 'trick', 'deceive', and 'lie'—with all of the moral implications attaching to these words. The question arises whether Homeric poetry uses these words with the same moral overtones and whether they are interchangeable or if each of them indicates a different type or degree of deception. In this discussion, I will focus on one category of Homeric deception—that which is designated by words with a *pseud*-root. If the use of a *pseudo*- word indicates a lie, what is the nature of that lie? What is the standard of truth against which the lie is measured? What are the intent of the speaker and the result of the telling? When, and if at all, do "lies" in the moral sense become "fictions" in a generic sense? When, and if at all, does Homeric vocabulary recognize the difference? Are there any implications for our understanding of the poems?

Louise Pratt writes of Greek *pseudea* ψεύδεα that they "do not necessarily imply that the speaker deliberately seeks to deceive the hearer; they denote only the objective falsity of what is said."[1] Although this formulation might be the case for *pseudo*-words in later usage, which reflects legal and philosophical discourse, it does not apply to Homeric usage. Examination of *pseudo*-words in context suggests that Homeric *pseudea* depart from Pratt's scenario in three fundamental ways: first, the "objective falsity" of Homeric *pseudea* is measured not against any historical reality but only against the reality established by the main narrative, usually in the narrator's own voice; second, the speaker of Homeric *pseudea* intends to deceive, at least to the

---

1. Pratt 1993:56.

extent that the speaker of an oath, omen, promise, or narrative account designated by a *pseudo*-word signals awareness that the promised outcome or reported event is not consistent with events as they will play out, or have played out, in the reality established by the main narrative; third, at least in the case of narrative *pseudea*, the speaker intends to gain an advantage or win a prize as a result of the telling. Forethought is therefore implied and attaches at least as much to the strategic advantage of the telling as to its artfulness. Indeed, these tales may be marked by what seems to be their lack of artfulness[2] despite the fact that most of them are transmitted in some kind of narrative frame and often to the delight of the listener who recognizes the *pseudea* as fictional narrative intended to divert or even entertain.

Gregory Nagy has explored a phenomenon by which the "myth-making mind can become critical of variants in myth."[3] I suggest that a similar phenomenon operates in Homeric poetry where *pseudo*-words applied to narrative sequences tag material deemed inappropriate for inclusion for one of two reasons: they transmit either a variant version of material accepted elsewhere by the text or "low" material not usually accommodated by epic transmission—material more suited to prose genres like folk tales, wanderer's tales, and nursery stories, that is, material that cannot claim an identifiable and reliable source. Not only do the speakers of narrative *pseudea* vie for some sort of advantage in an agonistic setting but even the material itself seems to compete for the ultimate prize of approval by, and inclusion in, the Homeric poetic tradition.

Common Factors in Homeric *Pseudo*-Words

Pseudo-words occur twenty-six times in our received text of Homeric poetry, seventeen times in the *Iliad*[4] and nine in the *Odyssey*.[5] Their use can be broken down into four general categories of association: an omen at *Iliad* 2.349,[6] four oaths or promises, also in the *Iliad*,[7] and nineteen instances of

---

2. See Pache (this volume).
3. Nagy 1990a:57.
4. *Il.* 2.81, 349; 4.235, 404; 5.635; 6.163; 7.352; 9.115; 10.534; 12.164; 15.159; 18.46; 19.107; 21.276; 23.576; 24.222, 261.
5. *Od.* 3.20, 328; 4.140; 11.366; 14.125, 296, 365, 387; 19.203.
6. *Il.* 2.349.

"false" information comprising part of a narrative.[8] The last group is the focus of this discussion, but it can be said of all these categories that the ultimate arbiter of what is *pseudo-*, and what is not, is the main narrative. All omens and oaths to which *pseudo-*words are applied are judged to be *pseudo*, or not, only as measured against the reality established by the larger narrative.[9] Omens and oaths fulfilled in the narrative are not "false," not *pseudo-*, but, when events seem to be running contrary to expectations based on oaths or promises, characters worry that those oaths and promises will prove to be "false," and a *pseudo-*word is used. When the same standard is applied to narrative sequences characterized by *pseudo-*words, the same rule holds: narrative accounts corroborated elsewhere in the main narrative are not characterized by a *pseudo-*word while those not verified elsewhere are suspect. This pattern holds whether the narrative is the repetition of a message, the report of an experience like an ἀγών *agôn* 'a contest or struggle' of some kind, the report of a dream, or the telling of a tale. A closer examination will demonstrate that in all of these instances, the applicability of a *pseudo-*word is measured by the yardstick of the overall narrative, not any historical or moral reality that might exist outside or beyond the narrative. Hereafter, therefore, in this discussion, "false" will indicate information not verified elsewhere in the narrative, usually by the narrator.

Twelve of the nineteen Homeric narrative sequences designated by a *pseudo-*word share the common element that they are, or refer to, fictionalized accounts contrived and spoken in some kind of agonistic setting where the speaker intends to gain an advantage.[10] In the remaining narrative sequences, where no contest is involved and no prize at stake, a negated

---

7. *Il.* 2.349; 4.235; 7.352; 19.107.

8. *Il.* 2.81; 4.404; 5.635; 6.163; 9.115; 12.164; 15.159; 21 276; 23.576; 24.222, 261. *Od.* 3.20, 328; 11.366; 14.125, 296, 365, 387; 19.203.

9. Two instances of *pseudo-*words elude classification: the name of the nymph Ἀψευδής *Apseudês* in the catalogue at *Il* 18.46; the exclamation of surprise uttered by Nestor at *Il.* 10.534 and Helen at *Od.* 4.140, which I count as one in my total of twenty-six (ψεύσομαι, ἦ ἔτυμον ἐρέω; κέλεται δέ με θυμός 'Shall I make something up or shall I tell it like it is? My heart gives me an order'. All of these, however, can be included in the set of definitions, which assume that communication designated by a *pseudo-*word will contradict the evidence of the narrative.

10. *Il* 4.404; 5.635; 6.163; 9.115. *Od.* 3.20, 328; 11.366; 14.125, 296, 365, 387; 19.203.

pseudo-word designates 'not false'. It is worth noting that ψεύδομαι *pseudomai* is a middle verb and, as such, by definition, implies the self-interest of its subject. The subject of a middle verb is personally involved in its action and is by implication the beneficiary of any advantage incurred by that action. A middle form is not appropriate if the subject undertakes to do something for the primary benefit of someone else, which is why the unique active form ψευστήσεις *pseustêseis* at *Iliad* 19.107 seems odd but is notionally appropriate.

Iliadic Pseudo-History

It can be said in a general sense that all Iliadic *pseudea* are spoken in an agonistic setting, given that the entire *Iliad* is the account of a cataclysmic *agôn* 'contest, struggle' embracing a multitude of lesser *agônes*. The immediate contexts of narrative *pseudea* are agonistic as well. These include an exhortation to fight, a shouting match, and an athletic competition. In each case, there is a reward of some kind at stake, which the speaker hopes to win because of his *pseudea*. It may seem obvious that lies are told in order to gain an advantage, but an Iliadic speaker of *pseudea* doesn't just tell a lie like "the Trojans are retreating" when they are not; he tells a story whose telling is expected to bring a desired reward. Moreover, the stories themselves, or versions of the stories, seem to be in some kind of competition.

At *Iliad* 4.370-400, Agamemnon rebukes Diomedes and Sthenelos for holding back from the battle by telling a story that illustrates the courage and proficiency in battle of Diomedes' father, Tydeus, a hero from the past of whom Agamemnon admits to having no personal knowledge. Agamemnon acknowledges that "they say" is his source of information on Tydeus (*Il.* 4.374-375):

> <u>ὡς φάσαν</u> οἵ μιν ἴδοντο πονεύμενον· οὐ γὰρ ἔγωγε
> ἤντησ' οὐδὲ ἴδον· περὶ δ' ἄλλων φασὶ γενέσθαι.

> <u>So they say</u> who saw him toiling; for I myself neither
> met him nor saw him but they say he was beyond others.

Agamemnon wants Diomedes and Sthenelos and their companions to fight, but, instead of direct exhortation, he uses narrative to construct a standard of comparison against which Diomedes and Sthenelos are intended to feel shamed into performing better, into competing with the standard as narrated. At the end of his story Agamemnon says (*Il.* 4.399-400):

τοῖος ἔην Τυδεὺς Αἰτώλιος· ἀλλὰ τὸν υἱὸν
γείνατο εἷο χέρεια μάχῃ, ἀγορῇ δέ τ᾽ ἀμείνω.

Such was Aitolian Tydeus. But he begat a son worse
than himself in battle, but better in the assembly.

Diomedes' companion, Sthenelos, shouts back rebuking Agamemnon for telling *pseudea* in this account with its conclusion that the previous generation was better at fighting (*Il.* 4.404):

Ἀτρεΐδη, μὴ ψεύδε᾽ ἐπιστάμενος σάφα εἰπεῖν

Son of Atreus, do not tell false versions when you know
how to tell the story correctly.

It is not immediately clear from the text whether *pseudea* refers to the account of Tydeus' actions or the conclusion that Tydeus was more courageous than his son is, but I think it must encompass both. If the story is unreliable, then any conclusion based on it would be unreliable as well. This story belongs to the realm of the unreliable by virtue of the fact that it is not verifiable by any character living within the time of the main narrative: it seems to come from a stock of traditional material about Tydeus, not from Agamemnon's own knowledge. It is a kind of type-story of the sort that accumulates around heroes and legendary figures but that can no longer be verified by anyone who was present at the time. Homeric poetry abounds with hero tales. Richard Martin has suggested that the term μῦθος *mûthos* is used in Homeric poetry for such stories when they are told by heroes as remembered events.[11] I suggest that *pseudo*-words indicate this sort of type-

11. Martin 1989:47.

story when it is not a "remembered event" but one whose source cannot be identified, whose authority cannot be guaranteed, and/or which contains versions of epic material contradicted by the larger poem. Regardless of any objective falsity, it is their diversion from the narrative reality of the present poem that makes them false, makes them fiction rather than history for the characters within the poem and perhaps for the audience as well. We do not have any poems of the Theban Cycle against which to measure the differing versions in this exchange but the point here is that Agamemnon flings out a story in order to win a result, and he accomplishes his purpose. Diomedes understands and acknowledges the purpose of the story, awarding to Agamemnon the benefit he had sought. Diomedes returns to the fray, exhorting his companions to do the same. He says (*Il.* 4.412-418):

> τέττα, σιωπῇ ἧσο, ἐμῷ δ' ἐπιπείθεο μύθῳ·
> οὐ γὰρ ἐγὼ νεμεσῶ Ἀγαμέμνονι, ποιμένι λαῶν,
> ὀτρύνοντι μάχεσθαι ἐϋκνήμιδας Ἀχαιούς·
> τούτῳ μὲν γὰρ κῦδος ἅμ' ἔψεται, εἴ κεν Ἀχαιοὶ
> Τρῶας δῃώσωσιν ἕλωσί τε Ἴλιον ἱρήν,
> τούτῳ δ' αὖ μέγα πένθος Ἀχαιῶν δῃωθέντων.
> ἀλλ' ἄγε δὴ καὶ νῶϊ μεδώμεθα θούριδος ἀλκῆς.

> Be quiet, my friend, and obey my word.
> For I will not blame Agamemnon, shepherd of the host,
> for rousing the well-greaved Achaeans to fight.
> For glory will follow in company with this man, if ever
>   the Achaeans
> slay the Trojans and take sacred Ilion,
> but great sorrow will accompany him if the Achaeans
>   are slain.
> But come, let us concentrate on our eager battle prowess.

Agamemnon's *pseudea* have no known source and are never adopted by the poem's narrator. They seem to be in competition with some other version of the same material known to the characters involved, and they are told in an *agôn*, a contest or struggle, for the purpose of winning a hoped-for result.

Another *pseudo*-word turns up in another scene involving Diomedes. It occurs in a story embedded within the exchange of stories between Diomedes and Glaukos in *Iliad* 6. This is one of the few Homeric instances where such a word applies to the speech of a woman, Anteia, who is said to have told a lying story in order to get what she wants. The story is told that after Bellerophon had spurned her sexual advances, she avenged her shame by telling her husband that Bellerophon had tried to seduce her (*Il.* 6.163-165):

ἡ δὲ ψευσαμένη Προῖτον βασιλῆα προσηύδα·
"τεθναίης, ὦ Προῖτ', ἢ κάκτανε Βελλεροφόντην,
ὅς μ' ἔθελεν φιλότητι μιγήμεναι οὐκ ἐθελούσῃ."

Telling a false story, she spoke to the king Proitos.
"Would you die, Proitos, or kill Bellerophon who
wanted to have sex with me although I was unwilling."

In this instance, no full narrative is told but a narrative scenario is evoked by this short allusion, a scenario of attempted seduction, humiliation, revenge. We need only conjure the character of Euripides' Phaedra to appreciate the narrative possibilities of these few lines. Anteia's lie is a "typical" narrative response for a woman spurned and one of the few weapons available for a female character in an ancient literary setting to use against a male adversary. By telling this type of false story, a female character can prevail over a male opponent, can deal a destructive, even fatal, blow.

The contest between Anteia and Bellerophon is a struggle of will, not weapons, but is made more interesting by the larger frame within which it is told, which is the exchange between Glaukos and Diomedes in the midst of battle, a scene that Calvert Watkins (following Wackernagel) includes among Homeric passages that conform to old Indo-European narrative patterns (*Il.* 6.152-153).[12]

ἔστι πόλις Ἐφύρη μυχῷ Ἄργεος ἱπποβότοιο,
ἔνθα δὲ Σίσυφος ἔσκεν, ὃ κέρδιστος γένετ' ἀνδρῶν.

---

12. Watkins 1995:25.

> There is a city, Ephyre, in the heart of horse-pasturing Argos;
> there lived Sisyphos, craftiest of men.

Watkins quotes this line as his first example of "a widespread stylistic feature of (typically prose) folk tales, a text-initial, existential form of the verb 'to be' introducing the typical person or place."[13] Elsewhere he says of this line, "Stylistically we have left epic narrative behind, and we are in the domain of storytelling."[14] The story of Anteia's lie, employing stylistic elements of traditional folk tale and type story, is repeated in the context of a larger traditional story, which is itself told as part of a contest between two adversaries in battle, Glaukos and Diomedes. These two figures exchange armor and stories that they understand to represent events of the real history of the narrative world that they inhabit.[15] No *pseudo*-word is applied to either of their stories: only Anteia's story is *pseud*-, false, because it diverges from the facts adopted by the larger narrative that frames it, Glaukos' genealogy. Anteia's lie is part of a story already in the realm of legend when Glaukos tells it. It has apparently been passed down in some way but is not attributable to any authoritative source. This little story has been imported into the epic world of the *Iliad* but is not in itself Iliadic material.

Another battle exchange involving a narrative *pseudo*-word occurs at *Iliad* 5.634-646 between Tlepolemos, son of Herakles (making him the grandson of Zeus), and Sarpedon, son of Zeus. Tlepolemos taunts Sarpedon with a comparison to legendary figures of an earlier time. This is the same strategy employed by Agamemnon in exhorting Diomedes, but Tlepolemos uses it as a vaunting strategy:

> ψευδόμενοι δέ σέ φασι Διὸς γόνον αἰγιόχοιο
> εἶναι, ἐπεὶ πολλὸν κείνων ἐπιδεύεαι ἀνδρῶν
> οἳ Διὸς ἐξεγένοντο ἐπὶ προτέρων ἀνθρώπων·

---

13. Watkins 1995:25.
14. Watkins 1995:357.
15. Watkins 1995:387 discusses who wins what advantage in this exchange of armor in his observations on "potlach."

ἀλλ' οἷόν τινά φασι βίην Ἡρακληείην
εἶναι, ἐμὸν πατέρα θρασυμέμνονα θυμολέοντα·
(*Il* 5.635-639)

<u>They tell false versions</u> who say you are the son of aegis-bearing
Zeus,
since you fall far short of those men
who were begotten of Zeus upon former generations of men;
but such a man, they say, was Herakles the strong,
my father, bold spirited and with the heart of a lion.

The source of the stories about Sarpedon's divine ancestry is attributed to "they say" just as Agamemnon's story about Tydeus had been. Tlepolemos is suggesting that the source for this story is also not known, not reliable, and not acceptable. This too appears to be a "type" of story from some larger stock of traditional material that Tlepolemos chooses to reject—making ψευδόμενοι *pseudomenoi*[16] an appropriate label for those transmitting what Tlepolemos would like to consider an unacceptable version. His use of the term suggests that the story itself cannot be verified, nor can its source, at least within the narrative world of this poem. But Tlepolemos is wrong: the source of the story might be beyond knowing, and it might sound like a typical tale—but it is consistent with the narrative reality of the larger poem. This very scene had opened with the epic narrator's observation of the encounter between Sarpedon and Tlepolemos (*Il.* 5.630-631):

οἱ δ' ὅτε δὴ σχεδὸν ἦσαν ἐπ' ἀλλήλοισιν ἰόντες,
<u>υἱός θ' υἱωνός τε Διὸς</u> νεφεληγερέταο...

These, when they had come close against one another,
<u>the son and the son of the son of Zeus </u>the cloud-gatherer...

The narrator again corroborates the relationship in Book 16 as Zeus mourns the imminent death of Sarpedon at the hands of Patroklos:

---

16. Further discussion of this line is in the section on "Pseudo-Respectability."

64   Part I: Multigeneric Homer

αἱματοέσσας δὲ ψιάδας κατέχευεν ἔραζε
παῖδα φίλον τιμῶν, τόν οἱ Πάτροκλος ἔμελλε
φθίσειν ἐν Τροίῃ ἐριβώλακι τηλόθι πάτρης.
(Il. 16.459-460)

And he (Zeus) poured out bloody tears on the ground,
honoring his dear son, whom Patroklos was about to
kill in fertile Troy far from his father.

Zeus himself refers to Sarpedon as 'my own son, shining Sarpedon' (υἱὸν
ἐμὸν Σαρπηδόνα δῖον, Il. 15.67). There is no doubt in the larger narrative
that Zeus is the father of Sarpedon, but there are signs of competing traditions
about Sarpedon, especially about his maternal lineage. While giving his own
genealogy in Iliad 6, Glaukos declares that Zeus and Laodameia are the
parents of Sarpedon (Il. 6.198-199), and the catalogue of ships names
Sarpedon as ruler of the Lycians (Il. 2.876). Outside the Iliad, however, the
Hesiodic Eoiai make Sarpedon a king of Crete, son of Zeus and Europa and
brother of Rhadamanthus and Minos.[17] The Iliad names only Rhadamanthus
and Minos as offspring of this union. The word pseudomenoi at 5.635 does
not indicate the objective falsity of Sarpedon's divine parentage as much as
the refusal of the character Tlepolemos to accept a particular version that puts
Sarpedon one step closer to Zeus than Tlepolemos himself.[18] It may also
indicate his low opinion of what may be a non-hexameter story tradition,
perhaps even one originating in Asia Minor (Lycia). In any case, Tlepolemos
spurns the version adopted by the main narrative, and he also loses his life to
Sarpedon at the end of this encounter.

Before his demise, Tlepolemos had gone on to tell a story about an earlier
conquest of Troy by his own father, Herakles. This account, although it is a
hero tale that might seem to qualify as "legendary," is not labeled with a
pseudo-word because it is verified within the narrative world of the poem.

---

17. Scholia to Il. 12.292. This is also the tradition adopted by Aeschylus for the
Kares, fr. 99 R. See Gantz 1993:210-211.
18. This Tlepolemos leads the contingent from Rhodes and is fighting on the side
of the Achaeans (Il. 2.657). He is not to be confused with another Tlepolemos, a
Lycian character who is killed by Patroklos in Il. 16.416.

Sarpedon himself verifies the story in his retort. He shouts back to Tlepolemos:

Τληπόλεμ', ἤτοι κεῖνος ἀπώλεσεν Ἴλιον ἱρὴν
ἀνέρος ἀφραδίῃσιν ἀγαυοῦ Λαομέδοντος,
ὅς ῥά μιν εὖ ἔρξαντα κακῷ ἠνίπαπε μύθῳ,
οὐδ' ἀπέδωχ' ἵππους, ὧν εἵνεκα τηλόθεν ἦλθε.
(*Il.* 5.648-651)

Indeed, that man did destroy sacred Ilion
because of the heedlessness of noble Laomedon,
who reproached with base utterance the one treating him well
and did not hand over the horses for whose sake he (Herakles) had
    come from afar.

This story, along with other references in the poem to what seems to be the same incident involving Herakles and Laomedon,[19] may reflect a particular poetic, epic source familiar to the Homeric audience.[20]

In each of these three instances, a *pseudo*-word refers not to a simple lie but to a tale or narrative tradition, and each is told or evoked in an agonistic setting. Each of these stories draws on material from a time that is already in the legendary past at the time of its telling in the *Iliad*, and each involves characters about whom a rich and varied body of traditional material had evolved: Tydeus, who is a character in the Theban legends; Corinthian Bellerophon, who, by reason of his Lycian wanderings, became grandfather of both Glaukos and Sarpedon. These stories all contain elements designated by *pseudo*-words, but they are not so much "lies" in our sense of the word as they are "tales" told as if true but whose truth-value is not, or cannot be, entirely corroborated by the narrator, by the narrative reality of the poem, or by any character living within the time frame of the poem. Each of the stories is told to manipulate the emotions of the character to whom it is directed so that the character will behave in accordance with the will of the teller. In other words, the teller expects to win something as a result of telling the tale:

---

19. *Il.* 8.283-284; 20.144-148.
20. Gantz 1993:400.

Agamemnon wants Diomedes to return to battle, which is what happens; Anteia wants Bellerophon punished, which is accomplished when Proitos sends Bellerophon off to Lycia; Tlepolemos' attempt to unhinge Sarpedon by alleging that his credentials are *pseudea* backfires when he rejects the version adopted by the main narrative.

It appears, then, that tales are called *pseudea* not only when they are false from the point of view of the poem but when they are of a type often told, a type of story that seems very much like a true, verifiable account but cannot be corroborated, a type that may remain in the homier realm of prose folk tales rather than high poetry. Epic poetry must be selective in its accommodation of traditional material, and *pseudo*-words so far seem to signal references to lesser type-tales or discarded alternative versions of epic material. These stories are not really lies. Lies are the opposite of truth, but these stories are not the opposite of the truth: they are, in fact, so much like the truth, or some accepted version of the truth, or some recognizable human experience, that they invite belief or at least suspension of disbelief. In English, the prefix *pseudo-* still carries this sense, designating something that is very much like what it pretends to be but isn't. In the Homeric poems, *pseudo*-narratives are not received as reliable accounts of certifiable events although they seem very like other narrative accounts that are received as reliable. But the very presence of these tales in the poem, if only to be discarded, indicates that, like any good fiction, they are potentially acceptable, either by characters within the poem or by an audience outside the poem.

A good story, well told, resulting in suspension of disbelief is still said to be spellbinding, and it is this effect that worries Achilles in *Iliad* 21. Battered about by the river in which he expects to die, Achilles fears that he has been spellbound by Thetis' predictive narrative—that she has told him a tall tale in order to beguile him, a tale whose ending he fears will not be borne out by the narrative:

> ἄλλος δ' οὔ τίς μοι τόσον αἴτιος Οὐρανιώνων,
> ἀλλὰ φίλη μήτηρ, <u>ἥ με ψεύδεσσιν ἔθελγεν·</u>
> ἥ μ' ἔφατο Τρώων ὑπὸ τείχει θωρηκτάων
> λαιψηροῖς ὀλέεσθαι Ἀπόλλωνος βελέεσσιν.
> (*Il.* 21.275-278)

Not some other of the Uranian gods is responsible that such
   a thing befalls me
but my own dear mother who beguiled me with lies,
who said that under the walls of the breast-plated Trojans,
I would die by the swift shafts of Apollo.

The word θέλγειν *thelgein* 'to charm, bewitch' means to distract men's minds from reality by spells or trickery or words. Athena does this to the suitors (e.g., *Od.* 16.298), Circe does it with her drug (*Od.* 10.318, 326), Penelope with her appearance (*Od.* 18.212), Hermes with his wand (e.g., *Il.* 24.343; *Od.* 24.3). Words also can have this effect, which is how Penelope deftly solicits gifts from the suitors.[21] Singers also "charm."[22] Thus Penelope reminds Phemios that he knows 'many deeds, spellbinding for mortals, of men and gods which singers celebrate' (πολλὰ γὰρ ἄλλα βροτῶν θελκτήρια οἶδας/ ἔργ' ἀνδρῶν τε θεῶν τε, τά τε κλείουσιν ἀοιδοί [*Od.* 1.337-338]), and Eumaios uses the term twice to describe the effect of Odysseus' storytelling (θέλγοιτο *thelgoito* [*Od.* 17.514]; ἔθελγε *ethelge* [*Od.* 17.521]). We know, and the Homeric audiences no doubt knew, that Achilles would not die in the river and that Achilles' death scene would play out as described by Thetis but not within the frame of this particular poem. Neither the details of Thetis' prophecy nor its fulfillment are described in the *Iliad.* That Achilles will be short-lived is a recurring theme in the *Iliad,*[23] but the specific details are given only in prophecy form as here in Achilles' own complaint and in Hektor's dying words in Book 22 (356-360). In Book 9, Achilles quotes Thetis as having predicted either a short life with glory or a long life with contentment but not both (*Il.* 9.410-416). Death in the river

---

21. *Od.* 18.282-283: θέλγε δὲ θυμὸν / μειλιχίοις ἐπέεσσι, νόος δὲ οἱ ἄλλα μενοίνα 'She beguiled their hearts with honeyed words but her mind was bent on other things'.

22. Only gods and very special humans can do this: Zeus *Il.* 15.594, *Od.* 24 3; Poseidon *Il* 13.435; Apollo *Il.* 15.322, 21.604; Thetis *Il.* 21.276; Hermes *Il.* 24 343, *Od.* 5.47; Athena *Od.* 1.57; Circe *Od.* 10.291, 318, 326; Sirens *Od.* 12.40, 44; Odysseus *Od.* 14.387, 17.514, 521; Penelope *Od.* 18.282 Aegisthus *tried* to charm (iterative/conative form θέλγεσκεν *thelgesken*) Clytemnestra with words, but the text makes clear that it was not his words that finally persuaded her (*Od.* 3.264).

23. E.g., Achilles says so in *Il.* 1.352; Thetis in 1.416-418, 505; the horse Xanthus in 19.415-416; also 9.410-416, 18.95-126, 23.141-151; 24.130-132.

would accomplish neither. In a sense, then, Achilles is right to worry that Thetis' predictive scenario will eventually be considered *pseudea*. But the wider epic tradition corroborates Thetis' prediction: Achilles will not be trapped forever in a version of the Troy story that he would find unacceptable.

The Real Thing: Iliadic Narrative Not *Pseudos*

There are several instances in the *Iliad* where some form of narrative is specifically designated as not *pseud–*. Identification of what is not *pseud–* corroborates and clarifies what is. Reports of prophecies and dreams that are borne out by the narrative are not *pseudea*—nor are narrative sequences that recollect events already recounted in the poem.

The narrator describes Zeus' sending of Iris to Poseidon with a message and an admonition not to let her delivery of the message differ in any way from his original speech, lest she be a ψευδάγγελος *pseudangelos*:[24]

> βάσκ' ἴθι, Ἶρι ταχεῖα, Ποσειδάωνι ἄνακτι
> πάντα τάδ' ἀγγεῖλαι, μὴ δὲ ψευδάγγελος εἶναι.
> (*Il.* 15.158-159)

> Go, swift Iris, to the lord Poseidon, to report
> all these things and do not be a false messenger.

In *Iliad* 24, Iris visits Priam with the message from Zeus that he should go to Achilles with gifts to ransom the body of Hektor. In response to his wife's skepticism about the wisdom of such an expedition, Priam insists on the grounds of his own autopsy that the messenger was divine and that the message came from Zeus:

> οὐδέ με πείσεις.
> εἰ μὲν γάρ τίς μ' ἄλλος ἐπιχθονίων ἐκέλευεν,
> ἢ οἳ μάντιές εἰσι θυοσκόοι ἢ ἱερῆες,

---

24. ψευδάγγελος *pseudangelos* appears only here in Homer and not again until Aristophanes (*LSJ* 2019).

ψεῦδός κεν φαῖμεν καὶ νοσφιζοίμεθα μᾶλλον·
νῦν δ᾽ αὐτὸς γὰρ ἄκουσα θεοῦ καὶ ἐσέδρακον ἄντην.
(*Il.* 24.219-223)

> you will not persuade me.
> For if someone else ordered me, someone of mortals,
> either seers or diviners or priests,
> we might have called it false and rather dismissed it.
> But as it is, I myself heard the goddess and looked at
> her face to face.

The narrative verifies the content of the message given to Iris by Zeus at *Il.* 24.143-158. This message gives Priam an order while at the same time it tells him a little story predicting what will happen in the camp of Achilles. The accuracy of this predictive story is borne out by the later events of the poem. Priam's statement verifies not only the message but also the whole experience of receiving the message from Iris. He trusts the message because he can verify the source firsthand. Even if the entire sequence sounds like a type-tale, he acknowledges its reality.

Nestor had used the same line at *Il.* 2.81 with reference to Agamemnon's dream:

εἰ μέν τις τὸν ὄνειρον Ἀχαιῶν ἄλλος ἔνισπε,
ψεῦδός κεν φαῖμεν καὶ νοσφιζοίμεθα μᾶλλον
νῦν δ᾽ ἴδεν ὃς μέγ᾽ ἄριστος Ἀχαιῶν εὔχεται εἶναι·

> If some other one of the Achaeans told this dream,
> we might have called it false and rather dismissed it.
> But as it is, he who claims to be the best of the Achaeans
> has seen it.

Nestor cannot himself verify the content or experience of Agamemnon's dream, but the narrator does that for us. Agamemnon has recounted the event exactly as it occurred earlier in Book 2 (1-35). The dream sent by Zeus contains false information, but Agamemnon's retelling of his experience in having the dream is not *pseudos* because he tells it exactly as the dream happened. Nestor acknowledges that Agamemnon's story sounds like a type-tale but, because he trusts the speaker, he can maintain his belief at least in Agamemnon's belief.

In another exchange between Agamemnon and Nestor a narrative account is stipulated as not *pseudos*. At *Iliad* 9.115, Agamemnon reacts to Nestor's account of the events surrounding the taking of Briseis from Achilles by saying (*Il.* 9.115):

οὔ τι ψεῦδος ἐμὰς ἄτας κατέλεξας.

you have told no false version, recounting my madness exactly

Nestor's narrative represents events exactly as described by the narrator in Book 1 of the *Iliad*. His story is not *pseudos* because it is confirmed by the reality of the main narrative. The story is told as a report, not as part of a contest of some kind, and it is not phrased for the speaker's advantage. It is not *pseudos*. We can infer from Agamemnon's phrasing that κατέλεξας *katelexas* 'recount exactly' is the opposite of *pseudos*.

The notion that Nestor can be relied upon not to speak *pseudos* is picked up in the *Odyssey* when Athena says to Telemachus (*Od.* 3.17-20):

ἀλλ' ἄγε νῦν ἰθὺς κίε Νέστορος ἱπποδάμοιο
εἴδομεν ἥν τινα μῆτιν ἐνὶ στήθεσσι κέκευθε.
[λίσσεσθαι δέ μιν αὐτόν, ὅπως νημερτέα εἴπῃ·][25]
ψεῦδος δ' οὐκ ἐρέει μάλα γὰρ πεπνυμένος ἐστί.

But come now, go straight to (the palace) of horse-taming Nestor.
We know what astuteness he holds in his breast.
[Implore him to tell things in accordance with reality.]
He will not tell a false version for he is exceedingly shrewd.

Telemachus does what Athena advises, entreating Nestor to give an account of his father's activities exactly as he knows them to have occurred, to speak from personal memory rather than to invent some attractive tale:

---

25. Brackets as printed in Allen's edition indicate Bekker's deletion of line 19.

μηδέ τί μ' αἰδόμενος μειλίσσεο μηδ' ἐλεαίρων,
ἀλλ' εὖ μοι κατάλεξον ὅπως ἤντησας ὀπωπῆς.
λίσσομαι, εἴ ποτέ τοί τι πατὴρ ἐμός,
    ἐσθλὸς 'Οδυσσεύς,
ἢ ἔπος ἠέ τι ἔργον ὑποστὰς ἐξετέλεσσε
δήμῳ ἔνι Τρώων, ὅθι πάσχετε πήματ' 'Αχαιοί
τῶν νῦν μοι μνῆσαι, καί μοι νημερτὲς ἐνίσπες.
    (*Od.* 3.96–101)

Do not mince words, moved by feelings of pity for me,
but <u>tell me the affair exactly as you encountered the sight</u>.
I beseech you, if ever my father, the noble Odysseus,
undertook for your sake any word or deed
in the land of the Trojans, where the Achaeans suffered
    many woes,
recall these things now for me and tell them in accordance
    with reality.

Telemachus is asking Nestor for one sort of heroic *mûthos*—identified by Martin as the account of remembered events.[26] Telemachus wants Nestor to perform essentially the same service for him that the singer requires of the Muse in the opening lines. The difference between the accounts of Nestor and the Muse, however, is that Nestor's reality is measured by the world of the narrative, but the Muse has broader horizons and, as we know from Hesiod, can tell all sorts of stories including those considered false, not acceptable, not in accordance with the reality of a particular poetic occasion (*Theogony* 27-28):[27]

ἴδμεν ψεύδεα πολλὰ λέγειν ἐτύμοισιν ὁμοῖα.
ἴδμεν δ', εὖτ' ἐθέλωμεν, ἀληθέα γηρύσασθαι.

We know how to tell <u>many false versions</u> like correct ones
but we also know, when we want, how to tell things that are true.

---

26. Martin 1989:47.
27. Further discussion of these lines to follow.

Nestor tells Telemachus a story that is not a fictionalized tale but that represents events as Nestor recalls them to have happened. We do not have the narrator's corroboration of all the details of Nestor's account but we also have no indication in the main narrative that Nestor is fabricating a fictional tale or relying on "they say" for his information. There is no reason to doubt Nestor's claim to be recounting from autopsy or to doubt Athena's assurance in the *Iliad* that Nestor does not tell *pseudea*.

This same line is repeated at *Od.* 3.328, where Nestor directs Telemachus to seek information from Menelaos with the same reassuring language with which Athena has directed Telemachus to Nestor. The presumption in each case is that the speaker will recount events as he personally knows them to have happened—without invention, embellishment, or elaboration. But Menelaos' speech seems to have elements of *pseudea*, folktales, or type-tales, because he claims to have had a conversation with the sea-god Nereus who had seen Odysseus in the clutches of Calypso. If the truth-value of an account were measured by its consistency with human experience, then we might suspect Menelaos of telling "tall tales," but if truth-value is measured by corroboration in the narrative, then Menelaos' tale is at least partially corroborated later by Odysseus. Whether Odysseus himself tells *pseudea* is a matter for discussion later in this essay. In any case, neither Nestor nor Menelaos tells his story in any kind of contest, and neither hopes to gain anything by the telling. Both seem free of *pseudea*.

Elsewhere Menelaos is careful to avoid being accused of telling *pseudea* to gain an advantage in a contest when he insists in *Iliad* 23 that Antilochus swear in public that Menelaos was not awarded the horse-prize in the chariot race because of some "tall tale" told about Antilochus' behavior during the race. Menelaos wants it known that the narrative reality of the poem supports withholding the prize from Antilochus:[28]

> μή ποτέ τις εἴπῃσιν ᾿Αχαιῶν χαλκοχιτώνων·
> ᾿Αντίλοχον ψεύδεσσι βιησάμενος Μενέλαος
> οἴχεται ἵππον ἄγων.
>
> (*Il.* 23.575-577)

---

28. *Il.* 23.398-441, voice of the narrator.

so that no one of the bronze-clad Achaeans says at some time that
Menelaos, <u>beating Antilochus by means of false versions,</u>
goes home taking the horse.

In each of these cases, speech described as not *pseudos* designates a
narrative account that does not differ from a version of the same account
given by the narrator elsewhere in the main narrative. To tell a story that is
not *pseudos* is to repeat exactly what the narrative reality of the poem
confirms, the inference being that *pseudea* are accounts that diverge from the
narrative reality established by the poem. The implications stemming from
speeches designated as *pseudos* and not *pseudos* are entirely consistent:
pseudo-words apply not to simple lies but to lying stories, narrative accounts
that are not verified elsewhere in the poem, fictions. They crop up in
agonistic settings where some advantage can be gained from their telling, and
they have the flavor of folk tales, fairy tales, or oft-told type-tales from the
distant past that have no identifiable source: tales of divine ancestry, heroic
feats, the tales of a woman scorned. In some cases, narrative accounts seem
so much like *pseudea* because of their "typicalness" that the narrative must
clearly identify them as not *pseudea,* as when a leader justifies what seem to
be irrational decisions by quoting orders sent by a god in a dream, or when
the loser of a race blames his loss on the unsportsmanlike behavior of his
opponent. Whether legend or type-tale, these stories labeled with *pseudo*-
words, though embedded in epic, would not by themselves have sufficient
epic gravity, importance, or reliability. Where epic claims veracity, *pseudea*
are left with verisimilitude.

Pseudo-Respectability

The entire epic world is an *agôn*, a contest or struggle: an epic character
derives his livelihood from winning in an *agôn*, whether it be a game where a
prize is awarded or a war where plunder is the prize. In the epic world,
singers hold a position of respect[29] and are rewarded for the performance of

---

29. In the *Odyssey* at least, only villains mistreat singers, e.g., the suitors who force
Phemios to sing 'under compulsion' (*Od* 1.154; 22.345ff); cf. also Aegisthus (*Od.*
3.270-271). The civilized Phaeacians treat Demodokos with great deference (e.g., *Od.*

their song. But Priam's outburst at *Iliad* 24.260-262 indicates that there is another type of entertainer whom he holds in low esteem. These are the ψεῦσται *pseustai* who are not, I suggest, liars but tellers of unacceptable versions or of lesser narratives like folk tales, fairy tales, or type-tales, maybe in prose form, probably of the sort any nurse or sailor could tell. Priam suggests that these storytellers do not give real value in exchange for prizes or advantages awarded them on the basis of their storytelling. Grieving for the heroic sons now lost to him, Priam says of those who survive:

> τὰ δ' ἐλέγχεα πάντα λέλειπται,
> ψεῦσταί τ' ὀρχησταί τε, χοροιτυπίησιν ἄριστοι.
> ἀρνῶν ἠδ' ἐρίφων ἐπιδήμιοι ἁρπακτῆρες
>
> (*Il.* 24.260-262)

> but the causes for shame are all left behind,
> tellers of false stories and dancers, the pride of those who
>   beat the ground in dance,
> thieves among their own people of lambs and kids.

There is nothing arbitrary about ἁρπακτῆρες *harpaktêres,* which, related as it is to ἁρπάζω *harpazô,* can only mean 'robbers'. They steal sheep and goats from their neighbors rather than their enemies, not by armed plunder, but by trading pseudea for prizes that ought to be reserved for a higher form of composition. This scornful dismissal of those who transmit tales rather than reliable, metrical accounts of accepted epic material echoes the scornful tone of Tlepolemos' similar dismissal of the ψευδόμενοι *pseudomenoi* who transmit stories about Sarpedon's ancestry. It is an echo that reverberates throughout the Odyssey, perhaps as part of an ongoing inter- and intra-textual dialogue about the worth of such tales and their place in epic poetry.

8.470-472), as does Odysseus himself in *Od.* 8.474-481, 488; 9.3-11 where Odysseus says καὶ μιν προσπτύξομαι 'I will greet him'. This is the same verb with which Telemachus intends to greet Nestor (*Od.* 3.22) and Penelope intends to greet the stranger who is, in fact, Odysseus (*Od* 17.509). This verb seems to imply a degree of protocol by which one who holds a position of respect might greet one who holds a position of greater respect.

Pseudo-Recollection in the Odyssey

In the Odyssey, pseudo-words are consistently applied to narrative accounts rather than oaths or omens or outright lies. Only Helen's exclamation at Od. 4.140 veers from the narrative pattern to which the other eight Odyssean pseudo-words belong. A brief digression on the exceptional elements of this line and its Iliadic twin (Il. 10.534) is in order.

Struck by the likeness of Telemachus to his father, Helen deliberates what her reaction should be. She debates making up a story to cover her astonishment at what her eyes confirm:

ψεύσομαι. ἦ ἔτυμον ἐρέω: κέλεται δέ με θυμός

Shall I make up something or shall I speak truly? My heart gives
   me an order.

This exact line appears also at *Iliad* 10.534, where Nestor expresses his hope that the sound he hears is the footfall of Odysseus returning safely.[30] Neither of these instances fits any other pattern of *pseudo*-words. There is no omen, oath, or narrative account, no contest or advantage to be gained, no conflict with traditional material. But it is interesting that this same phrase should be uttered by these two characters: Nestor, who, as we have seen, can be relied upon not to tell *pseudea,* and Helen, who seems the embodiment of variant versions, not only as their subject but as their speaker as well.[31] Both these lines place ἔτυμος *etumos* and ψευδ- *pseud-* in direct opposition, which seems to reflect a particular interpretation not only of *Odyssey* 19.203 but also especially of Hesiod *Theogony* 27:

ἴδμεν ψεύδεα πολλὰ λέγειν ἐτύμοισιν ὁμοῖα.

We know how to tell many false versions like true ones.

---

30. Iliadic line athetized by Zenodotus according to Scholia T.
31. See Jenkins (this volume).

This juxtaposition of ἔτυμος *etumos* with a *pseudo*-word occurs only this once in Hesiod, but it does appear elsewhere in Homer. The tales of the disguised Odysseus recounting his adventures to Penelope in *Odyssey* 19 (165ff) are described by the narrator in almost identical language (*Od.* 19.203):

ἴσκε ψεύδεα πολλὰ λέγων ἐτύμοισιν ὁμοῖα·

He knew how to tell many false versions like true ones.

In these instances, I suggest that 'true' can be understood to mean events that will, or have, come to fruition within the reality of the main narrative, corroborated by the narrator, and appropriate to epic poetry. In his tales to Penelope, Odysseus mingles biographical details of a non-epic fictional character whose persona he has temporarily assumed with details of his own life and appearance, which the narrator tells us (*Od.* 19.250) are corroborated by Penelope's own knowledge:

σήματ᾽ ἀναγνούσῃ, τά οἱ ἔμπεδα πέφραδ᾽ Ὀδυσσεύς.

she recognized the signs, the unmistakable ones, which
Odysseus indicated.

Details of "correct" epic material are mixed with wanderer's tales and perhaps some other tradition of an Odyssean sojourn in Crete. Odysseus not only tells fictional material as if true but he tells true stories at the same time. This ability to intertwine the two types of narrative into a moving performance is characteristic of Odysseus' storytelling.

Penelope uses ἔτυμα *etuma* in describing the gates of horn and ivory in *Odyssey* 19.562-569, but not in opposition to a *pseudo*-word:

δοιαὶ γάρ τε πύλαι ἀμενηνῶν εἰσιν ὀνείρων
αἱ μὲν γὰρ κεράεσσι τετεύχαται, αἱ δ᾽ ἐλέφαντι.
τῶν οἳ μὲν κ᾽ ἔλθωσι διὰ πριστοῦ ἐλέφαντος,
οἵ ῥ᾽ ἐλεφαίρονται, ἔπε᾽ ἀκράαντα φέροντες

οἳ δὲ διὰ ξεστῶν κεράων ἔλθωσι θύραζε,
οἵ ῥ' ἔτυμα κραίνουσι, βροτῶν ὅτε κέν τις ἴδηται.

There are two sets of gates for fleeting dreams;
one is made of horn and the other of ivory.
Of those that come through the gates of sawn ivory,
they deceive, <u>bringing words not to be fulfilled</u>.
But the dreams that come through the gates of polished horn,
<u>they are brought to pass</u>, when anyone of mortals sees.

Notice that the opposition here is between *etuma* and *akraanta* 'not to be fulfilled', not *pseudea*. The dreams that do not come to fruition are not labeled with a *pseudo*-word because Penelope is talking in general terms about dreams, not recounting any one particular dream: no narrative is involved. In Homeric poetry, it seems that a dream itself is never designated by a *pseudo*-word, but an inaccurate description of a particular dream or a false report of experiencing a dream qualifies for *pseudo*-designation.[32] A narrative element whose truth-value can be measured against another narrative seems crucial to the appropriate use of a *pseudo*-word.

The other eight instances in the *Odyssey* do refer to narrative sequences. Four of these occur in Book 14 and refer to various stories exchanged by Eumaios and Odysseus. All of these are wanderer's tales, and all of them are told with the expectation of a reward.

At *Odyssey* 14.122-133, Eumaios describes the sort of wanderer who comes to Ithaca telling tales to Penelope about encounters with, or reports of, Odysseus—reports that could never convince her, but that nonetheless make her cry and thus earn hospitality and maybe a cloak for the teller.[33] Eumaios says:

ὦ γέρον. οὔ τις κεῖνον ἀνὴρ ἀλαλήμενος ἐλθὼν
ἀγγέλλων πείσειε γυναῖκά τε καὶ φίλον υἱόν.
ἀλλ' ἄλλως. κομιδῆς κεχρημένοι. ἄνδρες ἀλῆται
ψεύδοντ' οὐδ' ἐθέλουσιν ἀληθέα μυθήσασθαι

---

32. See earlier discussion of Agamemnon's dream.
33. Most (1989:15-30) discusses Odysseus' "tales of woe" in Book 14.

ὃς δέ κ' ἀλητεύων Ἰθάκης ἐς δῆμον ἵκηται.
ἐλθὼν ἐς δέσποιναν ἐμὴν ἀπατήλια βάζει
ἡ δ' εὖ δεξαμένη φιλέει καὶ ἕκαστα μεταλλᾷ.
καὶ οἱ ὀδυρομένῃ βλεφάρων ἄπο δάκρυα πίπτει.
ἢ θέμις ἐστὶ γυναικός. ἐπὴν πόσις ἄλλοτ' ὄληται
αἶψά κε καὶ σύ. γεραιέ. ἔπος παρατεκτήναιο.
εἴ τίς τοι χλαῖνάν τε χιτῶνά τε εἵματα δοίη

Old man, no wandering man coming here,
bringing news of that man could persuade his wife and
    his son,
but wandering men, needing supplies,
do tell false versions, men who are not willing to tell true
    stories,
the sort of person who, wandering, arrives at Ithaca, and
    coming
to my mistress, tells fraudulent stories.
And receiving him well, she treats him with affection,
and she asks about each detail,
and the tears fall from her eyes as she mourns him,
which is right for a woman, when her husband perishes far
    away.
Perhaps, old man, even you could alter your speech,
if someone would give you a cloak or tunic or garment.

At the very beginning of this passage, Eumaios remarks that no traveling storyteller who tells 'false versions' (ψεύδοντ' *pseudont'*) could convince Penelope with reports about Odysseus, but he goes on to describe her reaction to these men when they come. She weeps, she mourns her lost husband, she welcomes the storyteller and rewards him, but she doesn't believe he is telling the truth, that he is giving her an accurate report of a person or event he witnessed for himself. Penelope does not reward these wandering storytellers for the accuracy of their information but for the suspension of disbelief that they afford. For a brief time she can imagine Odysseus alive, she can envision him in a particular setting, she can hope. It is the divergence between the version of the story she hears and the version she believes to be true that provokes her tears. She believes Odysseus to be dead and lost to her (and to epic glory) forever, but she is grateful for any well-told, more hopeful, version of the story of Odysseus' wanderings. In other words, she assumes that she is hearing what will be regarded as fiction, as the unaccepted version, but she welcomes the diversion.

Eumaios calls these tales *apatêlia*, which, related as the word is to ἀπάτη *apatê*, has overtones of cheating and fraud. Eumaios assumes that these men have no real grounds for their hopeful information about Odysseus and that they get better than they give. They tell the sort of outright lies that Odysseus does not tell; he even claims disdain for men who would tell *apatêlia* under the compulsion of poverty:

ἐχθρὸς γάρ μοι κεῖνος ὁμῶς Ἀΐδαο πύλῃσι
γίνεται. ὃς πενίῃ εἴκων ἀπατήλια βάζει
(*Od.* 14.156-157)

That man is as hateful to me as the gates of hell who,
yielding to poverty, says fraudulent things.

In the same passage, Odysseus says that he would welcome such gifts as a cloak, a tunic, or a garment—but only after his prediction of Odysseus' homecoming is proven out by the events of the poem. The implication here is that the stories that he tells to gain an advantage, his *pseudea*, are not told under the compulsion of poverty and are not lies about people and events that are real within the world of the poem: they are made-up stories about made-up characters, good yarns, recognizable as type tales. What he says about people and events that are real within the world of the poem will be corroborated, and what he predicts will come to fruition. Made-up stories about real people and real events are *apatêlia*—what we call lies; *pseudea* are what we call fiction, typical accounts of typical characters who can be recognized as such. Both types of story are told to gain some advantage, but the implication of Odysseus' remarks here is that *apatêlia* are not sporting.

Later in Book 14, Odysseus spins for Eumaios a yarn about the personal history of the Cretan character he has assumed as his disguise (*Od.* 14.191-359). Odysseus provides a life-story in fulfillment of his obligation as a guest to identify himself to the host who has welcomed him. Most of the details of the story did not happen, or at least are not reported elsewhere as having happened to Odysseus. They are not *apatêlia* because Odysseus is not giving false information about himself but about a character he has assumed who is fictional to begin with. Some details involving events at Troy reflect those transmitted by the epic tradition; others do not. Odysseus again demonstrates his gift for intermingling two different types of narrative, epic and folk.

Within this larger story is another story about the character's sojourn in Egypt and his foolish trust in a Phoenician, 'a man who knew many <u>deceiving words</u>' (ἀνὴρ <u>ἀπατήλια</u> εἰδώς [*Od.* 14.288]), who allegedly told *pseudea* to the Cretan (who Odysseus is pretending to be) so that the Cretan would accompany him but then be sold into slavery (*Od.* 14.296). These *pseudea* are promissory stories devised by a stereotypical Phoenician to get the better of the protagonist of the story and profit for himself. The Phoenician is shown to have painted a scenario for the Cretan in which the Cretan could envision profit for himself. In a sense, the Cretan and the Phoenician are subscribing to different versions of the scenario: the Phoenician is describing one scenario while subscribing to another. These *pseudea* entail not just false information but a narrative scenario in which the false information is couched, and they are told in a struggle of wills in which one man strives to gain advantage over another. Both the duped Cretan and the deceitful Phoenician seem to be stereotypical ethnic stock characters that might reflect a larger body of traditional folk-tales about foreigners.

Eumaios is moved by the old man's account of his alleged trials, his wanderer's tales, but he comments that there is something not "right" about them, 'not in order' (οὐ κατὰ κόσμον *ou kata kosmon*). Furthermore, he does not believe that subsequent events will bear out the old man's claims that Odysseus is alive and will return home. Taken all together, Eumaios judges Odysseus' narrative to be comprised of *pseudea*, folk material and false versions, but he cannot understand why the stranger would tell *pseudea* for no reason, with no expectation of advantage, with no competition. Eumaios says:

> ἆ δειλὲ ξείνων, ἦ μοι μάλα θυμὸν ὄρινας
> ταῦτα ἕκαστα λέγων, ὅσα δὴ πάθες ἠδ' ὅσ' ἀλήθης.
> <u>ἀλλὰ τά γ' οὐ κατὰ κόσμον, ὀίομαι, οὐδέ με πείσεις</u>
> <u>εἰπὼν ἀμφ' Ὀδυσῆι. τί σε χρὴ τοῖον ἐόντα</u>

μαψιδίως ψεύδεσθαι; ἐγὼ δ' ἐὺ οἶδα καὶ αὐτὸς
νόστον ἐμοῖο ἄνακτος, ὅ τ' ἤχθετο πᾶσι θεοῖσι
πάγχυ μάλ', ὅττι μιν οὔ τι μετὰ Τρώεσσι δάμασσαν
ἠὲ φίλων ἐν χερσὶν, ἐπεὶ πόλεμον τολύπευσε ...
καὶ σύ, γέρον πυλυπενθές, ἐπεί σέ μοι ἤγαγε δαίμων,
μήτε τί μοι ψεύδεσσι χαρίζεο μήτε τι θέλγε
οὐ γὰρ τοὔνεκ' ἐγώ σ' αἰδέσσομαι οὐδὲ φιλήσω,
ἀλλὰ Δία ξένιον δείσας αὐτόν τ' ἐλεαίρων.

(*Od*. 14.361-388)

O luckless stranger, you move my heart telling
each of these things, how much you have experienced
    and how far you have wandered,
but these are not right (in accordance with established usage),[34] I
    think, nor will you persuade me,
telling about Odysseus. But why should such a man
    as you are
make up false versions to no purpose? But I myself know well
the homecoming of my lord who was so much hated by all the
    gods
that they did not destroy him among the Trojans
in the hands of his comrades when he had carried out the war...
But you, much-suffering old man, since some god has
    led you to me,
do not delight me with false versions or beguile me,
for not because of these things will I respect you and befriend you
but because I fear Zeus, the god of hospitality, and I pity you

Eumaios equates 'delight' (χαρίζεο *kharizeo*) with 'beguile' (θέλγεο *thelgeo*), implying that there is a recognizable element of entertainment in Odysseus' performance. In this context, 'beguile' must mean 'cause me to suspend my disbelief'. Eumaios' use of the words ψεύδεσθαι *pseudesthai* 'to make up false versions' and ψεύδεσσι *pseudessi* 'with false versions' signals

---

34. Nagy (1990a:145) on κόσμος to mean 'arrangement of the words of their song'.

his recognition of two potentially variant versions of Odysseus' fate. Like Penelope, Eumaios fears that Odysseus has died somewhere without honor, without burial, and without the homecoming that should result in his epic glorification. The audience, both current and ancient, knows which version will be accepted and transmitted by epic poetry, but characters within the world of the poem like Eumaios and Penelope, like Achilles in the *Iliad*, must worry about what version will be embraced by poetic tradition. Eumaios anticipates that the other version will come to fruition. Clearly Eumaios thinks that Odysseus' performance is intended to delight and beguile—which seems to him a pointless effort outside the context of a competition. But a contest between versions is taking place, even if there appears to be no overt contest between characters. Of course, Odysseus does expect to win some advantage—if not the prize in a formal contest, at least the sympathy of his host and his hospitality.[35]

Eumaios has assured the disguised Odysseus of a safe haven regardless of the quality or believability of his stories, but still Odysseus has no cloak, so he improves upon his performance in order to persuade Eumaios, who is described as having 'an unbelieving heart in his breast' (ἦ μάλα τίς τοι θυμὸς ἐνὶ στήθεσσιν ἄπιστος [*Od.* 14.391]). Odysseus, in his assumed identity, tells a story (*Od.* 14.462-506) of going out on a night raid in Troy with a shield but no cloak and of Odysseus' devising a trick to gain a cloak for him. The story is remarkably reminiscent of the *Doloneia* in Book 10 of the *Iliad,* where it is Odysseus alone of all the combatants who has no cloak but is described by the narrator as going out only with his 'variegated shield on his shoulders' (ποικίλον ἀμφ' ὤμοισι σάκος θέτο [*Il.* 10.149]), this despite careful descriptions of the cloaks of other warriors involved in the *Doloneia* (*Il.* 10.23-24, 29-30, 133-134, 177-178).[36] No *pseudo*-designation accompanies this story: Eumaios characterizes Odysseus' tale as 'flawless speech' (αἶνος ... ἀμύμων [10.508]),[37] suggesting, I think, that he considers this event to have occurred (as, indeed, it did with certain details changed), or at least that it is composed of suitable epic material. Odysseus gets his cloak,

---

35. See Nagy (1990a:57, 66, 182, 188, 190, 265, 275) on κέρδος *kerdos*; Most 1989a, 1989b on "cloaks."

36. Muellner 1976:96n43.

37. Nagy 1990a:31 defines αἶνος as "authoritative speech: it is an affirmation, a marked speech-act, made by and for a marked social group."

or at least the temporary use of someone else's cloak, as a result of his performance but not in a context of direct competition of either performers or versions—hence no *pseudo*-designation.

Perhaps the most interesting and illustrative use of *pseudea* in reference to narrative occurs in Alkinoos' comments to Odysseus on his performance during its intermission in Book 11. Alkinoos says:

> τὸν δ' αὖτ' Ἀλκίνοος ἀπαμείβετο φώνησέν τε
> "ὦ Ὀδυσεῦ, <u>τὸ μὲν οὔ τί σ' ἐΐσκομεν εἰσορόωντες</u>
> <u>ἠπεροπῆά τ' ἔμεν καὶ ἐπίκλοπον</u>, οἷά τε πολλοὺς
> βόσκει γαῖα μέλαινα πολυσπερέας[38] ἀνθρώπους
> <u>ψεύδεά τ' ἀρτύνοντας, ὅθεν κέ τις οὐδὲ ἴδοιτο</u>
> <u>σοὶ δ' ἔπι μὲν μορφὴ ἐπέων, ἔνι δὲ φρένες ἐσθλαί,</u>
> <u>μῦθον δ' ὡς ὅτ' ἀοιδὸς ἐπισταμένως κατέλεξας,</u>
> πάντων Ἀργείων σέο τ' αὐτοῦ κήδεα λυγρά . . .
> . . . σὺ δέ μοι λέγε <u>θέσκελα ἔργα</u> . . .
> (*Od.* 11.362-374)

Then Alkinoos answered him and said,
"Odysseus, <u>on the one hand, we who are looking at you do
not suppose
that you are a deceiver (other than what you appear)</u>[39]

---

38. The word *polusperês* appears otherwise in Homer only at *Il.* 2.804 in Iris' description of the varieties of dialects employed by various Trojan allies and the need for each speech-group to be commanded by one of its own to reduce confusion. Its use here is a further indication that *pseudea* come from a wide range of traditions whose sources cannot be identified or considered reliable. See Nagy 1996b:49.

39. In Homeric poetry, words from the same root as ἠπεροπῆα often designate not just a 'deceiver' but one whose appearance is deceiving, e.g., Hektor's rebuke to Paris, which includes a comment on the difference between Paris' noble appearance and his cowardice (*Il.* 3.39-45); Helen accuses Aphrodite of deceiving her by adopting the appearance of an old woman (*Il.* 3.399); Odysseus accuses Athena of trying to deceive him in a context where her physical appearance belies her station (*Od.* 13.327); it is also the root of the verb used by the disguised Odysseus in recommending to Eumaios that he throw him from a cliff if his information about Odysseus proves "false": he describes "some other vagabond" like himself who might thus be discouraged from again 'deceiving' Eumaios with false versions. But

> or that you are clever, like many men
> such as the black earth nourishes, widely dispersed,
> putting into order various tales (*pseudea*), and from where
>   (*hothen*) they come, no one can know.
> But, on the other hand, there is form to your words, and a noble
>   heart in you,
> and you have recounted your *muthos* with know-how, like a
>   professional singer,
> the pitiful sufferings of all the Argives, and of yourself here
>   present . . .
> But tell me your wondrous deeds."

The language of this passage supports the observation that *pseudo*-words have special associations in Homer: they indicate narrative sequences unsuitable for a particular epic narrative either because they transmit a variant version of material adopted elsewhere in the narrative or because they transmit material unexpected in epic but more suited to the realm of folktales and type-tales; the speaker intends to deceive the listener, at least to the extent that the listener is beguiled and suspends disbelief; narrative *pseudea* are told in an agonistic context where the speaker expects to gain an advantage or win a prize. Odysseus' narrative in Books 8-12 interrupts the performance of the singer, Demodokos, and is so spellbinding that Odysseus, not Demodokos, is invited to continue performing through the night—at the end of which he is showered with gifts and goes home with all the prizes. Odysseus' performance is preferred to that of Demodokos, I suggest, because, speaking in the first person, recalling "remembered" events, he incorporates traditional epic elements, *muthoi*,[40] with non-epic and folk elements, *pseudea*, to the surprise and delight of the Phaeacians for whom he performs.

Since this passage invites different interpretations,[41] a brief explication of my reading of its language is in order. First, the passage is organized by the

---

Odysseus has not 'deceived' with his prediction that Odysseus will soon be home: his very presence is proof of the prediction's accuracy.

40. Discussion follows.

41. See Pache (this volume).

particles μέν *men* and δέ *de*; the statement introduced by *men* in line 363 is opposed by the statement beginning with *de* in 367; placement of σοί *soi* before *de* in 367 stresses the contrast between Odysseus and the supposition summarized by the τό that precedes *men* in 363;[42] the second *men* in 367 may either resume the thread of the first *men* clause after a brief digression[43] followed by two more *de* clauses (367, 368), which continue the opposition introduced by the original *de* in 367,[44] or it may simply emphasize a new statement, which it introduces. In any case, the sense of this passage must be, 'We are in awe. You don't appear to be a teller of *pseudea*, folk-type tales told to gain an advantage, but that is what you are doing except that you are telling them in poetic form, like a singer, using epic meter, investing them with epic gravity and authority'. By implication, Alkinoos suspects that Odysseus is in some way a 'deceiving' and 'clever' man, despite his appearance to the contrary.

Odysseus' appearance elsewhere is also deceiving,[45] misleading others into underestimating him: not only Penelope's suitors and Eumaios, but also Polyphemos (*Od.* 9.511-514); Circe (*Od.* 10.330-332); Antenor (*Il.* 3.220-224). In fact, almost everyone but his dog, Argos (*Od.* 17.292), and his nurse, Eurykleia (*Od.* 19.467), assumes him to be less than he is because of his appearance. If, in this passage, Odysseus appears to be less than he is, the inference must be that he appears to be less than the sort of storyteller described. Odysseus does not appear to be ἐπίκλοπον *epiklopon* 'a cunning man', the only sort of man who, according to Athena, could ever get the better of Odysseus. It is after Odysseus tells a disguised Athena one of his Cretan tales that she says to him with affection and admiration:

> κερδαλέος κ' εἴη καὶ ἐπίκλοπος, ὅς σε παρέλθοι
> ἐν πάντεσσι δόλοισι, καὶ εἰ θεὸς ἀντιάσειε.
> σχέτλιε, ποικιλομῆτα, δόλων ἆατ', οὐκ ἄρ' ἔμελλες,
> οὐδ' ἐν σῆ περ ἐὼν γαίη, λήξειν ἀπατάων
> μύθων τε κλοπίων, οἵ τοι πεδόθεν φίλοι εἰσίν.

---

42. Cf. Denniston 1934:371.

43. Monro 1902:315.

44. On μέν/δέ, see Denniston 1934:359-372, 384-85; Monro 1902:224-227, 304-307, 313-315.

45. See n39 on ἠπεροπῆα.

ἀλλ' ἄγε μηκέτι ταῦτα λεγώμεθα, εἰδότες ἄμφω
κέρδε᾽, ἐπεὶ σὺ μέν ἐσσι βροτῶν ὄχ᾽ ἄριστος ἀπάντων
βουλῇ καὶ μύθοισιν, ἐγὼ δ᾽ ἐν πᾶσι θεοῖσι
μήτι τε κλέομαι καὶ κέρδεσιν .

(*Od.* 13.291-299)

He would be a <u>crafty</u> and <u>cunning</u> fellow who could surpass
    you
in all your devising, even if a god opposes.
Incorrigible man, <u>varied in intelligence</u>, untiring of
    contrivances,
even in your own land you are not going to cease from the
beguiling and <u>artful speech</u> which is part of you from the tip of
    your toes.
But come, let us no longer discuss these things, we who both
    know
<u>craft</u>, since you are the best of all mortals
in planning and in speech, and I am famed among all the gods
for my artful intelligence and my <u>craft</u>.[46]

In light of this passage, *epiklopon* at *Od.* 11.362-364 cannot be an entirely
negative attribution. If Athena loves Odysseus, and identifies with him,
because of his 'crafty' nature, presumably she would not despise the man
who could rival him in this respect, a man she describes as *epiklopon*.

---

46. In translating this passage, I have in mind two important discussions by
Gregory Nagy: first, his definition of κέρδος *kerdos* as "'craft, craftiness; gain,
advantage, profit'; the same Greek word, in the diction of poetry, can refer to the craft
and the potential craftiness of poetry" (1990a.57); second, his observations both on
the programmatic implications of ποικίλος *poikilos* 'varied' in poetry and its
appropriateness as an epithet for the πέπλος *peplos* 'mantle' of Athena, "that ultimate
fabric, the *péplos* that the goddess Athena herself once made with her own hands
(πέπλον . . . ποικίλον [*Il.* 5.734-735]). It follows that the fabric of song is likewise
poikilos" (1996b.65). (The shield, which Odysseus carried with him in the night raid
of the *Iliad*'s *Doloneia* [10.149], his only protection, is also described as *poikilos*.)
Lurking under the surface of the language here may be a statement about the craft of
arranging words, about Athena's patronage of this craft, and about Odysseus' mastery
of it.

Elsewhere (*Od.* 21.397), Odysseus is said by one of the suitors to be *epiklopos* . . . *toxôn* 'cunning with bow and arrows' as he turns the great bow in his hands, contemplating both it and probably also his strategy for the slaughter to follow. At *Iliad* 22.281, Hektor accuses Achilles of being *epiklopos* . . . *muthôn* 'cunning with words', contending that Achilles has made up his prediction of Hektor's imminent death at Athena's hand. Hektor assumes correctly that Achilles is trying to rattle him, but the prediction is not wrong. In each instance, *epiklopos* implies intent to distract for the purpose of gaining an advantage, the same implication attaching to *pseudo*-words, and, in each situation, Athena is in control. There can be no doubt that Athena is present with Odysseus as he tells his stories among the Phaeacians, because she says to him (*Od.* 13.299-302):

> οὐδὲ σύ γ' ἔγνως
> Παλλάδ' Ἀθηναίην, κούρην Διός, ἥ τέ τοι αἰεὶ
> ἐν πάντεσσι πόνοισι παρίσταμαι ἠδὲ φυλάσσω,
> καὶ δέ σε Φαιήκεσσι φίλον πάντεσσιν ἔθηκα.

> but you did not recognize me,
> Pallas Athena, daughter of Zeus, I, who am always
> present for you and guard you in all your labors,
> and who made you dear to all the Phaeacians.

The epithets *epiklopon* ἐπίκλοπον and *êperopêa* ἠπεροπῆα,[47] describe a type of traveling storyteller in the first part of Alkinoos' remarks, but they also describe Odysseus elsewhere; he may not look like this sort of person but there is evidence in the main narrative that he is and that Athena admires these characteristics.

The wandering storytellers of Alkinoos' comment are said to 'put tales into order' (ἀρτύνοντας *artunontas*). Only here in Homeric poetry is ἀρτύνω *(artunô)* applied to the ordering of words, but it always means to put something into some kind of order: a plan, an army, an ambush, sailing

---

47. Cf. n39.

equipment, even bride gifts.[48] Alkinoos' teller of *pseudea*, then, is not entirely without art; essentially, he forms a composition. And his tales come from some unidentifiable source (ὅθεν κέ τις οὐδὲ ἴδοιτο [*Od.* 11.366] 'from where they come, no one can know'),[49] as do other Homeric *pseudea* that cannot be verified by the recollection of a hero still living within the narrative world of the poem and that transmit material, or versions of material, not embraced by epic or, at least, by a particular epic. But this is just the sort of tale Odysseus tells to the Phaeacians: a wonderful, colorful, multi-textured "text" of suitably epic Troy material laced with monster tales, sailor stories, the underworld, unpenalized love-making with nymphs, and so on. These sorts of events are not only outside the expected realm of an epic poem like the *Iliad* but they are outside normal human experience and expectation, surely as much for an ancient epic audience as for us. But Odysseus tells them 'like a singer', which must mean that he sings in hexameter and with the authority of recollection.

Most of this non-epic material is never corroborated by the narrator of the *Odyssey* or by any other character except Odysseus himself when he is briefly described as recapitulating these stories for Penelope in *Od.* 23.306-343. She, too, 'is delighted listening' (ἐτέρπετ' ἀκούσ' *eterpet' akous'* [*Od.* 23.308]), an appropriate reaction to a 'spellbinding' performance. For the Phaeacians (and later for Penelope), Odysseus has spun *pseudea* into his epic recollection—skillfully, metrically, with virtuosity. There is 'form to his words', and he has told his *mûthos* 'accurately, with know-how like a singer'.

Richard Martin has argued that *mûthoi* in the *Iliad* are "the full, exaggerated speech-acts of heroes" whereas *epea* (ἔπεα) "represent the means of conducting social life."[50] Martin observes that "the heroes and gods of the *Iliad* engage in only three types of *mûthos* discourses: commands, boast-and-insult contests . . . and the recitation of remembered events."[51]

---

48. E.g., *Il.* 2.55; 10.302; 11.215; 12.43, 86; 13.152; 15.303; *Od* 1.277, 2.196; 4.782; 14.469; 24.153.

49. It is more likely to be the tales whose provenance cannot be identified than the teller, since the epic world is insistent about the identification of strangers. The word *hothen* here at *Od.* 11.366 is unlikely to mean 'from which' since, elsewhere in Homeric usage, ὅθεν *hothen* is used adverbially to mean 'from where': *Il.* 2.307, 852, 857; 4.58; 10.200; 11.758; *Od.* 3.319; 4.358; 7.131; 17.206; 20.383; 21.142; 22.460.

50. Martin 1989:21.

51. Martin 1989:47.

Martin goes on to compare the hero's ability to recite remembered events to the performance of a poet. Both hero and poet speak *mûthos*, as Odysseus does here, but Odysseus has gone one step beyond Martin's Iliadic hero: he is not performing *like* a poet; for the moment he has taken over and *become* the poet in what constitutes a competition of entertainers, a kind of *agôn* that Martin contends is an element of all Iliadic *mûthos*[52] and that I suggest is an element of all narrative *pseudea*. In his performance, Odysseus accurately recounts "remembered" events of the Trojan War and its aftermath[53] (*mûthos . . . katelexas*)—material belonging to epic transmission—but interwoven with *pseudea*—material outside the parameters of epic. Odysseus tells both epic and non-epic material in his own voice, in the first person, expertly creating the illusion of remembering all these events, however improbable that may seem by any objective standard, modern or ancient. The suffering is real and remembered: the helplessness, the fear, the agony, and the loss. Odysseus' audience can identify with the experience of his suffering if not with all the events that cause it, events whose recounting might be dismissed if recounted by a less skillful teller. Alkinoos' use of the terms *mûthos* and *pseudea* in what seems to be opposition[54] indicates not only recognition of a difference in the two types of narrative but also appreciation of Odysseus' ability to tell both and to interweave them in such a way that disbelief is suspended, and the audience is "charmed."[55]

Odysseus' narrative is a tapestry, literally a fabrication[56] (as is appropriate for Athena's chosen hero), and he is rewarded as much for the skill with which he weaves his tale as he is for the nobility of the deeds he recounts or for the enormity of the sufferings he "recollects." Odysseus is not a deceiver here in any moral sense because of his *pseudea*; he is a spellbinding performer. In fact, because he is the better of the two performers in *Odyssey*

---

52. Martin 1989:220.

53. E.g., the sacking of the city at Ismaros (*Od.* 9.39-61) and the ensuing storm.

54. I do not claim that these two terms are always opposed in Greek poetry—surely not in Pindar—but that they seem to indicate very different types of material in Homer.

55. ὣς ἔφαθ᾽, οἱ δ᾽ ἄρα πάντες ἀκὴν ἐγένοντο σιωπῇ,/ κηληθμῷ δ᾽ ἔσχοντο κατὰ μέγαρα σκιόεντα 'Thus he spoke, and all were gripped by silence, held by a spell throughout the shadowy halls' (*Od.* 11.333-334; 13.1-2).

56. See Nagy 1996b.64n23 on weaving as a metaphor for songmaking in Homeric poetry.

8-12, Odysseus, and not Demodokos, is invited to continue, and, after his night of performance, Alkinoos orders (*Od.* 13.1-15) each man of the Phaeacians to add a 'great tripod' and a 'cauldron' to the collection of lovely gifts that had been laid out for Odysseus earlier (*Od.* 8.400-432). Odysseus, having given a delightful and innovative performance, goes home with all the prizes.

Conclusion

In all examples of narrative *pseudea* in Homeric poetry, common elements of context and implication can be identified: *pseudea* are "false" to the extent that they contradict the narrative reality of a particular poem—whether by altering the report of an episode described elsewhere in the poem (omens, prophecies, dreams) or, in the case of narrative *pseudea*, by transmitting a variant version of epic material or introducing non-epic material like folktales; the speaker of *pseudea* intends to distract his audience from "reality," to create at least suspension of disbelief, and sometimes delight; *pseudea* are told in agonistic situations where the speaker plans on a particular effect and intends to gain an advantage or win a prize by the telling of his tales. It is perhaps because of these common factors that *pseudo*-words acquire increasingly sinister connotations in the Greek language. But in its purest sense in Homer, I think, a *pseudo*-word most often indicates a story told to a listener who can recognize the story element and who understands that it is not intended to convey accurate information about living people and current events. The listener does not so much believe the story as he surrenders his disbelief—and often enjoys doing it.

A *pseudo*-word applied to a narrative sequence designates something more than a lie and something less. Stripped of the moral implications attaching to "lie" in English but amplified by the common associations outlined above, *pseudo*-words applied to narrative designate a particular kind of story told in a particular kind of situation for a particular purpose. These stories represent events that happen outside the boundaries of epic, outside the realm of events "remembered" by heroes, and, therefore, they help to define what belongs within those boundaries. They constitute variant versions rather than deceptions; fictions rather than lies. In the *Iliad*, such material includes variations in the legends of Tydeus, Herakles, and Bellerophon: material from a past that is already hazy and distant to the characters living within the poem. In the *Odyssey*, this material includes variant versions of the fate of Odysseus, told while his fate is still unresolved within the epic's own world, and type-tales—folktales, travelers' tales, monster tales, something for everyone. Non-epic material has found its way into hexameter epic, sparingly in the *Iliad*, where its exclusion would not much affect the overall picture but, in the *Odyssey*, Odysseus' ease in telling *pseudea* is central to his character, and the hero's own *pseudea* comprise significant pieces of the poem. They stand out, almost asserting themselves as not only appropriate for inclusion in epic poetry but also as the very foundation of a particular style of epic poetry, one which explodes the exclusive generic confines of epic as war poetry. The *pseudea* of the *Odyssey* are an important organizing element of its composition, and their skillful incorporation marks one way in which the *Odyssey* separates itself from, even competes with, a less inclusive, less varied epic style such as that of the *Iliad*.

In Homeric poetry, *pseudo*-words signal the inclusion of material expected to be excluded; the agonistic settings in which this material appears reflect not only a struggle between immediate contestants but also, and especially, an ongoing contest between versions and types of material vying for inclusion in epic, vying for a place in the genre. The off-hand translation of a *pseudo*-word as "lie" not only focuses anglophone attention on moral implications that are largely missing from Homeric contexts but also completely masks the generic implications. I suggest that, in most Homeric instances, a more informed and informative translation of a *pseudo*-word should convey a sense of variation rather than deception, thus attempting to indicate in English the sort of inter- and intra-textual generic dialogue that these words signal in the Greek of Homeric poetry.

II
DIACHRONIC HOMER

5

Penelope and the *Pênelops*

Olga Levaniouk

The search for the meaning of Penelope's name is an ancient one. Already Eustathius offers several conflicting versions, most of them attempts to connect Penelope's name with weaving, for example, Πηνελόπη *Pênelopê* from πένεσθαι *penesthai* 'to work' and λόπος *lopos* 'onion-shell', but metaphorically, Eustathius says, referring to λώπιον *lôpion* 'robe' [1] These folk etymologies clearly refer to the *Odyssey* by underscoring weaving as an instrument of Penelope's famous cunning. But alongside them, Eustathius cites the authority of Didymos for derivation of *Pênelopê* from the name of a water bird, πηνέλοψ *pênelops*—an etymology supported by modern linguistics. Here at least the ancient perceptions and the results of linguistic research coincide, yet this etymology has enjoyed little popularity in modern scholarship. The reason is a perceived lack of relevance to the *Odyssey*: in contrast with etymologies based on weaving, there is no immediately apparent link between Penelope and water birds, and the name seems, therefore, insignificant.

Eustathius himself addresses the problem of relevance by relating Didymus' explanation: Penelope used to be called differently, but on one occasion she was thrown into the sea by Palamedes and saved by the πηνέλοπες *pênelopes*, hence the change of her name. More will be said about this story later, but for now it is simply important to mention that it takes us beyond the Homeric *Odyssey*. Is there any connection between the πηνέλοψ *pênelops* and Penelope as we know her from Homer? In this essay I will discuss that question, suggesting some compositional connections between Penelope and the etymology of her name.

---

1. Eustathius on *Od.* 1.65.34-36. See also n81.

95

I. The Evidence

The main difficulty in interpreting Penelope's name lies in the scarcity of information provided by the Greek sources about the *pênelops*: less than ten lines is all that we have by way of description, and no certain identification of this bird has been made (although, to be fair, the volume of information is not always helpful for identifications—the birds of mythology need not conform to biological species). However, it is generally accepted that the *pênelops* is some species of wild duck or goose.

The *pênelops'* connection with ducks is based on a comment in the Scholia to Aristophanes' *Birds* that the *pênelops* is similar to a duck (νήττη μέν ἐστιν ὅμοιον),[2] a remark that is not sufficient to draw even a vague conclusion about the species of the *pênelops* itself. Besides, the passage in the Scholia is unclear for another reason: it goes on to say that the *pênelops* is about the size of a pigeon (περιστερή), but larger than the duck (νήττη). But pigeons are not larger than ducks, which makes the scholiast's description contradictory, as long as modern identifications of περιστερή and νήττη are correct (and they seem to be quite secure). The only conclusion that can perhaps be made from this passage is that the *pênelops* is of a relatively small size, since both the duck and the pigeon are relatively small.

Equally tenuous, but more abundant, evidence connects the *pênelops* with geese. The *pênelops* is named together with χήν 'goose', ὁ μικρὸς χὴν ὁ ἀγελαῖος 'small gregarious goose', and χηναλώπηξ 'sheldrake', in an Aristotelian passage.[3] However, about the *pênelops* specifically, Aristotle mentions only that they tend to live at sea. Similarly, Aristophanes places the *pênelops* next to χήν 'goose' in a list of birds [4]

In short, while it emerges clearly that the *pênelops* is a small water bird, a more precise identification remains problematic. Moreover, the scarcity of references in prose and the obscurity of descriptions may not be accidental: they may point to complex interactions between the *pênelops* of poetry and mythology and the *pênelops* of natural history. One might even wonder

---

2. Scholia to Aristophanes *Birds* 1302.
3. *Historia Animalium* 593b23. Sheldrake (χηναλώπηξ) is a species of duck, but it is goose-like in appearance and was seen as a goose by the Greeks.
4. *Birds* 1302.

whether the *pênelops* originated as a species or as a mythological concept, later identified with an observable bird. For this reason, its biological identification is of little significance for the purpose of this essay. What is more important is the poetic concept of the *pênelops*, or rather glimpses of it, preserved by the few surviving sources.

It should be noted here that several scholars have made a connection on the poetic level as well between the *pênelops* as a source for Penelope's name and the geese. In Book 19, Penelope dreams that an eagle has killed the geese in her house, and that she mourns for them. Penelope's delight in her geese and the extraordinary grief she displays at their destruction have long been noticed,[5] and Paul Kretschmer related this connection of Penelope with her geese to the *pênelops*.[6] Kretschmer argues that geese are traditionally regarded as faithful and loving mates, and it is this quality that connects them to Penelope, the proverbial faithful wife—and is signaled by the derivation of her name from *pênelops*. Further, Louise Pratt points out that geese were known in the Greek sources for their vigilance and prudence, especially in guarding their nest: Aristotle speaks of their ἤθεα αἰσχυντηλὰ καὶ φυλακτικά 'prudent and vigilant habits' and, in a Hellenistic epigram, a goose on a woman's omb is said to be a sign of δόμων φυλακᾶς μελεδήμονα 'careful guardianship of the house'.[7] Both prudence and guardianship of the house are, of course, two of Penelope's most prominent qualities.[8]

Inasmuch as the *pênelops* is associated with geese in some sources, it is possible that Penelope's name signals her fidelity and guardianship of the house. Still, it is to χήν 'goose' that these qualities are traditionally ascribed, not to the *pênelops*, and it is not from the root χην- that Penelope's name is formed. Moreover, no textual links have been noticed between the descriptions of the *pênelops* and those of geese as faithful guardians: the connection here is based entirely on the assumption that the *pênelops* is a type of goose. But does the name πηνέλοψ *pênelops* simply equal χήν *khên* 'goose'? And does the association between geese and the *pênelops* exhaust

5. For a way of reconciling Penelope's connection with her geese and Odysseus' identification of the geese with suitors, see Pratt 1994:149-151.
6. Kretschmer 1945:80-93.
7. Antipater Sidonius 7.425.7
8. In discussing the poetic relevance of Penelope's geese I rely on Pratt 1994.

the significance of Penelope's name? In this essay I suggest that there is a different poetic concept of the *pênelops*, which takes one far away from the geese and which can help uncover other connotations of Penelope's name equally meaningful in the light of her role in the *Odyssey*.

Glimpses of this poetic concept are preserved in two fragments of lyric poetry, which I cite here in full:

ὄρνιθες τίνες οἴδ' Ὠκεάνω γᾶς ἀπὺ πειράτων
ἦλθον πανέλοπες ποικιλόδειροι τανυσίπτεροι;
(Alcaeus 21)

What are these birds that came from the limits of the earth,
the long-winged *pênelopes* with varied[-sounding] throats?[9]

τοῦ μὲν πετάλοσιν ἐπ' ἀκροτάτοις
ἰζάνοισι ποικίλαι αἰολόδειροι
πανέλοπες ἀλιπορφυρίδες ⟨τε⟩ καὶ
ἀλκύονες τανυσίπτεροι
(Ibycus 8 317a)

On its topmost leaves sit variously colored
pênelopes with changeful[-sounding] throats,[10]
gleaming like the sea, and long-winged halcyons.

Unfortunately, the Ibycus fragment comes from an extremely corrupt and obscure passage in Athenaeus' *Deipnosophistae*, where it is cited in an unmetrical form.[11] The meter can be corrected by the transposition without significantly altering the syntax of the passage; the resulting word order,

---

9. For a justification of 'with varied-[sounding] throats' as a translation of ποικιλόδειρος, see Nagy 1996a:59n1 following Irwin 1974:72-73.

10. For a remark on the translation of αἰολόδειρος, see page 96. The square brackets in my translations of ποικιλόδειροι in Alcaeus and αἰολόδειροι in Ibycus are meant to represent the multiple sense of the Greek words, which are capable of referring both to color and sound.

11. Athenaeus 9.388d. The manuscript reading of the fragment is: τοῦ μὲν πετάλοισιν ἐπ' ἀκροτάτοις (Π ἐπακροτάτοισι) ξανθοῖσι (Β ξανθίαι) ποικίλαι πανέλοπες αἰολόδειροι αδοιπορφυρίδες (Β ἀδ) καὶ ἀλκύονες τανυσίπτεροι.

accepted in most modern editions, is the one cited here. But the most difficult problem of the fragment is the manuscript reading αδοιπορφυρίδες, which seems to the editors to be meaningless. Here I choose the reading ἁλιπορφυρίδες 'gleaming or flashing like the sea' suggested by Schneidewin[12] (and accepted by Hermann[13] and by D'Arcy Thompson).[14] Most editors prefer λαθιπορφυρίδες, suggested by Schweighauser.[15] But for several reasons it seems to me more problematic. First of all, not only does no manuscript read λαθιπορφυρίδες at this place, but this word is also not attested anywhere in Greek. The same passage of Athenaeus has the form λαθιπόρφυρας, but this is also not attested elsewhere. Λαθιπορφυρίς, then, is an editorial creation, a conjecture with regard not only to its occurrence, but even to its existence. Secondly, the meaning that the word is supposed to have seems unlikely. In the passage in question, Athenaeus describes a bird that he calls πορφυρίς; in the process he speaks about the secretive behavior of another bird, πορφυρίων, which feeds only where no one can see it. The word λαθιπορφυρίς is supposed somehow to reflect this behavior (Liddell and Scott translate this word as 'feeding in the dark'). But Athenaeus describes as secretive only the πορφυρίων, and his main point in this chapter is precisely that πορφυρίων and πορφυρίς are two different species, which seems to destroy the main reason for the existence of the word λαθιπορφυρίς. Moreover, as Schneidewin points out, other λαθι- compounds do not have the analogous meaning of 'secrecy', but rather of forgetting or bringing forgetfulness (e.g., λαθίπονος 'forgetful of sorrow'; λαθιπήμων 'banishing sorrow').

A separate question is whether one should take the -πορφυρίς compound in the Ibycus fragment as the name of a species, or whether it should be taken as an epithet either of the *pênelops* or the halcyon. The editors who take it to be the name of a species are obviously compelled by the fact that Athenaeus discusses a species πορφυρίς. But Athenaeus introduces the Ibycus passage with the following phrase: Ἴβυκος δέ τινας λαθιπόρφυρας ὀνομάζει διὰ τούτων 'Ibycus calls some birds *lathiporphurai* in the following words'. It

12. Schneidewin 1833:128-131.
13. As quoted by Bergk *Poetae Lyrici Graeci* 239 (on Ibycus 8 [13]).
14. Thompson 1936:46.
15. See Schweighauser on Athenaeus 9.388d.

seems to me that by saying τινας 'some', Athenaeus indicates that Ibycus is speaking not of the πορφυρίς, but, on the contrary, of some other birds. Perhaps the use of adjectival form with -πόρφυρας, rather than πορφυρίς in the introductory phrase, also suggests that Athenaeus regards the following πορφυρίς compound as an epithet and not an independently standing noun. One may object that Athenaeus, then, appears to be citing a fragment that has nothing to do with the object of his discussion. But Athenaeus' choice is understandable: he might have felt that it would be unfair to overlook a passage with a πορφυρίς compound in it, especially since πορφυρίς is such a rare word. In fact, Athenaeus cites virtually all the instances of it in the known Greek sources. However, he does not do more than adduce the passage as a piece of evidence, leaving judgment as to its significance up to the reader.

Finally, whatever the first part of the compound may be, the syntax of the fragment seems to point toward the *pênelopes* rather than the halcyons as the noun corresponding to the epithet -πορφυρίς. It is taken with halcyons by D'Arcy Thompson, who accepts the reading ἀλιπορφυρίς in our fragment, and even describes the word as "another name for the halcyon," but unfortunately he does not cite the fragment in full.[16] In all the readings known to me, the word ἀλιπορφυρίδες is separated by καὶ from ἀλκυόνες τανυσίπτεροι, a strange division if Thompson's reading is to be accepted: if it is another noun describing halcyons one would expect it to stand in apposition of ἀλκυόνες. On the other hand, ἀλιπορφυρίδες is not separated by any conjunction from πανέλοπες, so that it seems likely that it should be taken as an epithet of the *pênelops*.

II.   The *Pênelops*, the Halcyon, and the Nightingale

Whether or not this reconstruction is correct, in the Ibycus fragment *pênelopes* are mentioned together with halcyons. I think the joint occurrence is significant, especially since the two birds also come together in Aristophanes' *Birds* (298):

---

16. Thompson 1936:46.

οὑτοσὶ δὲ πηνέλοψ ἐκεινοσὶ δέ γ' ἀλκυών

This one is a *pênelops*, that one is a halcyon.

Given the scarcity of references to the *pênelops*, it is important that in two of them it is mentioned together with the halcyon. The two birds also share the epithets ποικίλος 'of varied color', τανυσίπτερος 'long-winged', and ἀλιπορφυρίς—if it should be restored in Ibycus. This restoration is important because ἀλιπόρφυρος is a fairly rare adjective, which is, however, consistently used of the halcyon and of birds closely related to it, for example the κηρύλος *kerylos*, whose name Thompson defines as "a doubtful, perhaps foreign, word, sometimes applied to the Halcyon, sometimes compared with it."[17] Sometimes the *kerylos* is regarded as the male counterpart of the halcyon, sometimes vice versa, and naturally they share epithets (not only ἀλιπόρφυρος, but also εἴαρος/ἐαρινός 'of spring' as in Alcman 12 (20):

οὔ μ' ἔτι, παρσενικαὶ μελιγάρυες ἰαρόφωνοι,
γυῖα φέρην δύναται· βάλε δή, βάλε κηρύλος εἴην
ὅς τ' ἐπὶ κύματος ἄνθος ἄμ' ἀλκυόνεσσι ποτῆται
νηλεὲς ἦτορ ἔχων ἀλιπόρφυρος εἴαρος ὄρνις.

My knees can not carry me any longer, O sweet sounding
maidens with loud voices. If only I could become a kerylos,
who flies together with the halcyons over the blossom
   of the wave,
a sea-gleaming bird of spring with a relentless heart!

Identified with kerylos as a male halcyon is another seabird, κῆυξ *kêyx* or κῆξ *kêx*, whose name, clearly onomatopoeic, also imitates the cry of a female halcyon.[18] The *kêyx* is a type of seagull or tern, according to D'Arcy

---

17. Thompson 1936:139; in the list of birds in Arisotphanes' *Birds*, quoted above, *kerylos* is mentioned immediately after the halcyon (*Birds* 299):
Pe. τίς γάρ ἐσθ' οὔπισθεν αὐτῆς;
Eu. ὅστις ἐστί: κηρύλος.
Note also that the halcyon is female.
18. Scholia on Lucian 1.178.

Thompson,[19] who, however, describes the name as a "vague, poetic, and even legendary word . . . hardly used as a concrete and specific bird-name." I suggest that, as a poetic concept, the *pênelops* belongs to the same group of birds as the *kerylos*, the *kêyx*, and the halcyon.

The poetic association between *pênelops* and halcyon calls, perhaps, for a few words about the latter. Among the fabulous birds of Greek mythology, the halcyon has a fair claim to first place because so much legendary and often mysterious information is associated with it. But for the moment I would like only to point out two features of the mythical halcyon that are relevant for the discussion of the *pênelops* and the *Odyssey*. First, halcyons are known for their mournful song, often described as a θρῆνος 'lament', a song of a female who has lost her mate. For example, Dionysius describes the halcyon thus:[20]

> ἀλκυών· εἰ τὸν ἄρρενα τελευτῆσαι συμβαίη, βορᾶς ἀπεχόμεναι
> καὶ ποτοῦ ἐπὶ πολὺ θρηνοῦσι καὶ διαφθείρονται, καὶ τὰς ᾠδὰς
> δ' εἰ καταπαύειν μέλλοιεν, κήυξ κήυξ συνεχῶς ἐπειποῦσαι σιγῶσιν.

Halcyon: if the male happens to die, they [the females] mourn for a long
time, abstaining from food and drink, and perish, and when
they are about to stop singing, they utter keyx, keyx at frequent intervals,
and then fall silent.

Second, for this song as well as for other features, the halcyon is often compared to the nightingale. In fact, D'Arcy Thompson observes that ἀλκυών 'halcyon' and ἀηδών 'nightingale' are easily confused.[21] For example, different manuscripts of Aristotle's *Historia Animalium* 8.593b9 give either ἀλκυών or ἀηδών. The Suda lists ἀλκυών between ἀηδών and κήυξ among the θαλάσσια ζῷα 'marine animals'.[22] And, most strikingly, there is a version of the Itylus-myth, preserved by Boios, where the mother of Aedon-nightingale is transformed into a halcyon.[23]

---

19. Thompson 1936:22.
20. Dionysius, *De Avibus* 2.7.
21. Thompson 1936:22.
22. Suda. s.v. Ἡμερινὰ ζῷα.
23. In Antoninus Liberalis 11. According to him and Athenaeus (9.393e), Boios is

But to return to the comparison, the voice of the halcyon is often described in the same terms as the voice of the nightingale, as 'sweet' (ἡδύς), 'shrill', or 'clear' (λιγύς), and also by a variety of adjectives with the underlying meaning 'mourning' (e.g., πολύθρηνος πολύδακρυς):

τῶν ἀλκυόνων δ' οὐκ εἴποι τις εἰς φωνὴν ὄρνεον ἥδιον.[24]

One couldn't name a bird with a sweeter voice than
    the halcyon.

πάντη δ' ὀρνίθων γενεὴ <u>λιγύφωνον</u> ἀείδει. <u>ἀλκυόνες</u>
περὶ κῦμα, χελιδόνες ἀμφὶ μέλαθρα, κύκνος ἐπ'
ὄχθαισιν ποταμοῦ, καὶ ὑπ' ἄλσος <u>ἀηδών</u>

The whole race of birds sings in a clear voice: halcyons
around the waves, swallows around houses, the swan
on riverbanks, and the nightingale under the cover of groves.

θαλαττία τις ὄρνις . . . <u>πολύθρηνος</u> καὶ <u>πολύδακρυς</u>,
περὶ ἧς δὴ παλαιὸς ἀνθρώποις μεμύθειται λόγος.[25]

[halcyon is] a sea bird . . . much lamenting and much crying,
about which an ancient tale is told by men.

Or at *Il.* 9.561:

τὴν δὴ τότ' ἐν μεγάροισι πατὴρ καὶ πότνια μήτηρ
Ἀλκυόνην καλέεσκον ἐπώνυμον, οὕνεκ' ἄρ' αὐτῆς

---

the author of the Ὀρνιθογονία (*Origin of Birds*), but there is some confusion about his identity. Some scholars think that the name is a re-interpretation of Boio, the name of an ancient Delphic priestess, to whom the Ὀρνιθογονία is apparently attributed by the antiquarian Philochoros (fourth-third century BCE). See *RE* s.v. Boio.

24. Dionysius, *De Avibus* 2.7.
25. Beginning of Lucian *Halcyon*.

μήτηρ ἀλκυόνος πολυπενθέος οἶτον ἔχουσα
κλαῖεν ὅ μιν ἑκάεργος ἀνήρπασε Φοῖβος Ἀπόλλων

And her father and honored mother in the halls called her
[Kleopatre] Alkyone, as a by-name, since her mother,
having the mournful voice of the halcyon,
wept because the far-reaching Phoebus Apollo had snatched her away.

Like the halcyon's, the nightingale's song is most often interpreted as a cry of lamentation. According to the myth, Aedon killed her own son Itylos, or Itys, and, after being changed into a bird by Zeus, continuously laments him, repeating his name. The Greeks believed that the refrain Ἴτυν, Ἴτυν 'Itys, Itys' could be heard in the nightingale's song.[26] The nightingale is traditionally described as δακρυόεσσα 'tearful' (Euripides, *Helen* 1109), βαρύδακρυς 'weeping grievously' (1110), and ὀδυρομένη 'lamenting' (Moschus 3.9); her song is called μινύρισμα 'warbling' (Theocritus, *Epigrammata* 4.11), πολύθρηνος 'much-wailing' (Euripides, *Phaethon* fr. 773.23), and πολύδακρος 'of many tears' (Aristophanes, *Birds* 211). All of these terms recall the halcyon.

In descriptions of the nightingale, epithets referring to the bird's song often merge with those referring to its appearance. For example, in *Works and Days* (203) it is called ποικιλόδειρος 'with varied throat', and Gregory Nagy has shown that this word refers not to the color of the bird's neck but to its variegated (ποικίλος) song, in this sense being synonymous with another epithet ποικιλόγηρυς 'with varied voice' that is given by the Scholia to the same passage.[27] Another interesting epithet of the nightingale is αἰολόδειρος (Nonnus 47.33), which probably stands in the same relationship to αἰολόφωνος 'shifting in sound' as ποικιλόδειρος to ποικιλόγηρυς. Liddell and Scott translate αἰολόδειρος as 'with sheeny neck', but there is more to the epithet: αἰόλος means 'swift, rapid, changeable', and by extension

---

26. The story of Aedon derives from Boios (in Antoninus Liberalis 11). The myth of Itylos, Philomele, and Procne is told in Eustathius on *Od.* 19.518 (cf. Apollodorus, *Bibliotheca* 3.14.8, where the names of the sisters are reversed) and mentioned in many sources, among others Aeschylus, *Suppliants* 60, *Agamemnon* 1142; Sophocles, *Electra* 107; Euripides, *Rhesus* 546.

27. Nagy 1996a:59n1.

'changeful of hue, glittering', so that the word could refer not only to the bird's color, but also to its voice, which in the case of the nightingale is more justifiable. It is through these characteristic epithets that the nightingale is linked not only with the halcyon, but also, more interestingly, with the *pênelops*. The *pênelops* is described as ποικιλόδειρος in Alcaeus' fragment and αἰολόδειρος in Ibycus, where it is also ποικίλος—another epithet connecting it with the halcyon, so called by Simonides (Aristotle, *Historia Animalium* 542b4).

Moreover, in Ibycus' fragment *pênelopes* and halcyons are represented as sitting πετάλοισιν ἐπ' ἀκροτάτοις 'on the topmost leaves', literally 'petals', a topos about the nightingale, who sings δενδρέων ἐν πετάλοισι καθεζομένη πυκινοῖσι 'sitting in the dense leaves (petals) of the trees' in the *Odyssey* (19.520). This might seem unremarkable, since many birds sit in trees, but in fact only particular creatures sit "in the petals." In the whole of Greek poetry outside of the Ibycus fragment, this expression is applied only to the nightingale, the swallow, the sparrow, the cuckoo, and the cicada, and only about the nightingale is it used repeatedly.[28] In every case, the image is that of a small and fragile creature, whose delicacy is matched by the delicacy of petals in which it hides.[29] And without exception, the creatures that sit "in the petals" sing in a voice that is like the nightingale's in its mournful tone. The swallow in Aristophanes' *Frogs* (682) 'twitters the tearful nightingale song' (τρύζει δ' ἐπίκλαυτον ἀηδόνιον νόμον), the cicada in Alcaeus 347 'echoes out of the petals' (ἄχει δ' ἐκ πετάλων), the sparrow in the *Iliad* (2.315) flies around her nest 'bewailing her dear children' (ὀδυρομένη φίλα τέκνα), reminding one of the nightingale in the *Odyssey* (19.522), who sings 'mourning her dear son Itylos' (παῖδ' ὀλοφυρομένη Ἴτυλον φίλον). The nightingale, about whom the expression ἐν πετάλοισι "in the petals" is used most often, is par excellence the tiny bird with a

---

28. *Od.* 19.520; Homeric Hymns 19.17-18; *Anthologia Graeca* 12.2.3, 12.136.3.

29. The only bird noticeably larger than a nightingale or a sparrow who is said to sit ἐν πετάλοισι is the cuckoo in *Works and Days* 486, and it is interesting that only here is the expression qualified: δρυὸς ἐν πετάλοισι 'in oak leaves': a larger bird calls for sturdier "petals." Note also that the cuckoo is also a bird with a remarkable voice, sometimes seen as a voice of lament in the Greek poetic tradition. Cf. Alexiou's list of birds who join the lamentation in Greek folksong: cuckoo, halcyon, nightingale, swallow, turtledove (Alexiou 1974:93-97).

musical voice, the main manifestation of a poetic figure of which the sparrow, the swallow, and even the cicada can be seen as variations.[30] The *pênelopes* and the halcyons, which sit on πετάλοισι ἐπ' ἀκροτάτοις 'the topmost petals' in the Ibycus fragment, are presented in the light of the same theme. Here, then, is another instance in which we see the nightingale, the halcyon, and the *pênelops* linked by poetic associations.

It goes without saying that it would be contrary to the poetic diction of the Ibycus fragment to see the *pênelops* here as a duck or a goose: in Greek poetry as much as in actuality, it is unusual for ducks or geese to sit even on trees, not to mention petals. But it is probably not an accident that the kingfisher, identified early on with the halcyon, is an exception among the water birds: only slightly larger than the sparrow, this bird lives on tree-covered banks of rivers and lakes and has a habit of sitting on the tips of slender branches, which project over the water, and diving off them [31]

III.   Penelope and the Birds

Now that some associations have been drawn between the *pênelops*, halcyon, and nightingale, it is time to ask how they apply to the *Odyssey*. On a surface level, Penelope herself establishes a connection by comparing herself to a nightingale in Book 19. Some people, Penelope says, find a relief from their sorrows in sleep, but for her the nights are full of grief. As the nightingale sings in the springtime, varying her voice, so Penelope spends sleepless nights, her mind divided whether to stay in Odysseus' house or to go away at last (*Od.* 19.515-523):

---

30. That the creatures who can sit "in the petals" do form a recognizable group is confirmed, for example, by the corresponding perception of Joannes Chrysostomus:
εἴ τις δὲ καὶ ἠχὴ γένοιτο. λιγυρὰ καὶ πολλὴν καταχέουσα τῶν
ἀκουόντων τὴν ἡδονήν ἢ γὰρ ὄρνιθες ᾠδικοὶ ἄκροις τῶν δένδρων
ἐφιζάνουσι τοῖς πετάλοις. καὶ τέττιγες. καὶ ἀηδόνες. καὶ χελιδόνες.
συμφώνως μίαν τινὰ ἀποτελοῦσι μουσικήν
'and if there also arises some sound, it is clear and it streams very pleasantly for those who hear it. For the song birds, sitting on the topmost petals of the trees, cicadas, and nightingales, and swallows, perform the same music in unison.'
31. Thompson 1936:46-47.

αὐτὰρ ἐπεὶ νὺξ ἔλθῃ, ἕλῃσί τε κοῖτος ἅπαντας
κεῖμαι ἐνὶ λέκτρῳ, πυκιναὶ δέ μοι ἀμφ' ἀδινὸν κῆρ
ὀξεῖαι μελεδῶναι ὀδυρομένην ἐρέθουσιν.
ὡς δ' ὅτε Πανδαρέου κούρη. χλωρηὶς ἀηδών
καλὸν ἀείδῃσιν ἔαρος νέον ἱσταμένοιο.
δενδρέων ἐν πετάλοισι καθεζομένη πυκινοῖσιν.
ἥ τε θαμὰ τρωπῶσα χέει πολυηχέα φωνήν.
παῖδ' ὀλοφυρομένη Ἴτυλον φίλον. ὅν ποτε χαλκῷ
κτεῖνε δι ' ἀφραδίας. κοῦρον Ζήθοιο ἄνακτος. .

But when the night comes and sleep takes all others,
I lie in my bed and the bitter cares, swarming around my heart,
torment me in my grief.
As when the daughter of Pandareos, the tremulous nightingale,
perching in the deep of the forest foliage, sings beautifully when
   the Spring has just begun;
she, frequently varying the strains of her voice,
pours out melody, mourning her dear son Itylos,
son of the lord Zethos, whom she once killed with bronze when
   madness was on her.

Penelope's grief, in general, seems to erupt at night: again and again, she
cries in bed until Athena sends her sleep. Introducing her nightingale
comparison, Penelope establishes an opposition between daytime when she
indulges in lamentation and pays attention to her work (i.e., weaving), and
nights, which she spends without sleep, "bitter cares" crowding around her
heart (*Od.* 19.513-520). And so pervasive is the theme of Penelope's
sleepless grief that the following formula (only one of the several used for
similar occasions) is repeated four times (*Od.* 1.363; 16.450; 19.603; 21.357):

κλαῖεν ἔπειτ' Ὀδυσῆα, φίλον πόσιν, ὄφρα οἱ ὕπνον
ἡδὺν ἐπὶ βλεφάροισι βάλε γλαυκῶπις Ἀθήνη

and then she bewailed Odysseus, her dear husband,
until grey-eyed Athena cast sweet sleep over her eyelids.

108 Part II: Diachronic Homer

Also telling are Penelope's own descriptions of her nights, not only in the nightingale passage, but also, for example, at the end of Book 19, where, still talking to Odysseus, she describes her bed as στονόεσσα 'sorrowful' and αἰεὶ δάκρυσ' ἐμοῖσι πεφυρμένη 'always wetted with my tears' (*Od.* 19.595-596).

Nightingales, of course, sing at night, and the sleepless nightingale is a topos in Greek poetry. The nightingale is called ἄμορος ὕπνου 'having no share of sleep',[32] and the expression ὕπνος ἀηδόνειος 'nightingale sleep' came to mean a very short sleep.[33] The nightingale is most likely alluded to in Sophocles' *Trachiniae* (105):

οἷά τιν' ἄθλιον ὄρνιν,
οὔποτ' εὐνάζειν ἀδακρύτων βλεφάρων πόθον

like some unhappy bird,
never to lay to sleep the longing of tearless eyes.

But the Scholia suggest that these lines refer to the halcyon—understandably, since, as has been mentioned, incessant mourning is a feature of the halcyon as well.[34]

If this comparison might seem superficial, it is strengthened by the fact that Penelope's crying in the *Odyssey* and the songs of the nightingale and halcyon in Greek poetry are described in very similar terms. It has been already mentioned that both nightingale and halcyon are described with the word λιγύς 'shrill', as well as λιγύφθογγος, λιγύφωνος 'shrill-voiced'. The same word, although not exclusively, is used to describe Penelope's crying (κλαῖε μάλα λιγέως in *Od.* 21.55). The halcyon's voice is described as πολυπενθής in the *Iliad* (9.563), and the same adjective, in one of its two attestations in the *Odyssey*, is used by Penelope about herself (23.15).[35] The epithet πολύδακρυς 'of many tears' has been shown above to belong to the

---

32. Aelian, *Varia Historia* 12.20
33. Nichochares, fr.16, Nonnus, *Dionysiaca* 5.411. Cf. Sophocles, *Trachiniae* 107, *Cyranides* s.v. εὐβοή, Suda s.v. οὐδ' ὅσον ἀηδόνες ὑπνώουσιν.
34. Among others: Lucian, *Halcyon* 2; Ovid, *Metamorphoses* 11.410; cf. Dionysius, *De Avibus* 2.7.
35. It is used about Odysseus in *Od.* 18.386.

halcyon as well as to the nightingale, and in the *Odyssey* it is used three times, each time about Penelope (*Od.* 19.213, 251; 21.55). The verb μινυρίζω 'complain in a low tone, whimper, warble', whose derivatives are used to describe the nightingale's song,[36] occurs in the *Odyssey* in the description of Penelope's crying when she learns that Telemachus has left Ithaca, and is, perhaps, noteworthy in spite of the fact that it refers not to Penelope herself but to her maids:

> τὴν δ' ἄχος ἀμφεχύθη θυμοφθόρον, οὐδ' ἄρ' ἔτ' ἔτλη
> δίφρῳ ἐφέζεσθαι πολλῶν κατὰ οἶκον ἐόντων,
> ἀλλ' ἄρ' ἐπ' οὐδοῦ ἷζε πολυκμήτου θαλάμοιο
> οἴκτρ' ὀλοφυρομένη περὶ δὲ δμωαὶ μινύριζον.
>
> (*Od.* 4.716-719)

Heart-destroying sorrow came over her, and she could
no longer sit on a chair, although there were many in
the house, but sat on the floor of the well-built room,
piteously weeping, and around her the maids were wailing.

The expression οἴκτρ' ὀλοφυρομένη 'piteously weeping', used here about Penelope, is significant as well. First, it is a metrical doublet of παῖδ' ὀλοφυρομένη 'bewailing her child' used to describe the nightingale in Book 19, and occupies the same position in the verse. Second, it marks an especially dramatic occasion, and here it emphasizes the unusual nature of Penelope's crying. The same expression is used only once about Odysseus' companions,[37] when they are panic-stricken and cry in despair for Odysseus, who has left to meet Circe: they are convinced that their leader, and with him any hope of return, has been lost, and when he does come it seems to them that they are in Ithaca again. Otherwise, this expression is used only about Penelope (*Od.* 4.719 and *Od.* 19.543) and about the Muses weeping at Achilles' funeral.

---

36. *Epigrammata Graeca* 546. 9; Theocritus, *Epigrammata* 4.11.
37. *Od.* 10.409.

ἀμφὶ δέ σ' ἔστησαν κοῦραι ἁλίοιο γέροντος
οἴκτρ' ὀλοφυρόμεναι, περὶ δ' ἄμβροτα εἵματα ἔσσαν
Μοῦσαι δ' ἐννέα πᾶσαι ἀμειβόμεναι ὀπὶ καλῇ θρήνεον.
(*Od.* 24.58-61)

Around stood the daughters of the Old Man of the Sea,
piteously weeping, and they had immortal clothes on.
And all the nine Muses, answering in a beautiful voice, mourned you
[addressed to Achilles].

The Muses' lament is of an extraordinary nature, and so is the sound of
their divine voice, here signaled by ὀπί—a word that is never used to denote
an ordinary human voice but always has a connotation of the supernatural.
Apart from the Muses, it is used about the voice of Cassandra (11.421),
Athena (24.535), the Sirens (12.52, 160, 185, 187, 192) and only one other
character—the crying Penelope, at a striking moment when, with the coming
of the dawn, her voice awakens Odysseus (*Od.* 20.92).

The sirens, in turn, were called ἁρπυιόγουνοι ἀηδόνες 'harpy-legged
nightingales' (Lycophron 653), and in Homer their song is described in terms
we have already seen used about the nightingale: λιγυρή 'shrill' (*Od.* 12.183,
208) and also μελίγηρυς 'sweet-voiced', an epithet applied to the nightingale
in epigrams.[38] The nightingale's song itself is often depicted as in some way
supernatural or even divine, and so is the song of the halcyon. An indication
of this is the word φθόγγος, which never denotes a human voice but is used
about Polyphemos (9.257) and repeatedly about the Sirens (12.41, 159, 198;
18.199; 23.326). It also describes the voice of the nightingale and the
halcyon.[39]

The use of ὀπί, linking as it does Penelope's crying with the Sirens' song,
does more, therefore, than indicate the extraordinary qualities of Penelope's
voice: it brings us back to the "supernatural" voice of the nightingale.
Penelope's crying is described in the *Odyssey* in special terms that associate
it with the divine voices of Sirens and Muses as well as with the mournful
songs of the nightingale and halcyon.

---

38. E.g., *Anthologia Palatina* 7.44, 9.437.
39. E.g., Euripides *Hecuba* (337); Tymnes in *Anthologia Palatina* 7.199.

The associations between Penelope and the *pênelops*-halcyon-nightingale group are matters not only of expression but also of plot. The elaborate nightingale simile comes in the momentous scene when Penelope and Odysseus are facing each other in conversation for the first time.[40] The respect Penelope pays to her guest, her striking dream about the geese, which predicts Odysseus' coming and which the queen asks the beggar to interpret—all the tantalizing details of this scene continue to attract the attention of critics. One of the most remarkable and often commented upon features of the scene is Penelope's sincerity in revealing her mind to the stranger—Odysseus. In the words of Norman Austin, Penelope "reveals her inner turmoil with astonishing candor, but candor shaped into three symbolic *mythoi*."[41] The first of these *mythoi*, the one about the nightingale, expresses aspects of Penelope's condition and personality that have been present from the very beginning of the *Odyssey*, and its relevance has been discussed in recent scholarship, in particular in Ioanna Papadopoulou-Belmehdi's book *Le chant de Pénélope*.[42]

To give an example, Papadopoulou-Belmehdi, following Norman Austin, discusses in detail the relevance of the nightingale comparison for illuminating the relationship between Penelope and Telemachus.[43] She points out that by concentrating on Telemachus' coming to maturity, the first books of the *Odyssey* throw light on Penelope's situation, as we enter the poem just at the moment when it becomes desperately difficult for her to remain in Odysseus' house: now that her son is becoming a man, he claims this house as his inheritance. Penelope's refusal to marry is the cause of tension between herself and Telemachus, who calls her "mother yet no mother."[44] Penelope responds to this discord with ambivalent emotions, and in Book 19 she expresses her torment most clearly by relating it to the story of Aedon—nightingale—a mother who killed her son. While her son was young, Penelope explains to the disguised Odysseus, he did not want her to leave the house; but now he asks her to go, vexed that the suitors are spending his wealth. This statement comes immediately after Penelope's

---

40. *Od.* 19.99-600.
41. Austin 1975:228.
42. Papadopoulou-Belmehdi 1994.
43. Austin 1975:228-9; Papadopoulou-Belmehdi 1994:153-160.
44. *Od.* 23.97.

nightingale comparison: the myth of the mother who laments her son expresses Penelope's own uneasy emotions, for in spite of Telemachus' insistence, and even after his very life has been threatened by the suitors, Penelope is unable to come to a decision to leave.

Much more can be said about the relevance of the Aedon myth for the *Odyssey*, but this is not the place to reiterate all the recent scholarly work on the matter. The point I hope to contribute in this essay is that the reference to the nightingale is more than just an apt comparison. Penelope's connection to Aedon is not occasional, but intrinsic: she is not only compared, but related to the nightingale. It is, therefore, no accident that out of all the mythological characters, Penelope chooses Aedon, and it is not surprising that the comparison fits so remarkably well. It is not the case that Aedon's accidental similarities to Penelope made her a suitable object for comparison: a more likely explanation is that the intrinsic relationship between the two figures led to both the similarities and the appearance of the simile in the *Odyssey*.

Moreover, Penelope's relatedness to Aedon can be extended to include the latter's two sisters, the younger daughters of Pandareos. A reference to the younger Pandareids at the beginning of Book 20 follows closely upon the Aedon simile, introduced at the end of Book 19. In Book 20, Penelope prays for a gentle death or disappearance and, explaining her wish, compares herself to the Pandareids, who were snatched away by the winds and taken to the streams of Okeanos to become the servants of the Erinyes (*Od.* 20.66-78). This collocation appears significant: the two comparisons are in close proximity, they are both introduced by Penelope herself, and in Book 19 Aedon is called Πανδαρέου κούρη 'daughter of Pandareos', the same words that are used to designate her younger sisters in Book 20. Nor is the genealogical relation between the three daughters of Pandareos within myth accidental; in fact, it can be shown to correspond to a thematic relation between their stories. Based on the suggested intrinsic connection between Penelope and Aedon one might expect to find Penelope in a similar relationship to the other Pandareids. That this is indeed so is confirmed by thematic connections in the *Odyssey*, which link the two younger daughters of Pandareos both to Penelope and to Aedon.

To appreciate the implications of Penelope's prayer and comparison with the Pandareids, it is easiest to resort to the help of the Scholia, which describe the daughters of Pandareos as ἄγαμοι 'unmarried' and in another passage as ὡραῖαι 'ready for marriage'.[45] It is at this moment that they are snatched away by the winds, and Penelope, herself on the brink of marriage, wishes for the same fate.[46]

Homer calls the Pandareids ὀρφαναὶ ἐν μεγάροισι 'orphans in the house' (*Od.* 20.68) and Eustathius, explaining their curious fate, uses the same word to emphasize the bereavement, due to which they became ἀνώνυμοι 'nameless':

> περικαλεῖς μὲν οὖσαι δι' ὀρφανίαν δὲ δυσπραγοῦσαι
> καὶ εἰς ὑποδύσκολον καὶ ὡς οἷον εἰπεῖν ἐρινυῶδες ἦθος
> μεταβληθεῖσαι τῇ λύπῃ ᾤχοντο καὶ διὰ τοῦτο καὶ ἀνέμοις
> ἐπαχθῆναι καὶ Ἐρινύσι παραδοθῆναι μυθεύονται.[47]

> although very beautiful, they were ruined by grief and changed into
> an unpleasant and, so to say, Erinys-like character, and because of this,
> they are said to have been transported by the winds and handed
> over to the Erinyes.

Eustathius connects the fate of Pandareos' daughters with their grief and ill luck as orphans, a grief that affects not only their "name" but also their beauty. Again one is reminded of Penelope, who says that she would have had both beauty and fame, but it all perished when Odysseus left for Troy.[48]

While among the living, the daughters of Pandareos enjoyed a contradictory fortune. Orphaned daughters of a criminal father, they were reared by the goddesses and endowed with many gifts, including beauty and prudence surpassing those of all other women.[49] But the Pandareids received this marvelous upbringing only to be deprived of life in their prime. Snatched away by the winds, they are taken to the streams of Okeanos and given as servants to the 'grim Erinyes' (στυγερῇσιν ἐρινύσιν).[50] This is indeed a fitting appointment, for with the Erinyes are associated the souls of those who

---

45. Scholia on *Od.* 20.66, 518.
46. *Od.* 20.74-78.
47. Eustathius on *Od.* 19.518.
48. *Od.* 19.124-126.
49. *Od.* 20.67-72.
50. *Od.* 19.78.

have died an untimely or violent death (ἄωροι, βιαιοθάνατοι), unmarried (ἄγαμοι), and childless (ἄτεκνοι), in other words, of those who left life too early, before they could make a name for themselves or leave behind progeny, and who do not find peace in Hades, but wander and cross the border into the world of the living.[51] The Pandareids as well are neither in the underworld nor among the living: theirs is a strange and uncertain condition that is as much death as it is immortality, but that, in any case, takes a person out of the sphere of an ordinary human life, out of the social framework and company of other people. In her ambiguous position, Penelope is like them: on the one hand, she is the wife of a famous hero, occupying a position of power in his house, sharing in his fame and very aware of it (φῆμις 'fame' is among the things she cannot bear to leave at *Od.* 19.527); on the other hand, it is not known whether she is a wife or a widow: her status—her name—is unclear. The fate of the Pandareids is comparable also to the one Odysseus himself repeatedly rejects during his travels in order to return to the land of the living and regain his name. But Penelope finds this strange fate in harmony with her condition. Had Odysseus not come back, the uncertainty of her position would have been irresolvable, except, as with the Pandareids, by a supernatural force. In this sense, Penelope is again comparable not only to the two younger daughters of Pandareos but also to Aedon, who was turned into a bird when a human resolution was no longer possible. It is important that transformation into bird form in Greek myth almost invariably takes place when gods take pity on a hopeless mortal: among other examples, both Alkyone's and Aedon's transformations are described in such terms.[52]

---

51. Roscher 1886-1903:1501; Rohde 1925:292n1, 373n1, 680, 651. Cf. what Penelope says about Telemachus when she learns that he has left for Pylos (*Od* 4.727-728):

νῦν αὖ παῖδ' ἀγαπητὸν ἀνηρείψαντο θύελλαι
ἀκλέα ἐκ μεγάρων. οὐδ' ὁρμηθέντος ἄκουσα.
'And now the winds have snatched away my beloved child,
without fame, from the house, and I did not hear when he set out'.

52. In the version of the myth deriving from Boios and preserved by Antoninus Liberalis 11, Zeus is moved by pity to transform Aedon and her family, including her mother Alkyone, into birds. Cf. for example, the sisters of Meleager, who did not cease mourning for their brother until Artemis pitied them and changed them into birds (Antoninus Liberalis 2).

Penelope tells the story of the younger Pandareids in some detail, and it can be used as a paradigm for revealing her own situation. The fact that the younger daughters of Pandareos were given in service to the Erinyes, for example, is significant. The reason they suffered such a fate, the Scholia explain, was Zeus' anger at their father. Once Pandareos was in Crete and stole a golden dog from the sanctuary of Zeus (note that Penelope's father is also a notorious thief).[53] Then Pandareos left the dog with Tantalus in Phrygia and fled, escaping divine vengeance, with his wife and two unmarried daughters.[54] But Zeus saw Pandareos, killed him and his wife, and made the daughters slaves to the Erinyes. The abduction of the Pandareids, then, is the result of Zeus' vengeance and of the inescapable memory of Pandareos' crime, represented by the Erinyes. The eternal memory of past evil is also the fate of Pandareos' other daughter, Aedon: even as a bird she forever remembers and laments the murder of her son. There is no need to argue here for the central place that the theme of memory occupies in the *Odyssey*: it is the implacable memory of Odysseus that prevents Penelope from marrying one of the suitors, that compels her to deny her son his inheritance and use her every resource to stay in Odysseus' house. It is for release from the power of this memory that Penelope prays in Book 20, complaining of her "evil dreams" in which she sees Odysseus just the way he looked when he left for Troy.[55] To use the expression of Papadopoulou-Belmehdi, Odysseus virtually turns into an "erinys" for Penelope.[56]

Penelope's stubborn memory of Odysseus is arguably the single dominant feature of her character. And it is this feature that conjures up the myths not only of the nightingale but also of the halcyon. The story of Aedon, which, within a single version, incorporates most of the elements relevant for the *Odyssey*, is the one told by Boios, where Aedon's mother is turned into a halcyon.[57] In this story Aedon is married to a skillful craftsman named Πολύτεχνος 'of many crafts'. Note the similarity to polÊtropow, literally 'of many turns', the most marked epithet of Odysseus and had an only son Itys

---

53. *Od.* 19.395-397.
54. The time of Aedon's marriage is given variously by different sources.
55. *Od.* 20.83-90.
56. Papadopoulou-Belmehdi 1994:137.
57. In Antoninus Liberalis 11.

(note the tradition in Odysseus' family of having only one son).[58] The marriage is very happy, until Aedon and Polytekhnos excite the envy of the gods by saying that they love each other more that Zeus and Hera. As a punishment, Hera incites Aedon and Polytekhnos to compete as to who will be able to finish first—she her weaving or he the chariot he has been making. When Aedon wins the competition, Polytekhnos is so angered that he resolves on revenge. He travels to Aedon's father, Pandareos, and asks him to send Aedon's sister, Khelidonis 'Swallow', with him for a visit. Unsuspecting Pandareos lets his daughter go, but Polytekhnos rapes the girl on the way back, changes her clothes, cuts off her hair, and, after threatening her with death if she discloses her identity, gives her to Aedon as a slave. But one day Khelidonis breaks down in wailing by a fountain, and Aedon recognizes her. As revenge, the sisters kill Polytekhnos' son, prepare a meal from his body, and serve it to his father. Then they flee back to Pandareos' house. When Polytekhnos learns about the crime, he pursues them, only to be captured by Pandareos' servants and subjected to punishment for Khelidonis' rape: his body smeared with honey, Polytekhnos is tied up and thrown among the cattle to be tormented by flies. But Aedon pities him for their former love, and keeps the flies away. This angers her father and brothers so much that they are about to kill her, but Zeus intervenes: before a worse evil can befall the house of Pandareos, he changes the entire family into birds—Polytekhnos into a woodpecker, Khelidonis into a swallow, Aedon into a nightingale, and her mother into a halcyon.

In Boios' version, Aedon's murder of her son coexists with a relentless love for her husband. It is the same love that is the most prominent feature of the halcyon in Greek mythology: if her mate dies, a female halcyon is said (in Dionysius' passage cited above) to abstain from food and drink, lament her bereavement, and finally perish with grief. In a later source, female halcyons are even said to carry the old males on their backs.[59] The song of the halcyon is understood precisely as lamenting her separation from her mate: it is in this quality of a female lamenting her husband that the halcyon is addressed in a choral ode in Euripides' *Iphigenia in Tauris* (1089-1095):

---

58. *Od.* 16.117-120.
59. Aelian, *Varia Historia* 7.17.

ὄρνις ἃ παρὰ πετρίνας
πόντου δειράδας ἀλκυὼν
ἔλεγον οἶτον ἀείδεις,
εὐξύνετον ξυνετοῖς βοάν,
ὅτι πόσιν κελαδεῖς ἀεὶ μολπαῖς,
ἐγώ σοι παραβάλλομαι
θρήνους, ἄπτερος ὄρνις

O halcyon, you who by the rocky sea reefs
sing your mournful fate,
a cry understandable to those who know,
because you cry for your husband in songs.
I, a bird with no wings,
sing my laments alongside you.

In connection with the halcyon as a bird of lament, it is worth considering here the example of Meleager's wife, Kleopatre, whose nickname, Alkyone, derives from ἀλκυών 'halcyon'.[60] Nagy observes that her name, expressing "the very essence" of πένθος 'grief', is in harmony with the role she plays in the story that Phoenix tells to Achilles in *Iliad* 9: when the Kouretes were fighting against Kalydon, Meleager, angry with his mother, refused to enter the battle (*Il*. 9.527-599).[61] All the Kalydonian nobles and his own family could not persuade him, until Kleopatre begged him in tears (ὀδυρομένη [*Il*. 9.591]) and listed all the troubles that befall a people whose city is taken: the men are killed, the city burned, the women and the children led away. Nagy compares Kleopatre's entreaty with the formal lament of Andromache (*Il*. 24. 725-745), which involves the same themes, and he calls to the reader's attention a description of the destruction of Corinth, where Nereids (the only ones who remain to mourn the city) are called halcyons: σῶν ἀχέων μίμνομεν ἀλκυόνες 'we remain as the halcyons of your sorrows'.

But while Alkyone's nickname is appropriate for her role, the reason she is called by this name is the fate of her mother Marpessa, who weeps because Apollo had 'snatched her away' (ἀνήρπασε) and who was reclaimed by her

---

60. *Il*. 9.561-564.
61. Nagy 1979:111.

husband Idas, the strongest man on earth at the time. For the sake of his bride, Idas even raises his bow against Apollo. It is hard to avoid thinking of Penelope, who (although she is not raped like Marpessa) is under threat of being "snatched away" by the suitors, and who is reclaimed by her husband, the divinely strong man with his famous bow (a marked choice of weapon in the heroic world, and so inseparable from Odysseus. Here, as in the case of Aedon, we find that the *Odyssey* draws on mythological patterns in a very sophisticated way: Penelope's relationship with Telemachus evokes the myth of Aedon, yet the conflict follows along the lines of the mythological plot only halfway, and its ultimate expression—murder—is far from the Penelope we know. Similarly, the rape present in the story of Marpessa remains only a possibility in the *Odyssey*.

Let us take a closer look at the several lines describing Kleopatre-Alkyone in the *Iliad* (9.556-564):

Κλεπάτρη
κούρη Μαρπήσσης καλλισφύρου Εὐηνίνης
'Ἰδεώ θ'. ὃς κάρτιστος ἐπιχθονίων γένετ' ἀνδρῶν
ὧν τότε καί ῥα ἄνακτος ἐναντίον εἵλετο τόξον
Φοίβου 'Απόλλωνος καλλισφύρου εἵνεκα <u>νύμφης</u>.
τὴν δὲ τότ' ἐν' μεγάροισι πατὴρ καὶ πότνια <u>μήτηρ</u>
'Αλκυόνην καλέεσκον ἐπώνυμον, οὕνεκ' ἀρ' αὐτῆς
μήτηρ ἀλκυόνος πολυπενθέος οἶτον ἔχουσα
κλαῖεν ὅ μιν ἐκάεργος ἀνήρπασε Φοῖβος 'Απόλλων

[with] Kleopatre,
the daughter of beautiful-ankled Marpessa, child of Euenos,
and of Idas, who was the strongest man on earth
in his time—he even took up his bow against
Phoebus Apollo for the sake of the beautiful-ankled <u>maiden</u>.
And her father and honored <u>mother</u> in the halls
called her Alkyone, as a by-name, since her
mother, having the mournful voice of the halcyon,
wept because far-reaching Phoebus Apollo had
    snatched her away.

These lines are not easy to read, and the source of the difficulty is clear: some pronouns refer to Kleopatre and some to Marpessa, and the context does not make it immediately evident which woman is meant. The reason is the fact that Marpessa is viewed as a maiden (νύμφη 560) and as a mother (μήτηρ 561) almost simultaneously. It is hard to resist thinking of Penelope, called μήτηρ repeatedly, but νύμφη by Eurykleia in *Od.* 4.743. Moreover, in the *Odyssey* we see Penelope not only mourning for Odysseus—like a halcyon for her mate—but we also see her grieving over her conflict with Telemachus and breaking down in tears when her son's life is threatened. So halcyons, famed in mythology for their conjugal love and grief, appear in epigrams and on epitaphs as symbols of mothers' bereavement:

αἰακτὰν δὲ θύγατρα κατεστενάχησε Στράτεια
οἷα τις εἰναλίη δάκρυσι ἀλκυονίς[62]

Strateia bewailed her lamentable daughter,
just like a sea halcyon with her tears.[63]

IV. Penelope and "Solar Myth"

There are also less explicit connections between the Homeric Penelope and the group of concepts associated with the halcyon, nightingale, and, by extension, *pênelops*. But discussion of these connections requires some preliminary comments. It has been mentioned above that sleeplessness and crying at night are prevalent features in the description of Penelope's grief. I see these features as linked to the diction of night and dawn, of the solar cycle, which is pervasive in the *Odyssey*.

---

62. Kaibel:205, as cited in Thompson 1936:47.
63. The halcyon may also be not a stranger to weaving, so prominent in the *Odyssey*, although the only evidence for this comes from an epigram by Antipater Sidonius (*Anthologia Palatina* 160), where the singing shuttle, dedicated by a young woman to Kore, is referred to as a halcyon:
κερκίδα τὰν ὀρθρινά. χελιδονίδων ἅμα φωνᾷ
μελπομέναν. ἱστῶν Παλλάδος ἀλκυόνα [σψ.Τελέσιλλα θήκατο]
[Telesilla dedicated] the shuttle, the halcyon of Pallas' loom, which
sings at dawn together with the swallows.

The various themes of sleeplessness and sleep, of consciousness and unconsciousness, of sunset and sunrise, are cognate with the theme of life and death, of disappearance and return, and all these themes are in turn connected with the solar symbolism of the *Odyssey*. This is not the place to reiterate the arguments in favor of this position; I simply refer to Nagy's article "Phaethon, Sappho's Phaon and the White Rock of Leukas: 'Reading' the Symbols of Greek Lyric," from which I quote: "In fact, the entire plot of Odysseus' travels is interlaced with diction that otherwise denotes the theme of sunset followed by sunrise. To put it more bluntly, the epic plot of Odysseus' travels operates on an extended solar metaphor."[64] Nagy refers to Douglas Frame's argument in favor of this interpretation, which shows, in particular, the association of Odysseus' absence with night and sleep and his return with the sunrise [65] This solar metaphor has as its foundation the basic concept of death and rebirth of the sun, sunset and sunrise. Sunset, archetypically the death of the sun, is described as its plunging into the waters of Okeanos (*Od.* 20.63-65, *Il.* 8.485) and also as going underneath the earth, into the land of the dead; the sunrise as its rising from the Okeanos (*Il.* 7.421-423; *Od.* 19.433-434). I refer to this concept as "solar myth" in the title of this section. I propose to explore this myth, together with associated themes and diction, in connection with both Penelope and the *pênelops*. I add that in referring to solar symbolism or solar metaphor, I am not equating it with the "meaning" of the *Odyssey*; this investigation is confined to the level of expression.

IV. 1.   Alkyone

It is necessary to keep in mind the solar metaphor in the *Odyssey* because both the halcyon and the nightingale have a relation to it. Outside the *Odyssey*, both birds are described with the epithet εἰαρινός/εἴαρος 'of spring'.[66] Moreover, the personified Alkyone was the principal star in the

---

64. Nagy 1990b:225.
65. Frame 1978:34-80.
66. Of the nightingale, among others: *Homeric Hymns* 19.16; Sappho 83; Simonides 73. Of the halcyon, Alcman 26. Thompson supposes that the myth of the nightingale's laments for Itys are "for the most part veiled allusions to the worship of Adonis or Atys; that is to say to the mysterious and melancholy ritual of the season

constellation of the Pleiades, whose celestial movement ancient astronomers connected with the increase of daylight in spring. According to ancient astronomy, the sun at the vernal equinox rose in conjunction with the Pleiades, and this moment was believed to be the starting point of the sun's yearly course. Another important astronomical event that can be seen as a turning point in the springtime return of the sun is the winter solstice, when, according to the ancient astronomers, the Pleiades culminated in the mid-heaven at nightfall. D'Arcy Thompson believes that the strange myth of the "halcyon days" has astronomical significance, probably in connection with the winter solstice.[67]

Solar symbolism plays an important part in some versions of the Alkyone myths. In Lucian's version (*Halcyon* 2), Alkyone and her husband Keyx[68] are descended from the morning star, which was believed to "lead" the sun back from the underworld. In another version of the myth, preserved by Ovid (*Metamorphoses* 11.410ff), Alcyone is a daughter of Aiolos,[69] married to Ceyx, son of the Morning Star.[70]

Ovid's version of the myth may be considered in more detail, because it offers, in my opinion, important points for comparison with the Odyssey. But since any comparison between Homeric poetry and Ovid is likely to be called into question, some methodological considerations are in order. First of all, although Ovid is known for an occasionally free handling of his Greek sources, there are cases when he is remarkably well attuned to the traditional essence of the myths he uses. The Greek sources for the details of Alkyone's story or stories are lost, but the basic elements of Ovid's plot are paralleled in Lucian's Halcyon, which suggests that there is a good chance

when women 'wept for Tammuz': 'Αδώνι' ἄγομεν, καὶ τὸν "Αδωνιν κλάομεν." (Thompson 1936:20-21). Cf. Nagy's suggestion that the myth of Adonis centers around the theme of death and rebirth and may operate on solar symbolism (Nagy 1990b:255).

67. Thompson 1936:49-51.

68. For the connection between halcyon and *kêyx*, see earlier discussion.

69. Aiolos is son of Hellên, according to Lucian (*Halcyon* 2). The name *Aiolos* may be significant: Aiolos son of Hellên is only partly separate from Aiolos the king of the winds. For the role of the winds in the context of the solar cycle, see the earlier discussion.

70. I change here to the latinized forms *Alcyone* and *Ceyx* to conform with what must have been Ovid's spelling.

that Ovid is being mainly faithful to his sources in this case. Secondly, the parallels adduced here are not textual, but thematic, and should be viewed against a background of basically similar plots. What I find remarkable is not only that similar details appear in the *Metamorphoses* and the *Odyssey*, but that this similarity in details is combined with striking parallels in plot. In both cases, there is an extraordinarily, proverbially faithful wife, whose husband leaves on a sea voyage against his will; she waits and cries for him, and the magnitude of her grief is exceptional; in both cases, the husband's fate is unknown for a long time, but the wife receives a prophetic dream directly before his return, dead or alive. It is important to stress that the starting elements and the first movements of the plot are essentially the same in both myths, but that two (the only two possible) variations on the ending are played out: Odysseus survives, Ceyx dies.

Let us now take a closer look at the story of Alcyone as depicted in the *Metamorphoses*. In Ovid's version, Alcyone and Ceyx live happily until they excite the jealousy of the gods by calling each other Zeus and Hera. As a result, Ceyx is compelled to sail to the oracle of Klaros and drowns on the way. But Alcyone keeps waiting and praying for him. Burdened by her idle prayers, Hera arranges for Alcyone to see a dream about Ceyx and learn her husband's fate. Alcyone sees Ceyx in a dream: dead, naked, and wet, he tells her of his death at sea. She cries and wakes up (11.673-680):

> ingemit Alcyone; lacrimas movet atque lacertos
> per somnum corpusque petens amplectitur auras
> exclamatur "mane! quo te rapis? ibimus una."
> voce sua specieque viri turbata soporem
> excutit et primo si sit circumspicit illic,
> qui modo visus erat; nam moti voce ministri
> intulerant lumen.

> Alcyone weeps and stretches out her arms,
> and trying to reach him in her sleep, she embraces only the air
> and cries: "Wait! Where are you disappearing? We shall go together."
> Disturbed by her own voice and his appearance,
> she wakes up and first of all looks whether he is there,

the one whom she has just seen; for the servants, awakened by her
   voice,
brought in the light.

After the dream Alcyone is sure that she has seen her husband's ghost, not
just a dream. She seems to have a particular sense that this vision was not an
empty one:

umbra fuit, sed et umbra tamen manifesta virique
vera mei. (11.688-689)

It was a shade, but even so it was clear and a true
shade of my husband.

She even looks for footprints at the place where the ghost of Ceyx stood.
   All of this is reminiscent of Penelope, who also receives prophetic dreams,
who cries at night, and who sees Odysseus in her dreams. In Book 20,
Penelope says in her prayer to Athena (*Od.* 20.88-90):

αὐτὰρ ἐμοὶ καὶ ὀνείρατ' ἐπέσσευεν κακὰ δαίμων
τῆδε γὰρ αὖ μοι νυκτὶ παρέδραθεν εἴκελος αὐτῷ
τοῖος ἐὼν οἷος ἦεν ἅμα στρατῷ αὐτὰρ ἐμὸν κῆρ
χαῖρ'. ἐπεὶ οὐκ ἐφάμην ὄναρ ἔμμεναι. ἀλλ' ὕπαρ ἤδη

But the god has sent me evil dreams.
For this night there was one who lay by me, looking like him
as he was when he went away with the army; and my heart rejoiced,
since I thought it was not a dream but a waking vision.

As in the *Metamorphoses*, the similarity of the ghost to the former
appearance of the husband is striking, and the dream leaves a distinct sense of
reality. Just as Alcyone asserts what she saw was, although a shade, a "true"
one, so Penelope contrasts her waking vision (ὕπαρ) with a mere dream
(ὄναρ). In the *Metamorphoses*, Alcyone awakens crying and wakes up the
servants. Similarly, in the *Odyssey*, Penelope awakens crying and wakes up
Odysseus.

For Alcyone, the dream is a foreboding of a coming resolution: the same morning (an emphatic *mane erat* in Ovid) she goes to the seashore and sees the body of Ceyx floating toward the beach. Reaching out to him, Alcyone jumps off a jetty and turns into a halcyon. Crying with a bird's cry, she touches Ceyx's body with her wings, and he is turned into a bird as well. Of course, there is no parallel to this scene in the *Odyssey*, but it is perhaps noteworthy that Odysseus, waking up at Penelope's crying, thinks that she has recognized him and stands near him. And this as well happens in the morning:

> ὡς ἔφατ'· αὐτίκα δὲ χρυσόθρονος ἤλυθεν Ἠώς
> τῆς δ' ἄρα κλαιούσης ὄπα σύνθετο δῖος Ὀδυσσεύς
> μερμήριζε δ' ἔπειτα. δόκησε δέ οἱ κατὰ θυμὸν
> ἤδη γιγνώσκουσα παρεστάμεναι κεφαλῆφι
> *(Od.* 20.91-94)

> So she spoke, and at once the golden-throned Eos came.
> Great Odysseus heard her voice crying and was in doubt,
> and it seemed to him in his heart that she had
> recognized him already and was now standing by his head.

Like Penelope, Alcyone wanted to follow Ceyx even as a shade: *ibimus una* 'let us go together!', she exclaims in her dream. With Ceyx dead, she does not find a place for herself in life, and an escape is granted her in the form of a transformation. We have already seen this pattern: an escape out of a grievous and humanly irresolvable situation is what Zeus bestows on Pandareos' family, turning them all into birds; what the snatching winds bestow on the younger Pandareids; and finally what Penelope prays for in Book 20.

IV. 2.   The Streams of Okeanos

Let us return to Alcyone's leap off the jetty. I have said that there could be no parallel for this in the *Odyssey*. Yet perhaps this jump can be seen as a reflex of a more general theme present in Homer as well. Here I refer again to Nagy's chapter "Phaethon, Sappho's Phaon, and the White Rock of Leukas," in particular to his discussion of the route by which the souls of the suitors are taken to the underworld in *Odyssey* 24.10-12. Led by Hermes, the souls pass by the stream of Okeanos, a rock called Leukas Petre 'white rock', the gates of the sun, and the "district of dreams." The mythical Leukas Petre has its material equivalent in a number of places in Greece—prominent rocks on the coast line that are called by the same name Leukas. Nagy discusses Strabo's description of one of these rocks, Cape Leukas (10.2.9C425). This rock had a custom connected with it: leaping from its heights into the sea below was believed to be a cure for love. According to Menander, Sappho jumped off it for the love of Phaon. But the first to jump was Aphrodite herself, out of love for Adonis. Nagy argues that the rock at Cape Leukas is like the white rock in *Odyssey* 24, and the plunge from it is somehow related to the sun's plunge into the ocean. This plunge is symbolic of leaving the realm of the day. Taken to the extreme, the plunge means death, but also falling asleep, unconsciousness, forgetfulness, and sexual release. To quote again: "In short, the White Rock is the boundary delimiting the conscious and the unconscious—be it trance, stupor, sleep, or even death."

The vertical plunge of diving sea birds is also like the solar plunge into the waters of Okeanos. Alcyone leaps off a jetty (into death but also into an immortality of a kind in bird's form, which is reminiscent of the sun's divided fate: nightly death, and yet eternal life. On the other hand, it can be compared to the death of Eumaios' Phoenician nurse in *Odyssey* 15.479: during a sea voyage, she is struck by a sudden, and gentle, death from one of Artemis' arrows, and she plunges vertically into the ship's bilge just like a sea bird κήξ kêx into the water:

ἄντλῳ δ' ἐνδούπησε πεσοῦσ' ὡς εἰναλίη κήξ.

And, falling, she plunged with a splash into the ship's
bilge, like a sea-kêx.

To repeat, the *kêx* or *kêyx* is inextricably tied to the halcyon, itself a diving bird. In Boios, Aedon's mother, after turning into a halcyon, immediately wants to plunge into the sea. In a myth reported by the Suda following Hegesandros, seven daughters of the giant Alkyoneus throw themselves into the sea off a headland rock after their father's death. In pity, Amphitrite turns them into birds and calls them, in memory of their father, Ἀλκυόνες 'the halcyons'—a story of orphaned girls, uncannily reminiscent of the Pandareids, also orphans, with their oceanic plunge.

The birds seem to have ties with the Leukas Petre as well. One may mention, for example, their role in a yearly ritual at Cape Leukas, described by Strabo. Every year a criminal would be cast off the rock 'for the aversion of evil' (ἀποτροπῆς χάριν). Wings and even birds would be tied to him, and fishing boats would be waiting at sea to fish him out. The details suggest a diving bird, but what kind of a bird would fit this context? The halcyon is one, and the pênelops, I think, is another. The information is supplied by the Scholia to *Odyssey* 4.797, where the scholiast is discussing Penelope's name:

Δίδυμος δὲ Ἀμειράκην φησὶ προσαγορεύεσθαι τὴν Πηνελόπην, ἢ Ἀρνακίαν. Ναυπλίου δὲ ῥίψαντος αὐτὴν εἰς θάλασσαν διὰ ποινὴν Παλαμήδους, ὑπὸ πηνελόπων αὐτὴν σωθεῖσαν οὕτως ὀνομασθῆναι.

Didymus says that Penelope used to be called Ameirake or Arnakia. But after Nauplios threw her into the sea out of vengeance for Palamedes she came to be called Penelope, since she was saved by the *pênelopes*. [71]

Penelope is like the person thrown off a rock at Cape Leukas, where wings and birds attend the oceanic plunge. It appears, then, that Penelope's name, through the sea bird, associates her with the same concept of sunset envisaged as a plunge into the streams of Okeanos that is involved in the myths of Alkyone and of Leukas Petre.

But the name of Penelope is only meaningful because it points to the themes that are operative and prominent in the *Odyssey*. Let us consider again the passage from Book 20, where Penelope compares herself to the two younger daughters of Pandareos. To repeat, the comparison is thematically relevant: oppressed by her bereavement and the inescapable Erinys of

---

71. The wording of the Scholia matches almost verbatim Eustathius' comment on *Odyssey* 1.65.34-36. Essentially the same account of Penelope's name is given in the Scholia on Pindar, *Olympian* 9.79d and in Tzetzes on Lycophron 792.

memory, Penelope finds herself trapped in an ambiguous position, comparable to the fate of the Pandareids and, before Odysseus' return, equally irresolvable on a human level. The comparison, or rather the myth of the Pandareids, is incorporated into Penelope's prayer, the object of which is death, or at any rate disappearance from the world of the living. Penelope wishes for a gentle death by the darts of Artemis;[72] alternatively, she wants to be taken away by a 'snatching wind' (ἀναρπάξασα θύελλα) that would drop her into the streams of the "backward-flowing Okeanos." Just as the daughters of Pandareos were 'snatched away' (ἀνέλοντο θύελλαι 66, ἅρπυιαι ἀνηρείψατο 77) and carried to the streams of Okeanos. This theme again brings us into the sphere of solar symbolism. Nagy discusses the topic in detail and convincingly argues that being carried away by the "snatching wind," described usually in the same terms as by Penelope here, is an image of death (or, in any case, of entering the realm of death) parallel to the sunset, since θύελλαι take their victims to the far west and drop them into the streams of Okeanos.[73]

The snatching winds (θύελλαι or ἅρπυιαι) perform many abductions, usually for the gods, most notably for Eos, known for snatching up youths, and for Aphrodite, Eos' counterpart in this function.[74] Through these snatching winds, Aphrodite has Phaethon abducted, and Eos has Kephalos, Tithonos, Kleitos, and Orion spirited away. The verb designating abduction is regularly ἁρπάζω 'snatch' or, occasionally, αἱρέω 'take away'. When Penelope worries about Telemachus, she thinks that the winds snatched him away (*Od.* 4.727). Telemachus says the same about Odysseus (*Od.* 14.371), and in both cases the same verbs are used. In her prayer, Penelope first imagines herself dropped into the streams of Okeanos, and we may suppose that other victims of the snatching wind would follow the same route. But later Penelope also mentions that she will be underneath the earth (*Od.* 20.80-81). Nagy comments that both themes, of falling into the Okeanos and of going underneath the earth, apply also to solar movements: the sun traverses the Okeanos and enters the underworld—thus it is also underneath the earth.

---

72. Cf. Eumaios' nurse (*Od.* 15.479) and see page 117.

73. Nagy 1990b:245-246.

74. For the discussion of such abductions by Eos and Aphrodite and their relation to the concept of death, see Vermeule 1979:145-178.

Since the setting of the sun is understood as its death, it travels along the same route as a human soul.[75] In the case of Pandareos' daughters, the snatching winds take them to the streams of Okeanos, but do not drop them in, and the girls suffer a curious fate: they do not die, but they do not belong to the world of the living any longer, and so remain on the very border between life and death. The solar pattern in the myth of the Pandareids finds an additional expression in the name of one of the sisters, Merope, a name derived from the bird name μέροψ *merops*, as Penelope from πηνέλοψ *pênelops*. Nagy proposes an explanation of μέροψ as 'he who has glowing looks', derived from the root *mer- as in μαρμαίρω 'glow, flash'.[76] Merops was the mortal father of Phaethon, whose divine father was Helios; Merope is a name of a star in Hesiod (F 169.3), and even the bird μέροψ *merops* 'bee-eater' seems to be associated with the solar cycle.[77]

The fate of the Pandareids can be compared to the fate of Alkyone in the *Iliad*, which brings us back again to the halcyon. The diction of abduction by snatching winds marks the already quoted passage (*Il.* 9.563) about Meleager's wife, Kleopatre, who was nicknamed Alkyone by her parents, and whose mother Marpessa was snatched by Apollo (ἀνήρπασε).

Did Apollo carry Marpessa to the streams of Okeanos, as the diction of the passage suggests? And may one assume that the halcyon, through its connections to diving and the solar theme, is associated with the ends of the earth, where Okeanos flows? The association is implicit both in Homer and in Ovid. Throughout this essay I have been drawing on the halcyon's symbolism to find more detailed parallels for what is suggested by the scant

---

75. Nagy 1990b:246.

76. At the beginning of this essay I discussed the adjective ἁλιπόρφυρος 'flashing like the sea'. The meaning of this adjective depends on the interaction between two roots *porphur-* as in πορφύρα ('murex') and *porphûr-* as in πορφύρω 'to surge, boil, be agitated'. The adjective πορφύρεος derives from the word for shellfish and, strictly speaking, should mean 'red', but already in Homer it is affected by the verbal root and is used in the sense 'agitated' about the sea or, by extension, 'of changing color, sheeny' that evidently gives Latin *purpureus* 'bright, shining' as well as 'dark red'. Chantraine finds this use of the adjective surprising, especially since a formation in -*eos*, if it were to be derived from the verb, is anomalous. But it is interesting that the only parallel to πορφύρεος is the formation of μαρμάρεος 'sparkling', under the influence of μαρμαίρω 'to sparkle'.

77. Thompson 1936:s.v. μέροψ.

material on the *pênelops*. But the affiliation with Okeanos, only implied by the texts about the halcyon, is given about the *pênelops* quite explicitly. The Alcaeus fragment already quoted in this essay shows that the provenance of the *pênelops* is precisely the ends of the earth, the Okeanos, the region on the border of life and death where Penelope wants to be taken (Alcaeus 21):

ὄρνιθες τίνες οἴδ' 'Ωκεάνω γᾶς ἀπὺ πειράτων
ἦλθον πανέλοπες ποικιλόδειροι τανυσίπτεροι;

What are these birds that came from the limits of the earth,
the long-winged *pênelopes* with varied throats?

Moreover, there is an additional indication that the *pênelops*' affiliation with the streams of Okeanos is precisely solar. One of the characters snatched away by the winds is Phaethon, Nagy has convincingly argued, a mythological substitute for Helios (and his son by Klymene).[78] In Hesiod's *Theogony* 990, he is said to have been snatched up by Aphrodite; however, the best known story about him is that he was allowed to drive the chariot of his father Helios but could not control the team. Driving too close to the ground, Phaethon destroys everything in his way until he is struck down by Zeus and falls into the streams of Eridanos (which is mythologically identified with Okeanos).[79] We know from Pliny (*Natural History* 37.31-32) that in Aeschylus' version of the myth, Phaethon's mourning sisters are turned into poplars on the banks of the Eridanos. The same myth is alluded to by Euripides in *Hippolytos* 732-740.

ἡλιβάτοις ὑπὸ κευθμῶσι γενοίμαν
ἵνα με πτεροῦσαν ὄρνιν
θεὸς ἐν ποταναῖς
ἀγέλαις θείη
ἀρθείην δ' ἐπὶ πόντιον
κῦμα τᾶς 'Αδριηνᾶς
ἀκτᾶς 'Ηριδανοῦ θ' ὕδωρ

78. Nagy 1990b:235.
79. Nagy 1992:236-239.

ἔνθα πορφύρεον σταλάσ-
σουσ' εἰς οἶδμα τάλαιναι
κόραι Φαέθοντος οἴκτῳ δακρύων
τὰς ἠλεκτροφαεῖς αὐγάς.

Would that I were in the steep hiding-places of the rocks,
where the god would turn me into a winged bird and set me
    among the flying flocks.
I wish I could rise and fly to the wave of the Adriatic coast
    and the waters of Eridanos,
where the unhappy maidens weep in pity for Phaethon,
    dropping into the sparkling wave
the amber-gleaming rays of their tears.

Note that this myth of Phaethon's sisters functions in the *Hippolytos* in the same way as the myths of Aedon and the Pandareids in the *Odyssey*: it appears as a wish for an escape as a bird when a human escape becomes impossible: the chorus sings these lines while, behind the scene, Phaedra is preparing her suicide. But my main interest is in the last line, referring, of course, to amber, which was seen as related to the sun (in fact, the Greek word for amber, ἤλεκτρον, is a derivative of ἠλέκτωρ 'shining' used in *Iliad* 6.513 of the beaming sun). Amber is discussed at length by Pliny, who describes one of the amber-giving regions in the following passage:

Mnases Africae locum Sicyonem appellat et Crathin
amnem in oceanum effluentem e lacu, in quo aves,
quas <u>meleagridas</u> et <u>penelopas</u> vocat, vivere; ibi nasci
[sc. electrum] ratione eadem qua supra dictum est.
        (*Natural History* 37. 11. 38)

Mnases names Sicyon, a place in Africa, and the river
Crathis, which flows into the Ocean from a lake, where
birds called <u>meleagrides</u> and <u>pênelopes</u> live; [amber] is
formed there in the same way as was described above.

Here again we see the *pênelops* associated with a solar concept, and also with the imagery of the extreme west. Although the lake in Pliny's passage is in Africa, the association with amber generally points toward the land of sunset.[80] In the same chapter Pliny mentions another lake where the amber drips from poplar trees into the water, and this lake is situated in the extreme west—near the garden of the Hesperides. Nor is the occurrence of *pênelopes* in connection with amber accidental, especially since the other birds inhabiting the same lake, *meleagrides*, have a mythological reason for being there: according to Pliny, Sophocles stated that amber was formed from the tears of Meleager's mourning sisters who were changed into birds by Artemis out of pity—a myth that virtually duplicates the one about Phaethon's sisters.[81] The solar connotations of the Meleager myth, are, in fact, explicit, and we have already come across them in discussing his wife nicknamed Alkyone and her mother, snatched away by Apollo. The life of Meleager himself is inextricably joined with fire of the hearth and this, again, may point to the solar theme.[82]

IV. 3.   The Light of Sunset and Dawn

Returning from the *pênelops* to Penelope, one might add that her connection with solar symbolism and with imagery of the west seems to involve much more than her prayer in Book 20. In fact, some features of Ithaca link it to the fabulous places on the border of this world, such as Scheria, the island of the Phaeacians, and even the shore of Okeanos. For example, poplars, which are generally associated with death, and with sunset in particular, appear only in four locations in the *Odyssey*: on the shores of Okeanos, on Calypso's island, in Scheria, and in Ithaca.[83] The poplars mark

---

80. Cf. Aithiopia/Ethiopia in Africa vs. Aithiopes of the extreme East *and* West in e.g., the *Odyssey*.

81. Pliny, *Natural History* 37.11.40

82. In his chapter "The King and the Hearth," Nagy suggests that Greek words for dawn (Ionic ἠώς/ Aeolic αὔως) and for 'hearth' (ἑστία) ultimately go back to the same root meaning "shine" and observes that "the semantic connection between the macrocosm of dawn and the microcosm of the sacrificial fireplace is explicit in the *Rig-Veda*, where the coming of the dawn is treated as an event parallel to the simultaneous kindling of the sacrificial fire" (Nagy 1990b:148-150).

83. *Od.* 5.64,293; 6.78; 9.141; 10.510; 17.208.

these places as associated with the west and sunset—an association evoked, perhaps, by the shimmering effect of the sun on their trembling leaves.[84]

More important is the light imagery in the description of Ithaca and of Penelope as Ithaca's queen. In this sense, Ithaca is comparable to Scheria, and Penelope to Arete, the queen of Phaeacians. The palace of the Phaeacians is full of radiance: the gold, the blazing torches, and the repeatedly mentioned light of the hearth. Arete is described as sitting and weaving ἐπ' ἐσχάρῃ ἐν πυρὸς αὐγῇ 'by the hearth, in the light of the fire' (*Od.* 6.305). The only other person in the *Odyssey* who sits ἐν πυρὸς αὐγῇ is Penelope (23.89). The maids in the palace of Alkinoos are also weaving, their wool dripping with oil and shining in the torchlight, their fingers flickering. What is important is that this weaving is compared to the shimmering of the poplars' leaves: οἷά τε φύλλα μακεδνῆς αἰγείροιο 'as the leaves of the tall poplar' [*Od.* 7.106]). Even more interesting, the difficult epithet ἁλιπόρφυρος is used in the *Odyssey* only in the descriptions of Scheria and Ithaca. When Nausikaa—at dawn—comes to her parents, she sees Arete sitting by the hearth and weaving ἠλάκατα . . . ἁλιπόρφυρα 'turning the sea-gleaming wool on a distaff' (*Od.* 6.53). Directing Odysseus, Nausikaa predicts that he will find the queen at the same occupation (*Od.* 6.306):

> ὦκα μάλα μεγάροιο διελθέμεν, ὄφρ' ἂν ἴκηαι
> μητέρ' ἐμήν· ἡ δ' ἧσται <u>ἐπ' ἐσχάρῃ ἐν πυρὸς αὐγῇ</u>
> <u>ἠλάκατα στρωφῶσ' ἁλιπόρφυρα, θαῦμα ἰδέσθαι,</u>

> Very quickly cross the hall until you come to
> my mother; she will be sitting <u>by the hearth in the fire light,</u>
> <u>turning the sea-gleaming wool on the distaff, a wonder to see.</u>

This word ἁλιπόρφυρος is of course the epithet of the halcyon and may also refer to the *pênelops* in Ibycus' fragment. In the *Odyssey*, it appears one more time, in the description of the cave of the nymphs in Ithaca where the

---

84. The association with the extreme west entails one with the extreme east as well, through the *coincidentia oppositorum* 'the falling together of the opposites'. A clear example of it is Circe's island, which is located simultaneously in the extreme west (*Od.* 10.135) and in the extreme east (*Od.* 11.1-4). See Nagy 1990b:237.

Phaeacians leave sleeping Odysseus. [85] The nineteen-line description of the cave itself occupies an important place in the scene of Odysseus' arrival and is introduced by an emphatic reference to the dawn led out by the brightest morning star. The bay with the cave is sacred to Φόρκυς, whose name has a primary meaning of 'white' and derives from the root *bher- 'shining, clear'. Among the wonders of the cave there are stone looms for the Naiads to weave on:

ἐν δ᾽ ἰστοὶ περιμήκεες, ἔνθα τε νύμφαι
φάρε᾽ ὑφαίνουσιν <u>ἁλιπόρφυρα</u>, θαῦμα ἰδέσθαι.
(*Od.* 13.107-108)

inside there are great looms and there the nymphs
weave the sea-gleaming webs, a wonder to see.

The formula used here to describe the weaving of the nymphs is a variant of the one used in Book 6 about Arete, and shining fabric is an attribute that all of them share with Penelope, whose weaving is said to be no less than ἠελίῳ ἐναλίγκιον ἠὲ σελήνῃ 'like sun and moon' (*Od.* 6.24, 248) and who is addressed by Eurykleia as νύμφα φίλη 'dear maiden/bride/nymph' (*Od.* 4.743). And perhaps it is relevant to Homer's Penelope that Nereids are compared to the halcyons by Antipater Sidonius,[86] and that Theocritus describes the halcyons as "beloved of the sea nymphs."[87]

---

85. I am convinced that it means 'sparkling' or 'shimmering' rather than 'true purple of the sea' (Liddell and Scott), in spite of the fact that it derives from πορφύρα 'purple-fish, murex' rather than from πορφύρω 'to boil, be agitated'. Gregory Nagy has suggested to me that the two "roots" may actually be the same, by synecdoche: the murex is "seething" because of the purple it makes. In any case, πορφύρα and πορφύρω influence each other already in Homer, and πορφύρεος in Homer is applied to the gleaming sea. The addition of ἁλι-, I think, only strengthens this meaning (and ἁλιπόρφυρος is also used of water). Although in the *Odyssey* this epithet refers to fabrics, these fabrics are divine or nearly so, the type of cloth that is frequently described as shining in Homer; see Shelmerdine 99-107. For the discussion of ἁλιπόρφυρος, see Deroy 1948:3-10; Stanford 1985:437 (on *Od.* 13.85); Marzullo 1950:132-136; Hainsworth 1991:297 (on *Od.* 6.53).
86. Anthologia Palatina 9.151.
87. Theocritus *Idylls* 7.59.

Conclusion

An inquiry into Penelope's name connects her, through the *pênelops*, with the halcyon and the nightingale. Penelope's crying for Odysseus is comparable with the nightingale's mournful song for her son and the halcyon's for her mate, and as such it is a woman's lament not only for a dear one lost, but for her family as a whole and her life destroyed, the kind of mourning that is captured in the notion of a weeping bird. Tied to this theme is the escapist notion of bird transformation, a gracious release for a person, most often a woman, trapped in a social and psychological limbo.

Further, the mournful songs of the halcyon and the nightingale are particular instances of a more general theme of lamenting bird, which has survived in Greek tradition and assumes different forms. Throughout the history of Greek poetic tradition, the weeping birds appear most often in the context of laments for the fall of cities, such as the Hellenistic epigram on the fall of Corinth, where the Nereids are compared to the halcyons: σῶν ἀχέων μίμνομεν ἀλκυόνες 'we remain as the halcyons of your sorrows'.[88]

There are many other ramifications of the *pênelops*-halcyon-nightingale connection. For instance, it brings out the unusual nature of Penelope's voice and thus adds a new dimension to the comparison between Penelope and other characters of the *Odyssey*, such as Calypso and Circe, who are all known, as Penelope, for their remarkable weaving, but also for their singing. Michael Nagler, in his article "Dread Goddess Endowed with Speech"[89] has demonstrated that Penelope shares a number of features with these divinities whom Odysseus meets "in the other world." For example, Nagler compares the misfortune that Odysseus' companions suffer at the hands of Circe with the fate of Penelope's suitors: Penelope, just as Circe, is surprised by the suitors at the loom. In both cases, the intruders are enchanted: they lose self-control and, ultimately, are destroyed. The power of the "dread goddesses" centers on their songs, their looms, and their beds. Penelope's weaving and her bed, which is supported by a living olive tree, are clearly remarkable.[90]

---

88. This observation is made by Alexiou 1974:97. The epigram is by Antipater Sidonius, *Anthologia Palatina* 9.151.8.
89. Nagler 1977.77-85.
90. *Od.* 2.93-95; 24.128-130; 24.189-204.

The association with the nightingale and halcyon shows that her song is also extraordinary. This "more than human" side of Penelope brings her on a level with Odysseus: a woman whose voice can be described in the same terms as the voices of Sirens and Muses is a match for a hero who could stand to hear the Sirens' song. And if it is true that the contrast of the epic is between the hero and ordinary mortals, too weak to return from the dead, then Penelope, who could hold on to her position as Odysseus' wife through his long absence, is a match for the hero who could return.

Similarly, the ambiguity of Odysseus' position between life and death has been much discussed: he is alive, yet he is not in the land of the living; he has fame as a hero, yet even this fame is somehow obscured as long as nothing is clear about his life or death. The complex of poetic associations around the *pênelops* resonate with a similar ambiguity in Penelope's position: she is a wife and a widow, marriageable and not; she has a name, yet, like Odysseus' fame, it is uncertain, and she finds the strange fate of being taken alive to the land of the dead a fitting one for herself.

Finally, the etymology of her name links Penelope to the solar theme so pervasive in the *Odyssey*. The plunge into the waters of the Okeanos, longed for in Penelope's prayer and expressed in language used in the descriptions of sunset, is only one sign of this connection. Another is the prominence of sleep and wakefulness, of night and dawn in the descriptions of Penelope. Few would dispute the significance of Odysseus' wakefulness and sleep for his return, or doubt that sleep and death go hand in hand in Homer. Odysseus' sleep on Helios' island and on board the Phaeacians' ship is described by Frame as "a kind of passage through death."[91] Odysseus' return is associated with the dawn, the return of the sun, and with awakening from sleep. His wakefulness in travel is in contrast with his companions' weakness against the power of sleep. It is his unsleeping mind that allows Odysseus to gain "supernatural" knowledge and ultimately, to return. Comparison between Penelope and Alcyone in Ovid's *Metamorphoses* suggests that references to Penelope's sleep are related to the same general theme. The night, the time of the sun's absence, is the time of Penelope's mourning, and while Odysseus challenges sleep in the other world, she knows no sleep in Ithaca. And like Odysseus, Penelope has knowledge: her prophetic dreams

---

91. Frame 1978:75.

may be compared not only to the dreams of Alcyone, but also perhaps to Odysseus' communication with the shades in the underworld.

Names in the *Odyssey* are hardly ever arbitrary. Some of them, such as Calypso, are obviously descriptive; others, like Penelope, are less direct. Yet the meaning of Penelope's name resonates with a number of prominent themes in the *Odyssey*, among which is the solar theme and the theme of memory, Penelope's ambivalent state, her longing to escape, and the incessant grief for her lost husband, expressed as the mournful song of a bird of lament.

6

Odysseus Back Home and Back from the Dead

Brian W. Breed

During Odysseus' long absence from Ithaca, grief and worry have possessed the man's family. If he is alive, they do not know when or if he will return, and if he is dead, they are unable to mourn for him and bury him because they have no body. There is the fear of neglect, and this theme of concern for corpses runs through the poem. When Odysseus does finally return and rejoin his family, he confronts his father with these fears, using his last lying story and false names to raise the specter of neglect and its consequences. The false guise Odysseus presents to the old man in Book 24, I will argue, displays the essentials of the family's predicament on Ithaca: unable to bury their presumed dead son/father/husband, they have reason to fear divine wrath, which Odysseus' return from the dead could bring or banish.

For twenty years poor Laertes has suffered in his son's absence, and, even when Odysseus has returned and killed the suitors, still he must wait, wait for Odysseus to perform one last test, tell one last lie. Odysseus intends to test whether his father will recognize him (*Od.* 24.216-218). He has tested others of the household too, and they all passed. But when, posing as a wealthy traveler, he tells the old man a lie about entertaining Odysseus five years before and then sending him toward home under favorable omens, Laertes breaks down in grief. At this point Odysseus reveals himself truthfully, and, after proving himself in turn to his father, the son is welcomed home. Laertes' terrible expression of grief on hearing his son's testing story makes Odysseus reveal himself; in the old man's tears and wails Odysseus sees that he should put off his homecoming no longer. What of the test? Laertes, though he does not in fact recognize his son and reacts apparently wrongly to the good news that he was alive, in the hospitality of a wealthy house, and headed home only five years prior, in some sense passes his son's test. His grief serves as the proof of his fatherhood, the key to the reunion. Nor has Laertes ever been alone in this grief for his son; his daughter-in-law, grandson, and faithful servants weep with him awaiting Odysseus' return. In fact, much of the *Odyssey* is spent in tears: Odysseus weeps for himself, Menelaos for Agamemnon, Penelope for Odysseus, Odysseus' men for their fellows.

The shared grief of the *Odyssey*, however, is strangely hollow, unfulfilled. All the tears shed for Odysseus on Ithaca, in Sparta, at sea, are shed in uncertainty as to his actual fate. Laertes and his family can assume that Odysseus is dead and lost, when all the other surviving Greeks have returned from Troy, but they do not know, and, furthermore, in this state they suffer the pain of being unable to mourn properly for the man, to honor and bury him, to make their tears meaningful with funeral rituals. This is the predicament Laertes reveals to the questioning stranger (*Od.* 24.288-296):

πόστον δὴ ἔτος ἐστίν, ὅτε ξείνισσας ἐκεῖνον
σὸν ξεῖνον δύστηνον, ἐμὸν παῖδ', εἴ ποτ' ἔην γε,
δύσμορον; ὅν που τῆλε φίλων καὶ πατρίδος αἴης
ἠέ που ἐν πόντῳ φάγον ἰχθύες, ἢ ἐπὶ χέρσου
θηρσὶ καὶ οἰωνοῖσιν ἕλωρ γένετ' οὐδέ ἑ μήτηρ
κλαῦσε περιστείλασα πατήρ θ', οἵ μιν τεκόμεσθα
οὐδ' ἄλοχος πολύδωρος, ἐχέφρων Πηνελόπεια,
κώκυσ' ἐν λεχέεσσιν ἐὸν πόσιν, ὡς ἐπεώκει,
ὀφθαλμοὺς καθελοῦσα· τὸ γὰρ γέρας ἐστὶ θανόντων.

How many years is it, then, when you entertained him,
your poor guest, my son, if he ever once was,
evil-fated, whom far from friends and his fatherland,
either the fish ate in the sea, or on land
he has become food for beasts and birds. And his mother
did not wail for him, tending his corpse,
nor his father, we the ones who bore him,
nor did his wife, who brought many gifts, mindful Penelope,
grieve for her husband on his bier, as she should,
closing his eyes, which is the honor given the dead.

This is the end of the story; the same predicament, the inability of his family to mourn the believed dead Odysseus, appears also at the beginning.

The reader meets Telemachus, the first human character to enter the action, hoping that somehow, from somewhere, his father will return to scatter the suitors (*Od.* 1.114-117). But he is pessimistic, presuming Odysseus lost, as he shows in his first speech to Athena (*Od.* 1.158-177). Odysseus' bones are rotting on some beach, Telemachus thinks, or they are rolling on the waves (*Od.* 1.161-162); he is dead, deprived of his homecoming (*Od.* 1.168). Despite Athena's assurances that Odysseus is merely being detained and soon to return home, a look at the suitors' party in his house makes Telemachus persist in contemplating the death of his father (*Od.* 1.234-244):

νῦν δ' ἑτέρως ἐβόλοντο θεοὶ κακὰ μητιόωντες,
οἵ κεῖνον μὲν ἄϊστον ἐποίησαν περὶ πάντων
ἀνθρώπων, ἐπεὶ οὔ κε θανόντι περ ὧδ' ἀκαχοίμην,
εἰ μετὰ οἷς ἑτάροισι δάμη Τρώων ἐνὶ δήμῳ,
ἠὲ φίλων ἐν χερσίν, ἐπεὶ πόλεμον τολύπευσε.
τῷ κέν οἱ τύμβον μὲν ἐποίησαν Παναχαιοί,
ἠδέ κε καὶ ᾧ παιδὶ μέγα κλέος ἦρατ' ὀπίσσω.
νῦν δέ μιν ἀκλειῶς Ἅρπυιαι ἀνηρείψαντο
οἴχετ' ἄϊστος, ἄπυστος, ἐμοὶ δ' ὀδύνας τε γόους τε
κάλλιπεν· οὐδ' ἔτι κεῖνον ὀδυρόμενος στεναχίζω
οἷον, ἐπεί νύ μοι ἄλλα θεοὶ κακὰ κήδε' ἔτευξαν.

But the gods, angrily devising trouble, wanted otherwise,
who caused him, beyond other men, to be unheard of,
while I would not have grieved so for his death,
if he had been overcome in the country of the Trojans with his
    companions,
or in the hands of his friends, when he finished the war, then all
the Achaeans would have built him a tomb,
and in the future he would have created great renown for his son.
But now the Harpies have snatched him away without a word,
he has gone unheard of, unknown, and he left me pains and

> moaning; and grieving I do not mourn him alone,
> since now for me the gods have fashioned other terrible troubles.

It is not simply that Odysseus is dead but that he is lost, which causes the peculiar grief of his family. Dead at Troy, Odysseus would have been properly buried with the others, but now he is unseen, unheard of, unlamented. The result for Telemachus is only κακὰ κήδεα 'terrible troubles'.[1]

These two passages at the very beginning and very end of the *Odyssey* share the same concern, not merely the death of Odysseus, but also his lack of proper burial and family mourning. Such concerns appear elsewhere in the poem, in reference to Agamemnon, Menelaos and Orestes, Elpenor, even Telemachus himself. People in the *Odyssey* are worried about the proper care for the dead. There are consequences to be feared if a body is not properly disposed of, as Elpenor ominously reminds Odysseus in asking to be buried: μή τοί τι θεῶν μήνιμα γένωμαι ([*Od.* 11.73] 'so that I will not be a cause of the gods' wrath for you'). As Calvert Watkins has shown,[2] Elpenor's request, parallel to the request of Hektor to Achilles for a proper funeral (*Il.* 22.358), evokes the complex reciprocal relationship between men and gods. Men must obey divine ordinances (particularly to tend the dead properly) or face *theôn mênis* 'the gods' wrath'. "Le caractère funeste de μῆνις saute aux yeux. C'est une notion dangereuse, qu'il faut craindre; une notion sacrale, 'numineuse' (θεῶν), certes, mais dont même les dieux ont le souci de se débarrasser."[3] In a recent study Leonard Muellner expands on Watkins and defines *mênis* as "the sacred name of the ultimate sanction against taboo behavior, and epic personages invoke it to forestall people from breaking fundamental cosmic rules."[4] These fears, of both an ignominious end for the loved one's body and resulting consequences from the divine world, are quite alive in the world of

---

1. The word κῆδος also has the meanings of 'funeral' and in later Greek 'marriage connection', Chantraine s.v. κήδω; there is a verbal play on Telemachus' entrapment between burying his father and marrying off his mother. On epic *kêdea*, see Muellner 1996:163-164.
2. Watkins 1994a:582-584. The man who is θεῶν μήνιμα "est la cause de la colère potentielle des dieux exercée sur un autre homme" = θεῶν μῆνις.
3. Watkins 1994a:571.
4. Muellner 1996:194.

the *Odyssey*. Ultimately they appear in the context of the reunion of Laertes and Odysseus, influencing the test that Odysseus performs on his father, the particular reaction the old man has to his son's lies, and how finally the family is restored to happiness in part through their grief.

In the Homeric poems it does not always have to be this way, with families miserably unable to mourn properly. The *Odyssey* may emphasize the uncertainty and fear of unfulfilled grief, but it also hints at complete mourning, which is found in its fullness in the *Iliad*. Among Odysseus' many fits of weeping is one brought on by the stories of Demodokos; he weeps like a woman dragged away to slavery before she can mourn for her dying husband (*Od.* 8.523-531):

ὡς δὲ γυνὴ κλαίῃσι φίλον πόσιν ἀμφιπεσοῦσα,
ὅς τε ἑῆς πρόσθεν πόλιος λαῶν τε πέσῃσιν,
ἄστεϊ καὶ τεκέεσσιν ἀμύνων νηλεὲς ἦμαρ·
ἡ μὲν τὸν θνῄσκοντα καὶ ἀσπαίροντα ἰδοῦσα
ἀμφ' αὐτῷ χυμένη λίγα κωκύει· οἱ δέ τ' ὄπισθε
κόπτοντες δούρεσσι μετάφρενον ἠδὲ καὶ ὤμους
εἴρερον εἰσανάγουσι, πόνον τ' ἐχέμεν καὶ ὀιζύν·
τῆς δ' ἐλεεινοτάτῳ ἄχεϊ φθινύθουσι παρειαί·
ὡς Ὀδυσεὺς ἐλεεινὸν ὑπ' ὀφρύσι δάκρυον εἶβεν.

As a woman weeps falling over her own dear husband,
who has fallen before his city and his troops
warding off the dire day from the town and his children,
she seeing him dying and struggling for breath,
poured over him wails shrilly; but behind her
they strike her back and shoulders with spears
and lead her off to have labor and suffering;
and her cheeks are worn down by the most piteous grief,
so Odysseus shed a piteous tear under his brows.

The rupture between the woman and her husband is so sudden and violent that she is not even allowed to wait with him while he dies or see him properly buried. She is left with the "most piteous grief," believing, like a Penelope, that her husband has died but denied the certainty that comes only from attending the corpse. This simile shares diction with a comparable scene in the *Iliad*, Briseis mourning for Patroklos (*Il.* 19.282-286, 291-302):[5]

Βρισηὶς δ' ἄρ' ἔπειτ', ἰκέλη χρυσέη 'Αφροδίτη,
ὡς ἴδε Πάτροκλον δεδαϊγμένον ὀξέι χαλκῷ,
ἀμφ' αὐτῷ χυμένη λίγ' ἐκώκυε, χερσὶ δ' ἄμυσσε
στήθεά τ' ἠδ' ἀπαλὴν δειρὴν ἰδὲ καλὰ πρόσωπα.
εἶπε δ' ἄρα κλαίουσα γυνὴ ἐϊκυῖα θεῇσι . . .
"ἄνδρα μέν, ᾧ ἔδοσάν με πατὴρ καὶ πότνια μήτηρ,
εἶδον πρὸ πτόλιος δεδαϊγμένον ὀξέι χαλκῷ,
τρεῖς τε κασιγνήτους, τούς μοι μία γείνατο μήτηρ,
κηδείους, οἳ πάντες ὀλέθριον ἦμαρ ἐπέσπον.
οὐδὲ μὲν οὐδέ μ' ἔασκες, ὅτ' ἄνδρ' ἐμὸν ὠκὺς 'Αχιλλεὺς
ἔκτεινεν, πέρσεν δὲ πόλιν θείοιο Μύνητος,
κλαίειν, ἀλλά μ' ἔφασκες 'Αχιλλῆος θείοιο
κουριδίην ἄλοχον θήσειν, ἄξειν δ' ἐνὶ νηυσὶν
ἐς Φθίην, δαίσειν δὲ γάμον μετὰ Μυρμιδόνεσσι.
τῶ σ' ἄμοτον κλαίω τεθνηότα, μείλιχον αἰεί."
ὡς ἔφατο κλαίουσ', ἐπὶ δὲ στενάχοντο γυναῖκες,
Πάτροκλον πρόφασιν, σφῶν δ' αὐτῶν κήδε' ἑκάστη.

Briseis then, resembling golden Aphrodite,
when she saw Patroklos wounded by the sharp bronze,
poured over him, wailing shrilly, and beat her breast with her
    hands
and her smooth neck and lovely face.
And then the woman similar to the gods spoke weeping,
" . . . my husband, to whom my father and mother gave me,
I saw before the city, wounded with the sharp bronze,
my three brothers, dear to me, whom our one mother bore,
who all followed the day of doom. And no, you did not

---

5. Most commentators in making the connection of the woman in the simile to the *Iliad* think primarily of Andromache, e.g., Podlecki 1971:86-87. Briseis is the more direct, appropriate, and powerful figure for comparison. See also Ebbott (this volume).

let me <u>weep</u>, when swift Achilles killed my husband
and sacked godlike Mynes' city, but you said that you
would make me the wedded wife of godlike Achilles,
    take me in the ships
to Phthia, and give me a wedding among the Myrmidons,
therefore without ceasing <u>I weep for your death</u>, you who
    were always kind."
<u>So she spoke weeping, and the women wailed in response,</u>
<u>for Patroklos as an excuse, but each for her own troubles.</u>

Briseis had been stolen away from her city, not allowed to mourn her husband and brothers killed fighting before its walls; she shares precisely the fate of the woman in the *Odyssey* simile. There is, however, for Briseis now at least the fulfillment of weeping for Patroklos, who had been kind to her, as an ersatz husband or brother. She and the other slave women weep for their own 'concerns', *kêdea*, and fulfill their need to mourn, in the tears shed ostensibly for Patroklos.

Elsewhere in the *Iliad,* the grief that Briseis would have displayed for her husband but must give instead to Patroklos is openly and properly offered to the dead by their friends and families. With the deaths of Patroklos and Hektor the focus of the poem becomes reaction to the loss of a loved one, both personal grief and public mourning. The rituals are all performed; this is best seen in *Il.* 24.719-804, where Hektor's family tends his corpse and mourns over it. The ritual performance is done "on stage" in the poem, complete down to Hektor's entombment and the family's funeral feast afterwards; so ends the *Iliad*.[6] The wailing over the body, the burning, and burial here properly performed are the acts that Briseis in *Il.* 19 can perform only for an ersatz husband and that Telemachus in *Od.* 1 and Laertes in 24 are unable to perform. The obsequies for Hektor show what kind of funeral honor Odysseus deserves and does not receive. Funeral rituals are greatly curtailed in the *Odyssey* as compared to the *Iliad*. The unwritten story of

---

6. Seaford 1994:70-78 sees the progress toward the complete funeral ritual as a unifying pattern in the *Iliad*; in the *Odyssey*, he sees the progress toward the "wedding" of Penelope and Odysseus. Cf. also Muellner 1996:168-175 on the resolution of the "*mênis* theme" at the end of the *Iliad.*

Odysseus' death at Troy, that is, in the context of the *Iliad* (1.237-239), is the paradigm for what is lacking in the *Odyssey*. Elpenor receives special treatment after being neglected originally; most of Odysseus' dead companions receive only some wailing from their fellows as they sail away, leaving the bodies behind (e.g., *Od.* 9.62-66). Mention is made of the need of Menelaos and Orestes to care for the corpse of Agamemnon because the circumstances of his death would allow for its neglect (*Od.* 3.258-261, 4.581-584).[7] These deaths occur away from home (or in Agamemnon's case in a hostile home) and in separation from battlefield companions, precluding Iliadic funeral honors. In worrying about the ultimate end of Odysseus at the beginning of the *Odyssey*, Telemachus states (*Od.* 1.234-244) that he grieves because Odysseus has not received the treatment of a Patroklos, as he would have if he had died at Troy; Laertes' sadness is that Odysseus has not died among his family, as Hektor did. In both cases Odysseus is believed, like some others in the *Odyssey*, to have been denied proper honor.

The parallels involving characters other than Odysseus maintain the concern for proper burial as a problem for the *Odyssey* as a whole. The most salient example is Elpenor: he best illustrates the fate of the untended corpse in the *Odyssey*. The proper burial he later receives (*Od.* 12.8-15) corrects the problem while pointing to its importance, and the *theôn mênis* with which he threatens Odysseus is one link between the *Odyssey* and the *Iliad*.[8] The connection between the deaths of Elpenor and Odysseus through the repeated symbol of the tomb mound crowned with an oar (*Od.* 11.75-78, 119-137) makes for parallel significance between Odysseus' presumed lack of burial and Elpenor's. When Elpenor requests burial from Odysseus, he pleads in the name of Odysseus' wife, father, and son (*Od.* 11.66-68), the figures in the poem most affected by the fear that Odysseus himself be unburied. If in his brief appearance in the poem Elpenor is a sort of double for the dead Odysseus, Telemachus too in the early books of the poem is repeatedly seen

---

7. Watkins 1994a:585-587. In the latter passage ring composition links κατέπαυσα θεῶν χόλον (4.583) to βούλοντο θεοὶ μεμνῆσθαι ἐφετμέων (4.353). The proper completion of Agamemnon's funeral rites = stopping the gods' wrath = remembering their commandments. "Nous voici en présence du même contexte thématique qu'avec Elpénor et Hector—assure-moi les funérailles, μνήσασαι ἐμεῖο, μή τοί τι θεῶν μήνιμα γένωμαι" (586).

8. Watkins 1994a.

to be resembling and modeling Odysseus. It is his badge of identity that he looks like his father. He even has a brief opportunity to have an "odyssey" of his own: the return voyage from Pylos to Ithaca while the suitors lie in ambush resembles in miniature Odysseus' sea wanderings. In this context, Telemachus faces death at sea and deprivation of burial like his father. Penelope recognizes the similarity (*Od.* 4.724, 727-728):

ἥ πρὶν μὲν πόσιν ἐσθλὸν ἀπώλεσα θυμολέοντα . . .
νῦν αὖ παῖδ' ἀγαπητὸν <u>ἀνηρείψαντο θύελλαι</u>
<u>ἀκλέα</u> ἐκ μεγάρων, οὐδ' ὁρμηθέντος ἄκουσα.

I who already lost my fine, lion-hearted husband . . .
and now <u>storms have snatched away</u> my beloved son
<u>aklea</u> from my home and I did not hear of his departure.

"Snatched away *aklea* 'without *kleos*'" means not only that there will be no sure report of Telemachus' death but also that he will not be memorialized, which is the function of entombment.[9] Penelope's words repeat in sense and diction Telemachus' first expression of the predicament of Odysseus (*Od.* 1.234-244). Here compare as well Odysseus' telling of his fears for himself when faced with death at sea (*Od.* 5.308-311):

ὡς δὴ ἐγώ γ' ὄφελον θανέειν καὶ πότμον ἐπισπεῖν
ἤματι τῷ ὅτε μοι πλεῖστοι χαλκήρεα δοῦρα
Τρῶες ἐπέρριψαν περὶ Πηλείωνι θανόντι.
<u>τῷ κ' ἔλαχον κτερέων, καί μευ κλέος ἦγον Ἀχαιοί</u>

Oh, to have died and met my fated end
on that day when so many Trojans threw their bronze-tipped
    spears
around the dead son of Peleus.

---

9. See Segal 1994:103-105 on *kleos* as the antidote for mortal decay, a kind of counterforce to the destructive power of Sirens and Harpies, 'snatchers' or Ἅρπυιαι; cf. *Od.* 1.241.

> Then I would have had my share of funeral rites, and the
> Achaeans would have handled my *kleos*.

He sees the same implication: no burial means no *kleos*, the final end of heroic life, where otherwise it would continue as *kleos*. The themes of *kleos*, death, burial, and memorialization cannot be separated in the heroic epic; the construct is among Homeric poetry's primary concerns. And one could not understand the problem of the death of Odysseus in the *Odyssey* without reference to epic poetry's self-referential manner of treating heroic deaths.[10] The *Odyssey*, particularly the Elpenor episode, however, does point to additional, less literary—one might say more religious or superstitious— ways of viewing the honors paid to a dead person: one who does not properly tend a corpse faces the wrath of the gods. The gods' wrath, *theôn mênis*, however, is a very literary idea, a central theme of both the *Iliad* and the *Odyssey*.[11] *Mênis* and *kleos* together figure in the making of the poetry and very much color understanding of Odysseus' strange status between death and life.

Elpenor receives no *kleos* from his burial and tomb;[12] or at least the poetry makes no mention of the idea in connection with Elpenor (or with Odysseus' parallel journey to the inland with the oar). One could say that despite his presence in the epic, Elpenor is not sufficiently heroic to receive *kleos*. He is after all the least of Odysseus' companions, neither a strong fighter nor a good thinker (*Od.* 10.552-553). But he is represented more fully than the other companions, and to be the least is to have a uniqueness, a certain superior status to the undifferentiated majority, which gives significance. Furthermore, there is the symbolism shared with Odysseus of the oar planted on the mound. So Elpenor cannot be discounted as an inconsequential or minor figure; his un-heroic type of death and burial is in the poetic tradition

---

10. For the connection between *kleos*, heroic death, and grief, see Nagy 1979:94-117. But Segal 1994:109 sees a "distanced, self-conscious, and ironic reflection on *kleos*" in the *Odyssey*. For discussion of another aspect of mourning in the *Odyssey*, see Levaniouk (this volume).

11. Muellner 1996 passim.

12. Granted, this is contradicted in a metaliterary way; Elpenor's death and burial have *kleos* by virtue of being an episode in the Homeric poetry.

for a reason. It is to draw attention to the issues of his fate after death because they are also meant to be seen in connection with Odysseus.

Elpenor, unique in the *Odyssey*, is suffering the consequences of his lack of burial. He does not say what unwanted fate specifically awaits him if he is left neglected, but the tradition holds that the unburied are denied entrance to the world of the dead. The consequences of Elpenor's neglect, however, extend beyond himself, and these he mentions. "I beg of you to remember me and not to go and return home leaving me unwept and unburied so that I will not become for you a cause of the gods' wrath," he says (*Od.* 11.71-73). This threat, as discussed above, raises the problem that those responsible for the care of a corpse could face punishment from the gods if they did not fulfill their duties. In Watkins' words, "Elpénor demande à Ulysse, un autre mortel, de *mettre et garder dans son esprit* ce que lui est dû dans l'ordre divin, l'ordre du destin des mortels dans l'autre monde, afin que cela ne retombe sur Ulysse, afin que lui, Elpénor, ne soit pas l'occasion de cette colère divine immanente."[13] Odysseus does avoid *theôn mênis*, of course, by returning to Circe's island and giving Elpenor his due. It is this reciprocal context of duties and consequences with regard to the care of the dead, which the story of Elpenor raises, that one should relate to the unknown fate of Odysseus and the pain of his family back in Ithaca.

Now we may return to the reunion between Odysseus and Laertes in *Odyssey* 24. Faced with a stranger asking questions about Odysseus, Laertes tells him of his and his family's inability to weep over and bury his son because he has died away from home and become food for beasts or fish (*Od.* 24.290-296). The mourning rituals that Odysseus' family want to perform for him, to bury him with the honors Hektor or Patroklos receives in the *Iliad*, are impossible due to the absence of Odysseus' corpse. This is a shameful and wretched state of affairs. Added to Laertes' shame and sorrow for his inability to bury Odysseus is also the fear both of the lack of repose for Odysseus' *psukhê* and of the wrath of the gods visited upon the neglectful family—the two eventualities held out by the Elpenor story. These concerns and their import are not conveyed on the surface level of the poetry. Laertes does not say to the stranger, "I have been unable to mourn for and bury my son, so I am worried about consequences for him and for myself from the

---

13. Watkins 1994a:585.

gods." The poetry does, however, preserve some such message within the linguistic fabric of the text. The language used in the communication between father and son, specifically Odysseus' false self-identification to Laertes (*Od.* 24.303-307), and the nonverbal but communicative message of Laertes' reaction to this story (*Od.* 24.315-317), can be unpacked to reveal just the same concerns that circle the Elpenor story. And this helps to explain why the reunion between Odysseus and Laertes takes the form it does.

The false name is one of the weapons in Odysseus' arsenal of μῆτις 'cunning intelligence', his salvation from the Cyclops for instance.[14] His use of one here, in reintroducing himself to his father, part of the test (*Od.* 24.216-218) he is performing, is puzzling (*Od.* 24.303-306):

> τοιγὰρ ἐγώ τοι πάντα μάλ᾽ ἀτρεκέως καταλέξω.
> εἰμὶ μὲν ἐξ Ἀλύβαντος, ὅθι κλυτὰ δώματα ναίω,
> υἱὸς Ἀφείδαντος Πολυπημονίδαο ἄνακτος
> αὐτὰρ ἐμοί γ᾽ ὄνομ᾽ ἐστὶν Ἐπήριτος

> Well then, I will tell you everything quite without confusion.
> I am from Alybas, where I have a well known home,
> the son of lord Apheidas, the son of Polypemon,
> and my name is Eperitos.

The first step to finding the significance of such a passage is to assign meaning to the *nomina loquentia*. And the parallel of the Οὖτις 'No one' in Book 9 would indicate that it is reasonable to expect false names to convey some meaning when used by *polumētis* 'much devising' Odysseus. The setting of the false names within the πεῖρα 'test' might even allow for understanding the names as a kind of riddle, a test of understanding. The audience for the test is immediately Laertes, but the Homeric audience also has a chance to answer.[15]

---

14. Peradotto 1990:143-170.
15. In what follows, it is the audience for the poetry whose understanding is key to unpacking the names. Whether one calls the associations evoked by the names "folk etymology" or sees them as poetic metaphor, scientific linguistics is not the proper tool to arrive at those audience-based associations; see West 1989:140n72.

One answer to the riddle has gained general acceptance. In his *Sprachliche Untersuchungen zu Homer*,[16] Jacob Wackernagel, following Wilamowitz and others,[17] argued briefly that the names mean "I am Select Man, *der Auserlesen*, the son of Not-sparing / Free-giving, *der nicht sparen muss / der nicht spart / freigebig*, the son of Many-possessions, *Vielbesitzer*." This interpretation involves taking Πολυπημονίδης as Πολυπαμονίδης (cf. *Il.* 4.433) and connecting Ἐπήριτος with the Arcadian Ἐπ-άριτοι (root as in ἀριθμός) while discounting association with ἔρις 'wrath'.[18] Many commentators have followed him on these points,[19] and this interpretation makes for a satisfactory integration of the names with Odysseus' claims of lavish hospitality to a stranger (*Od.* 24.266-279). The point would be "I am very rich." Wackernagel found further support for this in the place name Ἀλύβας, which he took as *Silberstadt* 'Silvertown'.[20] Perhaps one need not look for further significance in these lines, but in the context of Odysseus' test of his father and Laertes' reaction to his story, there seems to be a difficult disjunction. In Wackernagel's view, then, Odysseus says, "I am a wealthy man, from a rich land. I entertained your son very well and gave him expensive gifts and five years ago he left my home under favorable omens" (*Od.* 24.309-314). It is to this that Laertes reacts with such pitiful wailing that Odysseus abandons the false guise and declares his identity to his father. If any consistency is to be sought between Odysseus' lie and Laertes' reaction, under Wackernagel's interpretation it must be the five years' time that disheartens Laertes. But this rationale is quite weak, as Laertes has been waiting much longer than five years for Odysseus' return and should be glad to hear that relatively recently he was alive and with good prospects.[21] In order to preserve the context of Odysseus' *peira*, of the concerns Laertes has

---

16. Wackernagel 1916:249-251.

17. Wilamowitz 1884:70n1; Russo, Fernandez-Galiano, Heubeck 1992:395 have fuller bibliographical references for all the names in question.

18. Immisch 1911:457.

19. E.g., Heubeck (Russo, Fernandez-Galiano, Heubeck 1992:395), also von Kamptz 1982.

20. I will return to the question of the name of the town below.

21. One could speculate on various scenarios to explain the exchange, for instance that Laertes has recognized Odysseus and forces tears in order to elicit the declaration from him. But I hope that with what follows I can show that such speculation without textual basis is unnecessary.

expressed to the stranger, and of his extreme reaction to the lying story, Wackernagel's interpretation needs to be revised. In the words of John Peradotto, it "satisfies current state-of-the-art etymology and creates internal consistency among the four names but in the process renders them completely arbitrary within the framework of the entire narrative."[22] Fortunately, another interpretation, derived along the same linguistic lines as Wackernagel's, is available, and this reading not only accords better with the context but also helps to elucidate it.

Let us begin with the clearest name, Πολυπημονίδης. The simplest understanding of the meaning is 'son of many griefs' from πῆμα 'grief'; there is no need to restore α to make good sense. And if one accepts the derivation of 'Επήριτος from ἔρις 'wrath', which Wackernagel rejects,[23] these two names, of suffering and strife, in combination could suggest the connection between the name Odysseus and ὀδύσσομαι 'to rage',[24] and so the most central themes of the poem. The fictitious name of Odysseus' father, 'Αφείδας, is more difficult. The formation of the name is not a problem: elsewhere in Homer there appears Φείδας, beside 'Α-κάμας, 'Α-δάμας.[25] The name is a negation of the root φειδ-, which in Homer most commonly means 'spare';[26] so the accepted sense is 'not-sparing'. There is disagreement as to whether this should be taken as 'pitiless' with potential reference to the just accomplished slaughter of the suitors,[27] or as 'unsparing of possessions, lavish, generous', Wackernagel's preference. There is, however, a third possibility: that the name should actually be understood as 'neglectful', with specific reference to neglect of ritual propriety in the care for a corpse.

In post-Homeric poetic diction, the verb ἀφειδέω and the adjective ἀφειδής mean still 'to be unsparing of, lavish' but also 'to take no care for,

---

22. Peradotto 1990:144. He prefers, in part, the interpretation of the names that I will defend below.
23. On the basis that there are no other formations of ἔρισ + ιτος.
24. Noted by Monro 1901 at 304-306; cf. *Od.* 19.392-466 and, following on the passage under discussion, 24.328-335. See also the full examination in Dimock 1956.
25. Immisch 1911:456-457.
26. Chantraine s.v. φείδομαι.
27. φειδ- words appear often in Homer in contexts of sparing a vanquished enemy, e.g., *Od.* 16.185, 22.54. Cf. Herodotus 9.39: ἀφείδως ἐφόνευον and Hesychius: φείδεσθαι ἐλεεῖν.

neglect'.[28] There is a clear interconnectedness between meanings 'to spare not, to be lavish', 'not to have care for', and 'to neglect'. The intermediate stage of meaning 'to care for/not care for' of the φειδ- root is key to understanding how the name Ἀφείδας can mean 'neglectful' in Homer. There is a difficult passage in the *Iliad*, where Agamemnon agrees to a truce in order for the Greeks and Trojans to tend to the corpses on the battlefield, which have been lying uncremated while the fighting continued:

> ἀμφὶ δὲ νεκροῖσιν κατακαιέμεν οὔ τι μεγαίρω
> οὐ γάρ τις φειδὼ νεκύων κατατεθνηώτων
> γίγνετ', ἐπεί κε θάνωσι, πυρὸς μειλισσέμεν ὦκα.
>
> (*Il.* 7.408-410)[29]

Giving the key word φειδὼ its common Homeric meaning 'sparing', a paraphrase of the lines would be: "concerning the burning of the corpses I have no objection; for there is no sparing of dead bodies, whenever they die, of quickly giving them the honor of fire." The necessary sense is that during the fighting there has not been any opportunity to cremate the dead when they died, so a truce is called for. The paraphrase, however, would seem to yield the opposite: "no sparing of the dead of burning them when they died" should mean that the dead were burnt (unsparingly) when they died, as they certainly were not.[30] G. S. Kirk in his commentary is forced to take γίγνετο as meaning 'should be' in order to make the Greek say what he intuits it means: "the syntax is imprecise and proverbial but clear in implication (neither it nor

---

28. *LSJ*, s.v. ἀφειδέω. Chantraine, s.v. φείδομαι: "ἀ-φειδής 'prodigue, qui n'a pas souci de qqch.' et 'qu' on ne ménage pas'; . . . d'où le dénominatif ἀφειδέω 'être prodigue, ne pas ménager et 'négliger'." The relevant references are: Sophocles *Antigone* 414 (the object of neglect is the πόνου 'effort' of guarding the body of Polyneices, ironically so that it will not be buried); Apollonius Rhodius 2.98 (the object of neglect is the dead king Amycus); 3.360 (Medea "neglecting" her parents by choosing Jason). Interestingly, at both Sophocles *Antigone* 414 and A. R. 3.360, a form of ἀκηδέω appears as a variant reading for the form of ἀφειδέω.

29. For an attempted translation, see n31.

30. A gauge of the confusion can be found in Lattimore's translation, where there is recourse to an addition not in the Greek: "But about the burning of the dead bodies I do not begrudge you; / no, for there is no *sparing time* for the bodies of the perished, / once they have died, to give them swiftly the pity of burning" (emphasis mine).

e.g. φειδώ being particularly 'late'): 'there is [i.e., should be] no sparing in the matter of dead corpses, over quickly propitiating them in the matter of fire.'"[31] There is, however, an alternative solution to the problem. Another possible response would be to give φειδώ the sense 'concern, regard, care', which the root carries in ά-φειδέω and ά-φειδής. This interpretation would yield a paraphrase preferable in both sense and faithfulness to the Greek: "concerning the burning of the corpses I have no objection; for there is no concern/regard/care of the dead bodies, whenever they die, of quickly giving them the honor of fire." The prolonged fighting has not allowed the warriors to attend to the dead at the time they died, so a truce is called for.

The construction of abstract + γίγνομαι is a common one in Homer;[32] here the phraseology might carry ritual connotations.[33] Caring for the corpses has been lacking during the fighting; in other words, those responsible have neglected to gather and cremate them with the ritual propriety the situation demands. So this difficult passage in the *Iliad* bears on the interpretation of the name Ἀφείδας in *Odyssey* 24. For the sake of clarity and strict reading of the Greek, the word φειδώ at *Il.* 7.409 can be translated 'concern/regard/care' or even 'ritually proper attention'. In other words, Homeric usage allowed for the sense of the root φειδ- that, in post-Homeric poetic diction, is found in such words as άφειδέω and άφειδής.[34] These words mean 'neglect', a sense

---

31. Kirk 1990:285.

32. For other instances of this form (i.e., the construction with abstract noun replacing a verb and appearing as the subject), see Porzig 1942:11-23. The phrase οὐ γάρ τις φειδώ replaces precisely the verb άφειδέω.

33. The locution to some degree takes the form of a "taboo periphrasis"; for an example of such, in this case with regard to a fire ritual in the Iguvine Tables, see Nagy 1990b:164-170. Taboo periphrasis also figures in the story of "the Hero," the euphemistic appellation of a cult figure; see below n53.

34. Perhaps a similar connection between Greek φειδ- and concern for a corpse presents itself also in the *Odyssey* (9.277). The Cyclops says that if he did not want to, he would not 'spare' (πεφιδούμην) Odysseus and his men in order to 'avoid' άλευάμενος the 'hatred' (ἔχθος) of Zeus; here *ekhthos* could be a substitute for *mênis*. See Watkins (1994a:574-575) on "avoiding" *mênis* and the word's taboo status. Polyphemos' conspicuous lack of φειδώ involves not only failure to "spare" the lives of his suppliants (cf. 269), but also the most outrageous mistreatment of a corpse imaginable—eating it; cf. *Il.* 22.346-347, Achilles threatening to eat Hektor's corpse. This is breaking the ultimate taboo and shows the ultimate disrespect for the gods, their laws, and their sanctions (Muellner 1996:32-33, 168-169).

it is possible to accept also in the Homeric name 'Αφείδας 'neglectful', the one without proper (ritual) concern'.[35]

With the above interpretations, we have now arrived at another unified understanding of the fictitious names Odysseus gives himself in his lie to Laertes: "I am Strife, the son of Neglectful, the son of Many Griefs."[36] As Wackernagel's interpretation gave a consistent message of "wealth" conveyed by the names, this one reveals what could be seen as a sequence: neglect, strife, grief. Now one can see a clear relationship between the names and their context; they are directly related to Laertes' just expressed concerns about being unable to mourn for and bury his son. As the Elpenor story recognizes, neglect of a corpse can bring grief and strife (the wrath of the gods). And if the φειδ- of 'Αφείδας carries the sense of 'ritually proper concern', appropriate specifically to corpses, as the passage in *Il.* 7 might suggest, the contextual meaning could not be clearer. The names throw back in the face of Laertes just the worries he has expressed to the stranger a few lines previously (*Od.* 24.290-296); this rhetoric explains why the father reacts so negatively when he hears them, despite the good news appended to them.

The frightening message of neglected corpses, strife, and grief, furthermore, goes beyond the proper names Odysseus gives himself; the name of the town of origin he claims, 'Αλύβας, makes the same point, and in a very concrete way for Laertes, adding even more to the old man's misery. Wackernagel thought 'Αλύβας was 'Silvertown',[37] consistent with his understanding of the names; he tried to make the linguistics for this solution

---

35. I would compare the near synonymous names of the first Greek tyrant and his son (Herodotus 6.127): Φείδων and Λεοκήδης 'he who shows ritually proper concern' and 'concerned for the folk'.

36. Higbie 1995:186-187n66 is confident that this is the proper interpretation: "these names have clearly significant etymologies: Odysseus claims to be Strife, son of lord Neglect, son of Many-griefs." She does acknowledge that 'Αφείδας could also mean 'to be unsparing, lavish'. Though preferring 'Strife' for 'Επήριτος and 'man of much woe' for Πολυπήμων to Wackernagel's suggestions, Peradotto 1995:144 sees 'Αφείδας only as 'the unsparing', which "suggests the manner in which (Odysseus) has dealt with the suitors." He does not demand that all three names carry a single cohesive meaning.

37. Alybas presumed to be equivalent to the city at *Il.* 2.857: τηλόθεν ἐξ 'Αλύβης, ὅθεν ἀργύρου ἐστὶ γενέθλη. Cf. Euphorion fr. 6. Wackernagel 1916:251. See Watkins (1994b:707-709n13) on *Alybe*, silver, and the Hittites.

easier by proposing to read ἐκ Σαλύβαντος.[38] Other interpretations, however, are available. One offered by Peradotto is 'land of distress (or struggle)', from ἀλύω, though he thinks of this as only an association, not a true derivation: "even if only by poetic or folk etymology, giving Eperitos, like Calypso, metaphorical geography to match the condition signified by his name."[39] Both of these proposals maintain consistency with the names: Wackernagel's through an idea of wealth, Peradotto's through parallelism to ὀδυσσόμενος. Following in this vein of interpretation, I propose that 'Αλύβας, or at least the "metaphorical geography" and contextual associations of the name, should be understood in a way consistent with the fear of a neglected corpse and ensuing consequences, a fear that lurks in the names and animates the scene between Odysseus and Laertes.

The ancient scholarly tradition claimed that it knew the location of the town called *Alybas*; Eustathius records, at *Od.* 24.304, pp. 1961-1962, that *Alybas* was a South Italian town, the later Metapontum.[40] The *Etymologicum Magnum*, s.v. Μέταβος, has an explanation for the name change: Metabos is the eponym of Metapontum, and he was the son of Alibas the founder of Alybas, an eponymous relationship, though in two coexisting by-forms.[41] Odysseus' claim to have been driven ἀπὸ Σικανίης 'from Sicily' [*Od.* 24.307]) in coming from *Alybas* justifies, to some degree at least, attempts to locate the town, both for Homer and for the historical period, in that part of the world. And the evidence from all sources would indicate that this is correct. Odysseus' town *Alybas* then is at least notionally in south Italy, in the area of the later Metapontum.

Etymologicum Magnum gives the name of the eponymous founder of the place 'Αλύβας as 'Αλίβας; likewise, Hesychius, in using 'Αλύβας as a place

---

38. Likewise at *Il* 2.857: ἐκ Σαλύβης.

39. Peradotto 1990:144.

40. This and nearly all the other references in the following discussion of *Alybas* and *alibas* were brought to my attention by Lawson 1926. Basically the same information is clearly summarized in the note of Pearson to Sophocles fr. 790; Radt 1977:539 does not add anything.

41. Lawson 1926:121. The variation in spelling *Alybas/Alibas* (which also occurs in Hesychius) is of importance to the argument that follows. Part of the legitimacy of locating Alybas in Magna Graecia is the presence of the *-as* termination in several local place names: Taras, Akragas, as noticed by Wackernagel. There are others, e.g. the river Gelas, for which Gela is named, Thucydides 6.4.

name, conflates it with Ἀλίβας.[42] It is possible to say with confidence that for this word a "variation of spelling therefore existed, at any rate in South Italy."[43] Now *alibas* was a word that in antiquity gathered much speculation as to its meaning.[44] Whether it in fact derived from α + λειβ-/λιβ- 'without moisture' as the lexicographers maintain, its primary usage, among others, was as a word for 'corpse', παρὰ τὸ μὴ λίβαδα ἔχειν 'because [a corpse] has no moisture'.[45] But *alibas/alybas* is not used for simply any corpse. The attestation of the word in Plato (*Rep.* 387c) carries strong connotations of otherworldly terrors; *alibantas* are to be banished along with *kokutous te kai stugas kai enerous* and all the other *deina te kai phobera* 'terrible and frightening words'. For Plato an *alibas* or an *eneros*, but not every *nekros* 'corpse', is a frightening thing. "Ἀλίβαντες then are a class, and in some way a terrible class, of νέκροι."[46] J. C. Lawson used comparative material from modern Greek folklore about the dead and their bodies and an examination of the lexicographic information about *alibantes*, including the popular etymology of "juiceless" corpses, to reach the conclusion that an *alibas* was to an ancient Greek a *revenant* corpse, a horrible, withered thing of physical substance (not an incorporeal ghost), which, in its complementary guise of *alastôr*, could wreak damage on the living.[47] He also reached the conclusion that a corpse could become an *alibas* when it was not properly

---

42. See Pearson on Sophocles fr. 994, with note. Radt 1977:605.

43. Lawson 1926:118.

44. And it has not stopped: Chantraine s.v. can examine the ancients' "explication qui n'est qu'une étym. populaire" and modern hypotheses that "ne valent guère mieux" without reaching a decisive conclusion.

45. Chantraine: "Le sens attesté le plus anciennement est 'vinaigre' mais ce doit être par hasard et les Anciens pensent que le sens originel est 'mort', le vinaigre étant un 'vin mort.'" Cf. Wilamowitz 1919:64-65.

46. Lawson 1926:54. The use in Plato follows on a literary context; he has just discussed condemning frightful underworld elements in Homer. Banishing *alibantes*, and the other words that "make all the listeners 'shudder' (φρίττειν)," is then the next step. The setting in which these words create this frightening effect, unfortunately, is perhaps corrupt in the text. Plato's wording refers not to the text of Homer, which the discussants have left, but could this still refer to some poetic/song performance, literary or subliterary? Or are they merely ghost stories?

47. Lawson 1926:56-58 finds this not only as an element of folklore but also alive in the literary context of the *Oresteia*.

buried or cremated.[48] To support this belief he attributed to the ancient Greeks, Lawson adduced a remarkable story of an *alibas* (actually in this case spelled *alybas*).[49]

The story is recorded most fully in Pausanias (6.6.7-11) and concerns a combat between a historical personage, Euthymos of Locri, the Olympic victor in boxing in 484, and an *alibas*. The story begins when Odysseus on his wanderings put in at Temesa in south Italy. One of his crew got drunk, raped a local girl, and was stoned to death by her townspeople; Odysseus and his men abandoned their comrade in their haste to get away. Thereafter the citizens of Temesa were beset by the vengeance of the dead man; people were killed indiscriminately until they built him a temple and annually offered him the prettiest girl in town. He was called simply "the Hero."[50] Euthymos came to Temesa during the time of giving the Hero his yearly offering and defeated the δαίμων 'superhuman entity'—in a boxing match presumably) to win the girl for himself.

This story is consistent with all of Lawson's conclusions about an *alibas*. Odysseus' sailor had become an *alibas* both because he died an untimely and violent death and because his corpse was neglected. Within the story, however, Pausanias does not call the man an *alibas*, only the Hero or *daimôn*. But he says that he did see a painting of the story, with places and characters labeled. For the label of Euthymos' terrible opponent on this painting the Loeb text and most modern editions of Pausanias read ὄνομα Λύκαν τὰ ἐπὶ τῇ γραφῇ γράμματα 'for the name the letters on the painting are Lykas' (meaning 'Wolfman'), which would be justified by the figure's wearing a wolfskin]). This name Lykas, however, is the product only of Bekker's emendation of the text and should be removed. The text actually gives: ὄνομα λύβαντα ἐπὶ or ὄνομα λύβαν τὰ ἐπὶ. As several editors before Bekker realized, a double haplography should be posited here, and the text properly emended to: ὄνομα ᾽Αλύβαντα τὰ ἐπὶ. The painting labels the

---

48. Lawson 1926:52: "the most humane way of treating them is to burn their bodies," securing repose. "[C]auses of such a condition are threefold—lack of burial, sudden death, and execration or deadly sin deserving it."
49. Lawson 1926:116-121.
50. See below n52 on the taboo convention surrounding this hero's name.

vengeful Hero of Temesa as an *alybas*,[51] alternate spelling of *alibas*, his behavior according quite well with Lawson's understanding of the belief. Further confirmation of this comes from the *Suda*, in which the entry for Euthymos says: οὗτος ὁ Εὔθυμος ἠγωνίσατο καὶ πρὸς τὸν ἐν Τεμέσῃ ἥρωα Ἀλύβαντα 'this Euthymos also fought the Hero of Temesa, Alybas'.[52]

The *alibas/alybas* in short was the horrible, murderous, vengeful *revenant* corpse of a neglected dead man. As Plato knew, *alibantes* scared people; one shuddered even to hear the word. Those who neglected to tend the dead could be afraid that they would face consequences, perhaps even death at the hands of the neglected corpse itself.[53] This is the real power of the place name *Alybas*, carrying associations with all of the above, at *Od.* 24.304.

51. Probably to be understood as a proper name, Alybas, as indicated in the *Suda*; see below.

52. This Hero of Temesa/Alybas/*alibas* is in many ways an interesting figure in the story of Greek hero cult. Fontenrose 1968 looks at a peculiar type of Greek hero, a victorious athlete prone to terrible violence; in the case of Euthymos, his heroically violent side is assigned instead to the Hero, so that the two figures together form the "hero as athlete." At Temesa Euthymos clearly inherited the cult honors given first to the Hero. Brelich (1958:136n188) takes the anonymity of the Hero as appropriate for an eponymous hero; he could just as well be called Temesios and should be understood as the hero of Temesa's city cult. Note the eponymous relationship between Alibas/Alybas and Metapontum, which is in roughly the same region as Temesa. Lawson 1926:121 speculates that a founder cult of Alibas/Alybas remained after the city took the name Metapontum, spread to the nearby city of Temesa, and at some point required an explanation for the name. The euphemistic appellation "the Hero" could also reflect a taboo on the hero's actual name (Alybas?). See Brelich 1958:156-158 for heroic figures, such as Hesychos, Euphemos, Sigelos, whose euphemistic names represent cult practice of ritual silence. The attestation of the story of the Hero in Strabo (6.1.5) gives the name of Odysseus' dead sailor as Polites. This again is an appropriate name for the heroic founder figure of a city, "the Citizen." Priam's son Polites in the *Iliad*, who stands watch for Troy on a hero's tomb (*Il.* 2.791-794), is a figure who "seems to personify the garrison defense of Troy" (Scully 1990:55-56); see also Seaford 1994:111-112. The Polites in Odysseus' crew is strongly characterized (*Od.* 10.224-225) as "leader of men, who of my companions was the dearest to me and most cared for," that is precisely *not* one Odysseus would neglect to bury: *kêdistos* 'most dear' carries the sense 'one whose funeral (*kêdea*) I would attend to'; cf. *Il.* 19.293-294. The epithet *kednotatos* 'most cared for' is perhaps related; see Chantraine ss.vv. κήδω and κεδνός. Any direct connection between the story of the Hero and our *Odyssey* is, of course, obscure, though for Eustathius (p. 1379.22-24) the story of the Hero proves that Odysseus went to Temesa.

53. See the Appendix for a discussion of the Hero in proverbs and a proposal for an emendation in the text of Strabo.

The test that Odysseus presents his father in Book 24, he says, is one of recognition (*Od.* 24.217-218), but what Odysseus asks Laertes to recognize is not himself but his vengeful spirit, returned to punish Laertes for neglect. He says to the old man, "I am from Revenant-corpse-town, where I have a well-known home, the son of lord Neglectful, the son of Manygriefs." At these words, after having just expressed his grief for Odysseus in terms of his inability to mourn, Laertes is naturally overcome with suffering. And in revealing these emotions, the guilt and sadness of not having buried his dead son and the fear of having to face an *alibas* as punishment, Laertes passes Odysseus' test. The reunion can proceed.[54]

Odysseus' last test and last lies do interrupt what should be a smooth course toward his completing his reintegration into the family on Ithaca. Verses 24.327-348 show how father and son were ultimately able to reunite as one would expect. The *peira*, however, is not superfluous or otiose; it directly addresses concerns that have animated the entire poem, that is, the grief of the absent Odysseus' family, which connects the action away from Ithaca to the action on Ithaca. The fears of Odysseus' family have been in the air since 1.234-244, and these are forcefully summoned up and then finally put aside just before the poem ends.[55] In a way, by returning to Ithaca after

---

54. Through the exchange of symbols (24.328-348), just as Odysseus was made known previously to Eurykleia and then to Penelope.

55. The resolution of the problem of the disposal of Odysseus' corpse may add to the arguments in favor of accepting *Od.* 23.297 and following as an integrated part of the entire poem. See Russo, Fernandez-Galiano, Heubeck 1992:342-345 for a discussion of the large bibliography concerning the "Epilogue." West 1989:115-118 would favor removing Laertes entirely from the poem as a later addition, save perhaps Antikleia's description of him in Book 11; see 125-128 for problems particular to the scene between Odysseus and Laertes (*Od.* 24.205-411) and n72 on Odysseus' false names. For Seaford 1994:38-42, the end of the poem is a later continuation, but also necessary to conform to an emerging public sense that the city-state requires a solution for a "public" problem, the expected vengeance of the suitors' families. How the very private reunion between father and son would figure in this he does not say. Muellner 1996:41-45 well defends the text: "the concluding scene of the *Odyssey*, which effectively puts a seal on a morally selective, socially integrating revision of the *mênis* theme, seems to belong where it is as a statement of the identity of the *Odyssey* as against the *Iliad*" (45). He is referring to the failure, ensured by Zeus, of the Ithacans to avenge the dead suitors, but this could equally well accord with a deflection of the theme of *mênis* provoked by neglect of a corpse fashioned by

so many years and so much doubt, Odysseus came back from the dead. Fortunately for his family it was not in the horrible form they feared.

Appendix: Strabo and the Hero of Temesa

In this appendix, I offer a proposal for an emendation in the text of Strabo. In the section of his work on southern Italy, the geographer mentions Temesa and the Hero of Temesa (6.1.5):

> ἔστι δὲ πλησίον τῆς Τεμέσης ἡρῷον, ἀγριελαίοις συνηρεφές,
> Πολίτου τῶν 'Οδυσσέως ἑταίρων, ὃν δολοφονηθέντα ὑπὸ
> τῶν βαρβάρων <u>γενέσθαι βαρύμηνιν</u>, ὥστε τοὺς περιοίκους
> <u>δασμολογεῖν αὐτῷ</u> κατά τι λόγιον, καὶ <u>παροιμίαν εἶναι πρὸς</u>
> † <u>αὐτοὺς μηδεὶς</u> † <u>τὸν ἥρωα τὸν ἐν Τεμέσῃ λεγόντων</u>
> <u>ἐπικεῖσθαι αὐτοῖς</u>.

Near Temesa there is the hero shrine, surrounded by wild olives, of Polites, one of Odysseus' companions, who was treacherously slain by the barbarians and <u>became a heavy burden of wrath</u> (<u>barumênin</u>), so that following an oracle, the local people <u>paid him tribute</u>, and <u>there is a proverb concerning the † † that "they have to deal with the Hero of Temesa."</u>

Two emendations for the crux have been offered: πρὸς τοὺς ἀνηλεεῖς 'concerning the pitiless' (Buttman, Kramer, [Berlin 1844]; Müller & Dübner [Paris 1853-58]) and πρὸς τοὺς ἀηδεῖς 'concerning the unpleasant' (Meineke [Leipzig 1852]).[56] I propose that, given the sense of the proverb and the fact that the Hero is an *alibas* taking vengeance for the neglect of his corpse,[57] the proper reading is πρὸς τοὺς ἀκηδεῖς 'concerning the neglectful'. It is the careless, heedless, neglectful who

---

Odysseus' successful reunion with his father. Neither the Ithacans nor Laertes have to face the *mênis* of Odysseus.

56. As reported in the *apparatus* of Jones 1924, Lasserre 1967.

57. See above on Pausanias' version of the Hero's story.

have to face the wrath of the Hero, that is to say, of the *alibas*. Furthermore, *akêdês* is redolent of the "care" particular to corpses.[58] If this solution is not to be accepted, the 'pitiless', taken in a similar sense, is at least preferable to the 'unpleasant.

Eustathius would seem to offer some help in emending the phrase, as his reportage of the Hero story takes Strabo (i.e., ὁ γεωγράφος 'the geographer') as its direct source (at *Od.* 1.185, p.1409.12-16). He uses Strabo's words for the city foundation background, the shrine surrounded by olive trees, Polites being treacherously killed, becoming a *barumênis*, and exacting tribute (*edasmologei*). His version of the proverb, however, is different: ὅθεν ἐπὶ τῶν ἀγριαινόντων ἔξω καιροῦ παροιμία κεῖται, ὁ ἐν Τεμέσῃ ἥρως, ἤγουν ὁ ἐν οἷς οὐ δεῖ ἀγριώτατος 'whence comes the proverb concerning those who are angry beyond measure, 'the Hero of Temesa,' that is, one who is extremely angry against those he should not be'. Emenders have been misled by this report into thinking that Strabo's text requires some word near in sense to *agriôtatos* 'extremely angry', but it is rather the case that Eustathius has incorporated a different version of the proverb from some other source.[59]

Other versions of the proverb occur in (Pseudo-) Plutarch ii.31(CPG I.342), Suda (s.v. ὁ ἐν Τεμέσῃ ἥρως, quite close to the Plutarch), and Aelian (V.H. 8.18); these all share a financial concern. Either one who calls in a debt but is himself found to owe money is called "Hero of Temesa" (Plutarch, Suda) or one who makes a profit improperly (literally, 'unprofitably' [ἀλυσιτελῶς]), faces the Hero (Aelian). A potential connection exists between these versions and Strabo's in that the geographer says that the Hero "exacted tribute" from the local people. This refers, however, not to financial tribute but precisely to the annual dedication of a girl of Temesa to the Hero as recorded by Pausanias (6.6.7-11).

A fragment of Callimachus helps to explain how the proverb could evolve in significance from the superhuman wrath that faces those who neglect corpses to a tag about square dealing in financial matters. Callimachus told the story of Euthymos in Book IV of the Aetia (fr.98-99 Pfeiffer). One obscure line survives, but this section of the poem is covered by the fragmentary Diegesis that has been found. This summary (Dieg. IV.6-15) makes it clear that the 'tribute' (ἐδασμοφόρει 7) is precisely the virgin girl the Hero demands from the people. Euthymos freed Temesa from paying this tribute (12-13): τὸν δὲ / δ[ασ]μὸν [τοῦτ]ον ἀπέλυσεν Εὔθυμος. At some point the δασμός 'tribute' mentioned in the story of the Hero of Temesa was interpreted in

58. Chantraine, s.v. κήδω.
59. As inferred by Lasserre 1967:131.

a literal, monetary sense; this allowed the Hero proverb to evolve into the form Pseudo-Plutarch and Aelian knew. Pausanias, however, knew that it was not money that the vengeful spirit of the neglected corpse at Temesa demanded; Callimachus also recorded the story similarly. Strabo was closer to these latter two than the others. Originally an *alibas*, a *barumênis* like Odysseus' dead sailor Polites, came to face not financial misdealers, 'or those who could not control them, but those who had neglected the corpse.

III

VISUAL HOMER

7

Artemis and the Lion: Two Similes in *Odyssey* 6

John Watrous

σφαίρῃ ταὶ γ' ἄρα παῖζον. ἀπὸ κρήδεμνα βαλοῦσαι·
τῇσι δὲ Ναυσικάα λευκώλενος ἤρχετο μολπῆς.
οἵη δ' Ἄρτεμις εἶσι κατ' οὔρεα ἰοχέαιρα,
ἢ κατὰ Τηΰγετον περιμήκετον ἢ Ἐρύμανθον,
τερπομένη κάπροισι καὶ ὠκείῃς ἐλάφοισι
τῇ δέ θ' ἅμα Νύμφαι, κοῦραι Διὸς αἰγιόχοιο,
ἀγρονόμοι παίζουσι, γέγηθε δέ τε φρένα Λητώ
πασάων δ' ὑπὲρ ἥ γε κάρη ἔχει ἠδὲ μέτωπα,
ῥεῖα δ' ἀριγνώτη πέλεται, καλαὶ δέ τε πᾶσαι·
ὡς ἥ γ' ἀμφιπόλοισι μετέπρεπε παρθένος ἀδμής.

(*Od.* 6.100-109)

And the women were playing with a ball, casting aside their veils;
and white-armed Nausikaa was the leader of their dancing
game. As Artemis who rains down arrows descends from the
    mountain
along either lofty Taugetos or Erymanthos,
delighting in her bears and in her hinds;
and with her the Nymphs play, daughters of aegis-bearing Zeus
who roam the wilds, and Leto rejoices in her heart;
and her head and brow rise above all her companions,
and she stands out, and all are lovely;
so the young woman stood out among her attendants.

βῆ δ' ἴμεν ὥς τε λέων ὀρεσίτροφος, ἀλκὶ πεποιθώς
ὅς τ' εἶσ' ὑόμενος καὶ ἀήμενος, ἐν δέ οἱ ὄσσε
δαίεται· αὐτὰρ ὁ βουσὶ μετέρχεται ἢ ὀίεσσιν

ἠὲ μετ' ἀγροτέρασ ἐλάφουσ κέλεται δέ ἑ γαστὴρ
μήλων πειρήσοντα καὶ ἐς πυκινὸν δόμον ἐλθεῖν
(*Od.* 6.130-134)

And he set out like a mountain-bred lion, trusting in
    his prowess,
who walks rain-soaked and wind-tossed, and his eyes blaze;
he moves among cattle or sheep or wild deer; and his stomach
    prompts him
to try his luck with the sheep and enter a secure house.

These two similes occurring within thirty lines of each other in Book 6 of the *Odyssey* jointly illustrate the story of the meeting of Nausikaa and Odysseus. The first simile compares Nausikaa to Artemis at the moment before Odysseus emerges from his hiding place, crusted with salt and grime and battered from his journey. The second simile figures Odysseus as a lion, but a strangely bedraggled and hungry one. Although there is little extraordinary about either simile taken individually, their proximity, and the fact that they describe the same event (an encounter between strangers) from two points of view, suggest that they ought to be read together. This essay attempts to give such a reading, paying close attention to the ways in which each simile responds to the other, creating an intricate web of half-spoken meanings and double entendre that subverts the normal expectations of a heroic simile in Homer. The spirit of play with which the first simile begins suffuses the whole and demotes the Homeric lion from savage predator to an object of sport for young girls.

The first simile, comparing Nausikaa to the goddess Artemis, is part of an overall narrative strategy that casts the story of Odysseus' and Nausikaa's acquaintance in terms of a thwarted romance. Athena sets the marriage theme in motion by reminding Nausikaa that her wedding day is fast approaching, requiring careful attention to her laundry.[1] The marriage motif is perhaps most explicit in those passages where the characters themselves speak of it:

---

1. Doing laundry is one stage in the bride's preparation for her wedding. Everything must be cleaned, particularly the wedding clothes. "Laundry" may in fact have a special reference to the bride's outfit. See Austin 1991:238.

Nausikaa wishes for a husband like Odysseus (*Od.* 6.244-246); she imagines that a false rumor about her marriage to Odysseus will circulate if the Phaeacians see them ride to Alkinoos' palace together (*Od.* 6.276-277); and Alkinoos later wishes that Odysseus would remain on Phaeacia as his son-in-law (*Od.* 7.311-314).[2] This is how the marriage theme will develop; in the meantime, however, laundry provides an excuse for a day in the country in the company of other young women. This excursion removes Nausikaa and her companions from the safety of Alkinoos' house and creates a narrative context for the two similes that, as we will see, suggests the possibility of abduction and rape. After having set the wash out to dry, Nausikaa and her maids eat their lunch *al fresco* before they begin a dance performed with a ball.[3] During the course of their dance they remove their veils, and Nausikaa becomes the leader of the dance.

It is as the leader of the dance that Nausikaa is compared to Artemis dancing in a secluded mountain spot, accompanied by a band of dancing *numphai* 'nymphs', 'brides', whom she overshadows because of her greater stature (πασάων δ' ὑπὲρ ἥ γε κάρη ἔχει ἠδὲ μέτωπα [*Od.* 6.107]). Nausikaa's youthful beauty and her stature are the focus of the comparison. Artemis is used elsewhere in the *Odyssey* as an exemplar of feminine beauty. We might expect Helen to be associated with Aphrodite, her patron deity in the *Iliad*, but it is in fact Artemis to whom she is likened at *Od.* 4.122. Penelope, on the other hand, is twice compared to both goddesses (*Od.* 17.31, 19.54), and at *Od.* 20.71 Artemis is the divinity who bestows stature on young women. The erotic overtones of the comparison deepen if one reads the simile in the tradition of the *eikasia*, which is the comparison of a *numphê* 'bride' to a goddess or a heroine, that is a typical motif in Greek wedding songs.[4] This interpretation becomes more attractive in light of *Od.* 6.150-152,

---

2. The theme of Odysseus remaining behind is an important element common to Nausikaa's wish (καὶ οἳ ἅδοι αὐτόθι μίμνειν. [*Od.* 6.245]) and Alkinoos' (αὖθι μένων. *Od.* 7.314), implying a threat to Odysseus' *nostos* 'homecoming'.

3. σφαίρῃ ταί γ' ἄρα παῖζον *Od* 6.100. Similar is Anacreon 358, where a dance involving a ball takes place in an erotic context. Compare also *Homeric Hymn to Aphrodite* 117ff where the nymphs are "playing" in a circle of Artemis.

4. See Hague 1983.132ff, esp. 136, where she attempts to show that Odysseus' supplication speech (*Od.* 6.149-185) exhibits some of the same structural features found in Greek wedding songs. In addition to the *eikasia*, which I mention above, Hague finds a *makarismos* 'blessing' in the praise that Odysseus lavishes on

where Nausikaa is once again compared to Artemis, this time by Odysseus in a speech that closely follows the pattern of an *eikasia*.[5]

The simile, however, does not simply pay tribute to Nausikaa's youthful beauty, but represents that beauty in a context of implied threat, for secluded dances are rarely safe from the watchful eyes of a potential attacker. But who is really in danger? The dancing circle of Artemis seems to have been a notorious locale for the abduction of young women. Artemis is dancing in the company of other goddesses when Hades spies Persephone and drags her down to the underworld (*Homeric Hymn to Demeter* 424). Hermes in particular seems susceptible to this kind of impulse: at *Il.* 16.183 he falls in love with a woman participating in the dances of Artemis and conceives a child with her, and Aphrodite capitalizes on his bad reputation when she pretends to be a woman kidnapped from Artemis' dancers by the sex-crazed Argeiphontes (*Homeric Hymn to Aphrodite* 117ff).[6] The Artemis simile suggests the possibility of such a crime on peaceful Scheria, and it transforms Nausikaa's winsome beauty, the very attribute it celebrates, into a potential incentive for violence. The simile makes clear, however, that the danger is not directed at Nausikaa, for in every instance it is one of the goddess' *numphai* votaries, and not Artemis herself, who is spirited away by a lustful attacker; Artemis remains ever inviolate. At the same time that it establishes a perception of danger, the comparison implies that Nausikaa herself will emerge intact.

The lion simile must be viewed in the light of a multitude of similar comparisons in the *Iliad* and *Odyssey*. The bulk of these similes lurk among the verses of the *Iliad*, where they are most commonly applied to warriors in

---

Nausikaa's parents (*Od.* 6.154-161) and identifies the blandishments at the conclusion of his speech with a traditional wish for the bride's happiness (*Od* 6.180-185). Wedding language is present in the Artemis simile as well, but in a strangely refracted way.

5. εἰμὲν τις θεός ἐσσι, τοὶ οὐρανὸν εὐρὺν ἔχουσιν.
'Αρτέμιδί σε ἔγω γε. Διὸς κούρῃ μεγάλοιο.
εἶδός τε μέγεθός τε φυήν τ' ἄγχιστα ἐΐσκω.
(*Od.* 6.150-152).
Notice that here too stature is one of the primary points of comparison.

6. Note especially the key words 'nymph' and 'play' from the latter passage.

the heat of battle to express their ferocity, deadliness, eagerness for killing, and superior strength. It is perhaps the close association of the lion with war that accounts for its greater frequency as a creature of metaphor in the *Iliad* as compared to the *Odyssey*, where there simply are not enough battle scenes to support a burgeoning population of lion similes.

The seven lion similes that occur in the *Odyssey* deviate in interesting ways from the patterns of their Iliadic congeners. In four instances lion similes are applied in a fairly conventional way (from the standpoint of the *Iliad*) to Odysseus as he takes vengeance or is imagined to be taking vengeance on the suitors.[7] In one departure from the typical Iliadic simile, Penelope, besieged by the suitors, is compared to a desperate lion surrounded by a crowd of hunters.[8] This is unusual on two counts: no other woman in the *Iliad* or *Odyssey* is made the subject of a lion simile, and Homeric lions are rarely at bay.[9] A further instance is even more bizarre: Polyphemos *eats* like a mountain-bred lion, gulping down innards and bones along with the flesh.[10] There are numerous instances in the *Iliad* where a hungry or feeding lion represents a warrior hungering for battle,[11] but a feeding lion never represents a man (or a monster) eating; Iliadic similes simply cannot stomach such a literal vehicle-tenor relationship. These two instances transfer the lion from his natural Iliadic habitat of war to a strange new country of metaphor, where lions are stripped of their nobility and cease to function as vehicles for

---

7. *Od.* 4.335=17.126; 22.402=23.48.
8. *Od.* 4.791-792.
9. But cf. *Il.* 5.554-558, where the death of Krethon and Orsilokhos is represented by the slaughter of two young lions.
10.   ἤσθιε δ' ὥς τε λέων ὀρεσίτροφος, οὐδ' ἀπέλειπεν,
        ἔγκατά τε σάρκας τε καὶ ὀστέα μυελόεντα.
                                    (*Od.* 9.292-293).
11. At *Il.* 3.23ff, Menelaos approaches Alexander eagerly, like a 'hungry' (πεινάων) lion that comes upon a corpse and begins 'to feed upon it' (κατεσθίει); at *Il.* 5.782-783=*Il.* 7.266ff the Achaeans huddle around Diomedes like flesh-eating lions or boars; Agamemnon kills Trojans like a lion (*Il.* 11.176=*Il.* 17.64, with Menelaos as the lion); Patroklos and Hektor are like hungry lions (*Il.* 16.756ff); and the Aiantes protect Patroklos' body from Hektor the way shepherds will drive a hungry lion from its kill (*Il.* 18.162).

kleos glorification in epic song. Their audacity and fierceness become desperation and barbarity.

The lion simile at *Od.* 6.130-134 is a curious blend of the traditional Iliadic simile and the exotic Odyssean. As with the lion similes at *Od.* 4.791-792 and 9.292-293, the narrative context is not a battle scene, but an impromptu dance that resembles the city of peace from Achilles' shield more closely than the city at war. It seems that the lion is an intruder, and surely this is the point of the comparison; whereas Nausikaa is singled out by her beauty, Odysseus, naked and crusted with sea foam, is outlandish, monstrous, and uncanny, a stranger on an island seldom visited by outsiders. Neither he nor the creature that represents him belongs—and yet, precisely because they disrupt the dance, they are exactly the sort of intrusion into the narrative that the Artemis simile, brimming with erotic energy and intimations of danger, demands. The intrusion of war into the city of peace had already been anticipated by the narrative prior to the appearance of the lion simile.[12] Martial language draws the idyllic scene of innocent laughter and play into the sphere of heroic poetry. The sound that awakens Odysseus is the shrieking of Nausikaa and her companions when they lose their ball in the river, but this cry takes on a decidedly martial overtone with the expression θῆλυς ἀυτή 'female cry' (*Od.* 6.122), since ἀυτή in the *Iliad* is normally used of a war cry, or even metonymically of war itself. As Odysseus advances he covers his genitals with a branch held with a heavy hand (χειρί παχείῃ [*Od.* 6.128]), a formula that normally applies to the hand of a warrior carrying a weapon or shield. Perhaps the most outrageous mixture of heroic and erotic expression is reserved for the bridge leading from the simile back to the narrative, where Odysseus is prepared to encounter the young women:

ὡς Ὀδυσεὺς κούρῃσιν ἐϋπλοκάμοισιν ἔμελλε
μίξεσθαι, γυμνός περ ἐών. [13]

---

12. Lattimore 1969:89ff.

13. *Il.* 5.143 provides a parallel. Diomedes, having been compared to a lion, fights against the Trojans: ὡς μεμαὼς Τρώεσσι μίγη κρατερὸς Διομήδης 'thus enraged, powerful Diomedes engages with the Trojans'. Because of the univocal meaning of μίγη in this line, Diomedes' intention to fight is reported in the aorist as an accomplished fact, whereas Odysseus' resolution to "mix it up" with the Phaeacian maidens is never carried out, hence the use of μέλλειν with the future.

So Odysseus was ready to mingle with the
lovely-haired women, naked as he was.

(*Od.* 6.135-136)

The double entendre arises from the identity of Odysseus' adversaries: young women with lovely coifs. The combination of erotic and heroic themes demands that μείγνυμι mean both 'fight' and 'have sexual intercourse', while the phrase γυμνός περ ἐών plays on the Iliadic theme of fighting 'without a shield' (and hence naked). These phrases cast an ironic light on the reality of Odysseus' situation, which is that a naked hairy man on a beach poses a sexual threat to a group of young women.

Given the playfully ambiguous narrative within which it is embedded, it is no surprise that within the simile we find similarities to conventional lion similes alongside less strictly Iliadic features. The λέων ὀρεσίτροφος 'mountain-bred lion' is a popular subject for lion similes, and the phrase ἀλκὶ πεποιθώς 'relying on one's prowess' is common as well.[14] Line 134 is identical to *Il.* 12.301, where Sarpedon's eagerness to breach the Achaean wall is compared to a lion anxious to enter a farm and steal some sheep. The motivation is different, however: in the Sarpedon episode, it is the lion's proud spirit that drives him (κέλεται δέ ἑ θυμὸς ἀγήνωρ 'his proud spirit prompts him' [*Il.* 12.300]), but Odysseus' lion acts at the prompting of his belly (κέλεται δέ ἑ γαστήρ [*Od.* 6.133]). The difference is an important indicator of the distinction between lion similes in the two poems. Odysseus' lion, like Polyphemos', is a slave to his hunger, and, like Penelope's, he is in desperate straits (ὑόμενος καὶ ἀήμενος 'rain-soaked and wind-blown' [*Od.* 6.131]). Most important, like both he is cut off from the possibility of winning *kleos*; the similarities to Iliadic lions serve to remind us that he is in a radically different situation, where the lion is no longer king.

I wish to conclude this essay by suggesting a connection between the two similes discussed above and a figure not very prominent in epic, the *Potnia*

---

14. Lattimore 1969:90. Very close to *Od.* 6.130 is *Il.* 12.299 βῆ ῥ' ἴμεν ὥστε λέων ὀρεσίτροφος. 'Sarpedon advances like a mountain-bred lion' and *Il.* 17.61 ὡς δ' ὅτε τίς τε λέων ὀρεσίτροφος. ἀλκὶ πεποιθώς, where Menelaos is the lion. For ἀλκί πεποιθώς compare *Il.* 5.299, Aeneas in a lion simile; *Il.* 13.471, Idomeneus in a boar simile; *Il.* 17.728 of the two Ajaxes.

Thêrôn 'Mistress of Wild Beasts'. I have already alluded to Artemis' role as a divinity deeply involved in the maturation of young women, but there are many other aspects of this complex goddess, some of which are represented in Homer.[15]

Although the *Potnia Thêrôn* was a prominent figure in cult she is generally ignored in Homeric epic.[16] In her guise as *Potnia Thêrôn*, Artemis exercises a control over the world of nature that assumes two forms. In the first place, she is a nurturer and protector of wild animals, whose fructifying influence matters to those who depend on uncultivated land for their livelihood. Conversely, she is the fiercest and deadliest of hunters, and is frequently represented iconographically with the weapons of her sport in the act of tracking, slaying, and collecting her prey. There is only one explicit reference to the *Potnia Thêrôn* in all of Homer,[17] but her association with nature in general and hunting in particular is constantly present in Homeric poetry[18] and may furnish a dim reflection of this conception of Artemis.

As *Potnia Thêrôn*, Artemis is commonly depicted without the bow, dominating wild animals through sheer physical strength. Although she is a hunter in epic, in sculpture and vase painting she *tames* the wildest of beasts—lions, wolves, stags, and boar—sometimes appearing at the center of a pair of beasts heraldically arranged on either side of her, often grasping them firmly by a leg, antler, or by the neck.[19] A lekythos by the Amasis painter, dated 550-525 BCE, treats this subject in a typical manner (Fig. 1).[20]

---

15 Artemis, in both poems, is the goddess who slays women with her arrows, as Apollo kills men. In the *Iliad*, she is said to have killed Bellerophon's daughter (*Il.* 6.205), Andromache's mother (*Il.* 6.428), and Niobe's children (*Il.* 24.606). Achilles wishes that she could have averted his quarrel with Agamemnon by killing Briseis (*Il.* 19.59). In the *Odyssey*, Penelope prays to Artemis for death to release her from her sorrows (18.202; 20.60-61, 80); Odysseus asks his mother if Artemis was responsible for her death (11.172); Artemis slays Ariadne (11.324) and Eumaios' nurse (15.478).

16 See Burkert 1985:149.

17 *Il.* 21.043.

18 At *Il.* 05.051 she is the hunting instructor of Skamandrios; at *Il.* 09.529, she sends the Calydonian boar; in *Hymn to Aphrodite* 118ff, she prefers hunting to erotic pleasures.

19 *LIMC* s.v. Artemis 2, 11-56, 64.

20. Louvre F71. For the date, see *LIMC* Artemis 34; for attribution, see Beazley 1978:154n49.

In the center of the composition, a winged *Potnia*, shown in profile with her arms extended, holds two lions by the hind leg, while two youths armed with spears look on from either side. The heraldic composition focuses the viewer's attention on the *Potnia* in the center, which towers over the smaller lions held captive in her tight grip. This mode of representation was already of venerable antiquity in the geometric period, extending back in time at least as far as Bronze Age Greece,[21] but though it coexisted for several centuries with the long oral tradition that lies behind the Homeric poems, this vision of the *Potnia Thêrôn*, the goddess who grapples with animals and tames them, does not explicitly enter into the Homeric conception of Artemis as a goddess who hunts animals and even occasionally commands them—as in the case of the Caledonian boar.

Figure 1. *Potnia Thêrôn* c. 550-525 BCE. Louvre, Paris

Although epic does not explicitly acknowledge the connection between Artemis and the *Potnia Thêrôn*, a connection that is well attested in cult and that would be familiar to the audience of epic, there are other female

---

21. Depictions of the *Potnia Thêrôn* from Mycenae and Crete are discussed in Nilsson 1968:355ff; *LIMC* Artemis 2.

characters who behave in ways evocative of the *Potnia Thêrôn*. Circe can be considered in this light. She is a goddess who subverts the order of nature by transforming men into animals and imprisoning them—perhaps, at least in the case of men changed into swine, to be consumed later. The fate of her victims is all the more troubling because the memory of their lost humanity persists even though their physical forms have been altered.[22] The reconnaissance party from Odysseus' ship first meets Circe surrounded by an uncanny entourage of enchanted wolves and lions who fawn on their mistress like dogs fawning on their master.[23] It is curious that wolves and lions should appear in this context, particularly since they are the two most common subjects for animal similes in Homer. It is worth considering the implications of Circe's activity for the system of beast similes in the *Iliad* and the *Odyssey*. Homeric similes are parallel narratives that affect the main narrative by analogy, without ever establishing direct contact with the story. Hektor or Achilles may be like lions, and Paris is like a man who sees a snake, but there is never any danger that the creatures of the similes will break free of their own realm and burst into the main narrative, or that the heroes of the Trojan

---

22 *Od* . 10.240.
23 ...ὡς δ' ὅτ' ἂν ἀμφὶ ἄνακτα κύνες δαίτηθεν ἰόντα
σαίνωσ· αἰεὶ γάρ τε φέρει μειλίγματα θυμοῦ·
ὣς τοὺς ἀμφὶ λύκοι κρατερώνυχες ἠδὲ λέοντες
σαῖνον· τοὶ δ' ἔδεισαν, ἐπεὶ ἴδον αἰνὰ πέλωρα.
(*Od.* 10.216-219).
It is not perfectly clear whether these beasts have been transformed from men or are wild animals that have been tamed. In *Od.* 10.212 wolves and lions are called 'mountainous' (ὀρέστεροι), which might mean that they are wild animals that lived in the mountains before Circe enchanted them, or that they were originally men who have taken the form of wolves and lions that live in the mountains. In *Od.* 10.433 Eurylokhos warns Odysseus that Circe will transform the remaining members of his crew into pigs, wolves, and lions. A passage with verbal similarities to *Od.* 10.216-219 is *Hymn to Aphrodite* 68ff, where Aphrodite tames wolves, lions, bears, and leopards:
Ἴδην δ' ἵκανεν πολυπίδακα, μητέρα θηρῶν.
βῆ δ' ἰθὺς σταθμοῖο δι' οὔρεος· οἳ δὲ μετ' αὐτὴν
σαίνοντες πολιοί τε λύκοι χαροποί τε λέοντες
ἄρκτοι παρδάλιές τε θοαὶ προκάδων ἀκόρητοι
ἰσαν.
In addition to the verbal echo σαίνωσ/σαίνοντες, note Aphrodite's epithet μητέρα θηρῶν 'Mother of Beasts', which is similar to *Potnia Thêrôn* but emphasizes Aphrodite's procreative power.

war will leap into a simile and begin hunting down the animals. Narrative coherence is preserved by an unstated but impermeable barrier that separates vehicle from tenor and prevents the *Iliad* from turning into *The Purple Rose of Troy*. From this perspective Circe's island presents a special danger to Odysseus and his men, for the spells of the goddess threaten to collapse the separate realms of simile and literal narrative. In an eerie foretaste of their imminent subjugation, Odysseus' men encounter mountain wolves and lions, the proud and savage creatures of the Homeric simile, now made submissive to the mistress of the isle. This first breach of the barrier between figurative and literal narrative appears to them as a frightful prodigy, and is followed by a terrifying sequel, as they themselves are transported into the world of similes by being transformed literally into beasts and forced to live as the brutish creatures of simile. It is only through the timely intervention of the master shape-shifter Hermes that Odysseus is able to resist Circe's spells and force the goddess to restore tenor and vehicle to their rightful places by returning his men to their human forms.

The iconography of Circe tends to depict her at the moment when she is handling the drugs with which she transforms men into animals, often in the presence of her victims, who have already assumed some of the physical features of the animals they will become. Perhaps not coincidentally some of these images feature a heraldic arrangement of animals around Circe that recalls the type of Artemis as *Potnia Thêrôn*.[24] On a kylix from the Boston Museum of Fine Arts[25] Circe is in the center of the composition holding a cup in which she has presumably mixed the drugs she uses to transform her victims. The creatures approaching her from both sides are human from the torso down, but they have animal heads and forelegs: there is a boar-man, a bear-man, a dog-man, a ram-man, and a lion-man. Odysseus approaches Circe from behind (the left side) with sword in hand; behind the dog-man (far

---

24 *LIMC* Kirke 5 is a mid-sixth century lekythos from Taranto, with a view of Circe surrounded by creatures that seem human from the torso down, but with animal heads (a lion and a bull are in front of her, a pig and a wolf behind), and in some cases animal forelegs. The goddess is mixing what is probably the drug that she uses to ensnare her victims. Kirke 5 bis, a late sixth century amphora, shows Circe seated and stirring a kykeon, flanked by two ithyphallic men with asses heads and by two graceful cranes.

25. Boston MFA 94.518. See also *LIMC* Kirke 14.

right side) an unidentified man flees. Circe, like the *Potnia Thêrôn*, surrounds herself with the creatures she has tamed, but with this difference: whereas the *Potnia Thêrôn* subdues savage beasts through physical might, Circe uses magic first to create them and then to enslave them.

I mention Circe with reference to the *Potnia Thêrôn* in order to illustrate how a powerful female figure with the powers of the *Potnia* has the potential to disrupt the tidy categories of Homeric narrative. Artemis has a similar effect on the narrative in Book 6, where her appearance in a simile subverts Odysseus' attempt to respond to a crisis through heroic action, represented figuratively by the lion simile. Being 'mountain-bred' (ὀρεσίτροφος) is no advantage for this lion, since, after all, the mountains are Artemis' home-turf (κατ' οὔρεα). Nor is she one to dread lions, delighting, as she does, in wild boar and swift deer.[26] Whether her *terpsis* takes the form of hunting or nurturing is left ambiguous, but it is clear that wild beasts fall under her sphere of influence.

---

26. Lions as such are not mentioned, but the boar may function as a substitute. The two animals are closely associated in similes (see *Il.* 12.041ff; *Il.* 5.782-783=*Il* 7.266ff). The equivalence between the two animals is discussed in Scott 1974:58-59. See Muellner 1990: 63-64.

8

Homer's Leopard Simile

Fred Naiden

By a familiar alchemy, the Iliadic hero compared to a lion grabs his opponent by a vulnerable spot, the simile, and turns him into a lesser animal.[1] Even if the opponent was compared to a lion earlier, as Sarpedon and Patroklos were, he becomes a bull or a boar, still formidable, but decidedly inferior (*Il.* 12.299-306, 16.487-489; 16.756-758, 823-826). If the opponents are many, they become hunters or dogs, but it does them no good. Not one man or dog appears in the act of killing a lion, even when a lion's death is imminent (*Il.* 5.554-558), suggested (*Il.* 12.299-300), or forecast (*Il.* 12.41-99, 16.756-758). Unlike youths and suppliants, lions die offstage.[2]

As the lion of lions, Achilles ought to be invincible.[3] Rivers and gods will frustrate him or rescue their favorites, but no simile ever makes them prey or predators. They are outside the food chain. But one opponent very much inside the food chain does escape Achilles: Agenor. When Achilles attacks Agenor, Agenor escapes unscathed. A god intervenes, but does not truly rescue the Trojan. Rescue is Poseidon's favor to Aeneas: safe passage out of

---

1. Vermeule 1979:90ff. For similes as omens, see Lonsdale 1990:119. An earlier treatment of the influence of lion similes on narrative is Moulton 1977:139ff. For a prose statement of soldier as predator, see Xenophon *Cyn.* 1.1-3.

2. See Schnapp-Gourbeillon 1981:41, 57 on the lion's prestige as the comparandum of heroes. Hampe 1952:31-33 sees the lion less as a hero than as indestructible weaponry.

3. He sees himself as one (*Il.* 22.262-264), an opinion endorsed by Apollo (*Il* 24.041-403). The only other hero compared to a lion by someone other than the epic singer is Diomedes, so called by Paris (*Il.* 11.383). The choice epithet θυμολέων belongs only to Achilles, to two earlier heroes, Herakles and Diomedes, and to Odysseus in the *Odyssey*.

danger and then safe passage back to the front.[4] Agenor's god, Apollo, does only half the job. He gives Agenor safe passage out but never brings him back. Never mentioned by Homer again, Agenor is left hanging. Meanwhile Apollo pretends to be Agenor, the only time in Homer when a god is substituted for a participant in a two-man fight. Rather than rescue Agenor, Apollo has removed and replaced him.

The encounter between the Greek lion and the transformed god is just as unpredictable. Though he does not need to, the god runs away. Achilles gives chase and, for the first and only time, is outrun.[5] Meanwhile the rest of the Trojans are also running, but the other way. Only Hektor fails to take advantage of the situation indirectly created by Agenor, and his refusal dooms him.

A miscue for the lion, perhaps a parody, and a narrative turning point, the encounter between Agenor and Achilles features a simile that is as odd as the encounter itself. Agenor is compared to a big cat also, but to a leopard, and a female leopard at that. The leopard is the only animal in the *Iliad* that is always female when it is individual (*Il.* 21.573-579):

ἠΰτε πάρδαλις εἶσι βαθείης ἐκ ξυλόχοιο
ἀνδρὸς θηρητῆρος ἐναντίον, οὐδέ τι θυμῷ
ταρβεῖ οὐδὲ φοβεῖται, ἐπεί κεν ὑλαγμὸν ἀκούσῃ·
εἴ περ γὰρ φθάμενός μιν ἢ οὐτάσῃ ἠὲ βάλῃσιν,
ἀλλά τε καὶ περὶ δουρὶ πεπαρμένη οὐκ ἀπολήγει
ἀλκῆς, πρὶν γ' ἠὲ ξυμβλήμεναι ἠὲ δαμῆναι·
ὣς Ἀντήνορος υἱὸς ἀγαυοῦ, δῖος Ἀγήνωρ,
οὐκ ἔθελεν φεύγειν, πρὶν πειρήσαιτ' Ἀχιλῆος...

---

4. *Il.* 20.321-329.
5. Reflecting the leopard's superior speed noted by the hunters, see Turnbull-Kemp 1967:81; Roosevelt and Heller 1911:185. Turnbull-Kemp observes that the lion is superior in a stationary fight (48) and that lions chase what runs away from them (64). On the classification of epic lions as the surviving African breed, the extinct Persian breed, or as an emblematic mix, see Lonsdale 1990.103n10. Körner 1967:81 limits the leopard's ancient range to Asia Minor, showing the importance of oral report, although oral report is subject to cultural and poetic requirements.

As a leopard emerges from her lair in the deep woods
and confronts a huntsman, feeling no fear in her heart
and not taking flight, either, once she hears baying,
even if he stabs or throws first,
but though dragging a spear, she does not give up her courage
until she comes to grips or is beaten—
that's how bright Agenor, noble Antenor's son, was unwilling to
flee until he tested Achilles.

Modern scholarship has viewed this simile as a variant on the lion similes, a clue to Agenor's inferiority, or an illustration of how a simile may influence a hero's thoughts.[6] But to use the scholiast's words, 'Homer never had the nerve' (ὁ ποιητὴς οὐκ ἔτλη) to stage another such encounter, suggesting that the passage deserves attention for its boldness and uniqueness, which this essay will describe in the light of Leonard Muellner's 1990 study of the interplay of Iliadic animal similes.[7] Since leopards are scarce even if every mention of the leopard is included, the leopard skin, another kind of animal association, will also receive mention, as will Bronze Age iconography of leopard and lion.[8] Above all, the leopard simile will figure as a revision of one of the narrative habits that Lord said "is hidden, but felt."[9] The boldness and oddness of the leopard is that he challenges the habitual lion, hidden but felt, and routs him from the last three books of the *Iliad,* where lions seldom appear and never triumph.

6. Variant: Lonsdale 1990:37ff; Hampe 1952:18. Clue: Fränkel 1921:122; thought process: de Jong 1985:257-270.

7. Erbse 1969 on *Il.* 21.573. See Muellner 1990:76 for the variation and inversion of animal roles in similes; Muellner 1990:71 for the interpretation of seemingly irrelevant words or phrases by comparing their meaning in many similes.

8. A leopard inventory: compared to jackals and wolves by Ajax (*Il.* 13.103) and lions and boars by Menelaos (*Il.* 17.20-21), both prior to the only simile, Agenor's. For the lion, the pattern is substantially the reverse, with most of the comparisons made by characters coming later (*Il.* 11.383; 17.20; 22.262; 24.41). For brief surveys of Greek Bronze Age lion imagery, see Morgan 1988:45-49; Buchholz 1973:9-31. For Egypt, see Wreszinski 1932.

9. Lord 1960:97. For the similes as examples of oral composition, see Scott 1974:156-158.

Although this essay will confine itself to similes with finite verbs, since they are long enough to introduce hunters and prey, shorter similes do the service of grouping lions with two other species, boars and leopards. Shared epithets recruit two more species, wolves and the canines called θῶες 'jackals'.[10] But of all five, only lions appear as individual predators or in pairs.[11] The leopard, in contrast, is a lion manqué or a feline pack animal, and in either case might seem superfluous. But the leopard has two uses. If a hero appears as an undisguised or hidden lion, the leopard may face him without expecting to become prey, like a boar, or suffer defeat, like a hunter. A second use is one made of the leopard's skin, which may replace the living animal and protect a hero much as a simile does, though except in the *Doloneia* the skin and the simile are coordinated.[12] When a lion in a simile faces his first frustration, leopard skin will be the reason, as it will be when he meets his last, at the hands of Agenor who is compared to a leopard because he and his family use leopard skin as an emblem.

The first conjunction of lion and leopard will illustrate Muellner's thesis that animal similes influence story and will also show that a related aspect of narrative, the leopard skin, influences similes.[13] Let the simile come first and assert leonine military supremacy (*Il.* 3.21-28):

---

10. Lions and boars: *Il.* 8.342; 12.042. Common epithets: flesh-eating lion (*Il.* 5.782 , et al.); jackals (*Il.* 11.479); wolf (*Il.* 16.157); ravening lion (*Il.* 20.165) and wolf (*Il.* 16.353); ὀλοόφρων 'baleful' lion (*Il.* 15.630) and boar (*Il.* 17.021); ἀλκὶ πεποιθώς lion 'confident in his strength' (*Il.* 5.249; 17.61) and boar (*Il.* 13.471; 17.728). Leopards have no epithets, contributing to the surprise Agenor springs upon Achilles. None of the epithets listed is given to animals outside similes except in two special cases: shield decoration and the Chimera. The epithet αἴθων *aithôn* is used of large predators and other animals, in simile and narrative alike.

11. As noted by Helck 1979:9. Pairs of lions: *Il.* 5.554; 10.297; 13.198; 18.579. These are all male, leaving the leopard in search of a mate.

12. Where the leopard-man, this time Menelaos, is again superfluous, the lion-man, Diomedes, is central. For the epic poetics of lion and wolf, but without reference to the traits of the leopard, see Schnapp-Gourbeillon 1982:45-77.

13. For animal skin as a conveyor of identity, see Nagy 1973:179-180 translating Pausanias 9.2.3 ἐλάφου περιβαλεῖν δέρμα 'Ακταίων' as both 'clothe' and 'transform' the hero. Compare this likely quotation from Stesichorus with Aeschylus *Ag.* 1147 περέβαλον γάρ οἱ πτεροφόρον, meaning 'clothe' Procne in the body of a nightingale. See Gernet 1968:251-314.

τὸν δ' ὡς οὖν ἐνόησεν ἀρηΐφιλος Μενέλαος
ἐρχόμενον προπάροιθεν ὁμίλου μακρὰ βιβάντα,
ὥς τε λέων ἐχάρη μεγάλῳ ἐπὶ σώματι κύρσας,
εὑρὼν ἢ ἔλαφον κεραὸν ἢ ἄγριον αἶγα
πεινάων· μάλα γάρ τε κατεσθίει, εἴ περ ἂν αὐτὸν
σεύωνται ταχέες τε κύνες θαλεροί τ' αἰζηοί·
ὡς ἐχάρη Μενέλαος Ἀλέξανδρον θεοειδέα
ὀφθαλμοῖσιν ἰδών· φάτο γὰρ τείσεσθαι ἀλείτην·

Now as soon as war-loving Menelaos recognized him
striding before the army, he rejoiced
like a lion pouncing on a great carcass.
It has found a buck with horns or a wild goat
and it's hungry. It eats eagerly, although
swift dogs and vigorous young men rush it.
That's how Menelaos rejoiced when he laid eyes on god-like
    Alexandros,
for he said he would have the wrongdoer punished.

Nothing is said about Paris' battle with the lion-man and nothing needs to be said. Paris is as good as dead, so he is a corpse to be fought over.

But rival predators have appeared. Who is being compared to these hunters and dogs? In the end, it is Aphrodite, who will drag her favorite out of danger, just as the hunters in the simile may be expected to try to drag the carcass away from the lion. But Aphrodite is still in the background, so this additional or third term remains temporarily unactivated.[14]

Activating the third term will be Paris, who will use it to save his life. This hero boasts his own animal identity, conferred by a leopard skin. In the *Iliad* and *Odyssey* this is a rare accouterment, worn only by Paris and Menelaos, and outside the *Doloneia* by Paris alone. Like lion skin, it is conspicuous and, like lion skin, it is characterized in only one way. Leopard skin is *poikilê* 'spotted' (*Il.* 10.30), just as lion skin is *daphoinon* 'tawny' (*Il.* 10.23) and *poêenekês* 'man-sized' (*Il.* 10.23, 177).

---

14. For other descriptions of the role of hunters or herdsmen in lion similes, see Lonsdale 1990:Chs. 4-6; Krischer 1971:13-90; Shipp 1972:213-222.

It is, admittedly, an epithet used only once. When it is used elsewhere, moreover, it resembles Milman Parry's "generic" epithets, applicable to all heroes alike. The epithet *poikilê* thus applies to all kinds of valuable works of craftsmanship, including armor, arms, and women's embroidery on clothes and furniture.[15] For all these, *poikilê* is the only dactylic qualifier, save in a few instances where it is discarded for metrical reasons or for the sake of a striking effect. Like the constellation of other epithets that describe these nouns, it illustrates the principle of thrift.[16]

But *poikilê* should nonetheless be considered a "distinctive" epithet, a term Parry applied to adjectives qualifying one hero only. Here the epithet does not belong to one hero, but one kind of object—coverings. The military objects cover the body; the embroidered objects are coverings or surfaces on furniture. And all these coverings or surfaces are products of workmanship. The epithet *poikilê* has an air about it—an air of cleverness and disguise, female yet male.[17]

Applied to leopard skin, *poikilê* thus means more than 'spotted', which does not recognize the word's other uses. Instead it means 'wrought' in the sense of 'wrought as though the skin were a covering', that is, a visual definition to wear or discard. Since the skin is a visual definition anyway, as the skins of the *Doloneia* illustrate, *poikilê* is less an epithet than a gloss, reminding the listener that Paris' garb is a glamorous put-on. The reminder is useful whenever the skin appears, including this case, where *poikilê* underscores a distinction. The lion confers killing power, but animal skin

---

15. Parry 1971:164. The objects are τεύχεα (x7), ἅρματα (x6), ἱμάντα (x2), and ἔντεα, θώρηκα, σάκος, and δίφρος, all once, and among embroidered work, πέπλον (x2) and θρόνα once, as listed in Prendergast 1962.

16. Meter: *Il.* 7.222; 14.238; 16.107; 24.553. Visualization: ἀγκύλον δίφρον when a man is falling over the side (*Il.* 6.039). Irony: ἄμβροτα τεύχεα to frame Zeus' comment that even though Hektor now has Achilles' armor, he does not have long to live (*Il.* 17.194; 17.202). For "thrift," see Lord 1960:Ch. 3.

17. For "generic" epithets with unsuspected meanings, see Lowenstam 1993:13-59. For a survey of uses of δαίδαλος, meaning 'skillfully wrought', see Morris 1992:3-35. At *Il.* 18.590-592, *poikilê* and the name *Daidalos* occur in a description of a dance floor, the first being applied to Hephaistos, the second to the craftsman to whom Hephaistos is compared. Otherwise the two terms are not used in relation to the same object in the same scene, and *daidalos* is never applied to animal skin.

confers power to remake.[18] If this distinction reinforces the difficulty, which is that the lion is irresistible, it also defines the challenge. The leopard-wearer must remake what he cannot resist.

So Paris leaps away from Menelaos as though Menelaos were irresistible yet not a lion (*Il.* 3.33-37):

ὡς δ' ὅτε τίς τε δράκοντα ἰδὼν παλίνορσος ἀπέστη
οὔρεος ἐν βήσσης, ὑπό τε τρόμος ἔλλαβε γυῖα,
ἂψ δ' ἀνεχώρησεν, ὠχρός τέ μιν εἷλε παρειάς,
ὡς αὖτις καθ' ὅμιλον ἔδυ Τρώων ἀγερώχων
δείσας Ἀτρέος υἱὸν Ἀλέξανδρος θεοειδής.

It's the way it is when someone in mountain vales sees
a snake. Fear grabs his knees, he jumps back, and his
cheeks turn pale. That's how god-like Alexandros
slipped into the crowd of proud Trojans out of fear of
the son of Atreus.

This redefinition accompanies reversal. Paris is now the intruder with the height advantage—no lion, but more like the lion than the carcass he resembled before. Menelaos is now the creature below, the predator at his lowliest. The death threat is belittled, giving Paris an honorable excuse to withdraw.[19]

Paris' simile has redefined types, reversed roles, and reaffirmed *poikilê* as a gloss on the leopard-wearer's unpredictability. But the simile also operates in two dimensions reaching beyond the response of Paris to Menelaos.[20]

---

18. Cf. Schnapp-Gourbeillon 1981:Ch.1, who views the animal similes as "masques" shaped by the ideology of Heroic society. She does not assign a distinct role to the lion or leopard. For the opposite view, see Fränkel 1921:72-74, who regards animal similes as representations of recurrent natural phenomena.

19. Cf. Rahn 1953, who holds that every hero contains a repertoire of animal roles, though neither 'Tier' nor 'animal' corresponds to θήρ, a term that would include Menelaos' lion and snake similes. For the view that animals symbolize traits rather than assign or remove them, see Lloyd 1960:183-192.

20. As in Muellner 1990, anticipated by Fränkel 1921:65-66, who notes that Menelaos' lion does not hear the hunters approaching and is vulnerable to surprise. Cf. *Il.* 15.271, where the lion hears the hunters and surprises them instead.

First, it revises past action. Since Paris has jumped back, Menelaos is no longer closest to him, as the lion simile implied. Those represented by the hunters and dogs are closest. As a consequence, the lion will lose this prize, whereas before it seemed he would win it. Second, the leopard's craft creates new action. Reacting to Paris' excuse, Hektor forces a duel, the very kind of fight where Paris cannot do as he did with the snake and withdraw. Since Menelaos retains his deadliness, Paris must be rescued by Aphrodite. As noted above, she is a form of the third term, or the intruder who is neither predator nor prey.[21]

This third term is an important feature, overlooked in modern catalogues that classify similes by length, predator, and narrative purpose.[22] In the paradigmatic form of men and dogs, the third term appears in lion similes of all kinds, first keeping the lion from his prey and eventually defeating him through force of numbers.[23] In the first ten books, this third term is infrequent; men and dogs seldom appear together and never outfight a lion.[24] Even afterwards, they sometimes appear separately or fail to prevail. But in Book 11 comes the first victory for men and dogs. Save when Hektor is the subject, the lion declines thereafter. The low point will be Menelaos, who ends the simile story that he inaugurates. In the last simile before Achilles' reentry into battle, he becomes the only lion to do battle with humans, lose heart, and run.[25]

Menelaos was no doubt happier back in Book 3, and Diomedes was happiest of all. During his run of victory, the lion's only human foe runs and

---

21. For consecutive two-term similes, see Hesiod, *Shield* 168-177.

22. Length, Shipp 1972:211-212; predator, Lonsdale 1990:Chs. 4-6; narrative purpose, Krischer 1971:13-90.

23. For another view of the scarcity of lion similes after the shield of Achilles and of the virtual disappearance of them after Agenor, see Schnapp-Gourbeillon 1981.84-90.

24. Though they do hold their own against a θήρ (*Il.* 10.183); cf. *Il.* 15.324, 15.586. The common feature of all three occasions is that the herdsmen never lay eyes on their opponent. In the first two cases, the reason is the dark; in the third, the predator retreats before he is seen. Adopting the point of view of the herdsmen, the singer declines to identify the animals as lions. For another view, see Lonsdale 1990:39n2.

25. *Il.* 17.109, 657; retreat without loss of heart in *Il.* 11.548. For treatment of the similes as a "subgenre," see Marzullo 1954:312-314, quoted by Muellner 1990:60n1 with subsequent history of the term, here used as occasion to trace plot and characters.

hides, and either there are no dogs (*Il.* 5.136, 161) or they slink away (*Il.* 5.476).[26] By comparing minor fighters, the next pair of similes offers a contrast to the hero (*Il.* 5.553, 8.338). In the first simile, the lion's death is foreseen, but without mention of dogs or hunters or a description of the death-throes within the simile. When the time for death comes, a new simile turns the victims into pine trees (*Il.* 5.560).[27] In the second simile, the dog is in pursuit is Hektor and is snapping at the lion's heels, but again there are no hunters and thus no threat of death.

In the next stretch of similes, beginning in Book 10, various circumstances aid the lion. No men or dogs bother the favored Diomedes (*Il.* 10.485) or the marginal Agamemnon, who is only a forest or nocturnal lion (*Il.* 11.113, 172).[28] In the next simile Hektor is the huntsman, but the simile does not let him approach the lions, which, as in his earlier simile, may only be boars (*Il.* 11.293). With Hektor in the attacking role, lions benefit from a double chauvinism that protects them as well as the Greeks they represent.[29] Then comes a pause as Paris contributes a simile confirming Diomedes as a lion (*Il.* 11.383), and Ajax confirms the lion's superiority over θῶες 'jackals' who resemble dogs without masters (*Il.* 11.475). Up to this point, no simile has portrayed lions being defeated by men and dogs or even portrayed men and dogs holding the advantage. Here and there a lion's death has been predicted, but, unless the Chimera counts as a lion, no death has been reported as an accomplished fact, nor has any man or dog wounded a lion (cf. *Il.* 5.558).

Then the advantage shifts from lions to their foes. When Ajax becomes a lion a second time, men and dogs compel him to retreat from a sheep pen (*Il.* 11.548). Even a leonine Hektor finds himself surrounded by the same tormentors (*Il.* 12.42). This simile also contributes the new warning that the lion's "own courage (*agênoriê*) will kill him." This idea will recur (*Il.*

---

26. As in Moulton 1977:58–64. For other views, see Hampe 1952:19 and Schnapp-Gourbeillon 1981:Ch. 5, both relating the similes to immediate circumstances.
27. Schnapp-Gourbeillon 1981:71-77 emphasizes the youthfulness of both heroes and lions.
28. Schnapp-Gourbeillon 1981:71-77 holds that Agamemnon is marginal because royal and thus barred from more dangerous combat.
29. Van der Valk 1953; Lattimore 1951:30-33.

20.171–173), as will the related idea found in the next simile, Sarpedon's, that the lion must strike first or die (*Il.* 12.300 and the Agenor simile).

When the battle zigzags, the similes do as well.[30] Since no men are present, the lions representing the two Ajaxes snatch prey from dogs (*Il.* 13.138). Men without dogs fare no better (*Il.* 15.630), and Hektor dispatches Patroklos in the wild with no one to interfere (*Il.* 16.823). The death of Sarpedon marks the last successful entry of a lion into a herd, a bit of nostalgia for the non-human predators, just as it is a last hurrah for Patroklos (*Il.* 16.481).

As noted, this war within the similes often reflects the siege of Troy.[31] It also reflects the untold story of Greek plundering in the Troad. The climactic failure of Menelaos suggests a Greek raid (*Il.* 17.108-111):

αὐτὰρ ὅ γ' ἐξοπίσω ἀνεχάζετο, λεῖπε δὲ νεκρόν,
ἐντροπαλιζόμενος ὥς τε λὶς ἠϋγένειος,
ὅν ῥα κύνες τε καὶ ἄνδρες ἀπὸ σταθμοῖο δίωνται
ἔγχεσι καὶ φωνῇ· τοῦ δ' ἐν φρεσὶν ἄλκιμον ἦτορ
παχνοῦται, ἀέκων δέ τ' ἔβη ἀπὸ μεσσαύλοιο·

Menelaos backed off and left the dead man but kept
turning around like some great bearded lion that
dogs and men chase from the yard with spears and
shouts. The brave heart in the lion's breast freezes
and against his will he withdraws from the farm.

He tries again (*Il.* 17.664) and retreats in grief (τετιηότι θυμῷ). Meanwhile, the Ajax-lion finds that hunters are attacking his home, not he theirs, and he must defend his young (*Il.* 17.107).[32]

30. The same shift is noted by Lonsdale 1990:122, who relates the content of the similes to attacks or retreats involving fortifications and ships.

31. Hampe 1952:21; Lonsdale 1990:2. But no lion in a simile enters the field of battle except in the *Doloneia*, also unusual because its animal skins do not accompany similes. For a geometric image of such trespassing, see Vermeule 1979:86 Fig. 5.

32. A political interpretation of the fact observed by Shipp 1972:213, that lions are attacked only by "rustics" defending their flocks and homes or by hunters seeking other game and discovering lions by accident. On the importance of cattle as both sustenance and wealth, see Buchholz 1973:27-30.

So end the lion similes of the shepherds of the people. To use their own comparison, they might as well be Achaean lionesses and not Achaean lions. The real shepherds have beaten them.[33]

As the only description of lions, prey, and hunters outside a simile, the shield of Achilles encapsulates the change. The hunters are near, the dogs are nearer still. Meanwhile, the lions are devouring bulls in a feast recalling the reduction of Zeus' son, Sarpedon, to raw meat:

οἱ δὲ νομῆες
αὔτως ἐνδίεσαν ταχέας κύνας ὀτρύνοντες.
οἱ δ' ἤτοι δακέειν μὲν ἀπετρωπῶντο λεόντων,
ἱστάμενοι δὲ μάλ' ἐγγὺς ὑλάκτεον ἔκ τ' ἀλέοντο.
(*Il.* 18.583-587)

as the herdsmen sicced the swift dogs on them
(ἐνδίεσαν...ὀτρύνοντες). As for biting, the dogs
turned away from the lions, but stood very close,
bayed, and kept clear.

The lions are running out of time.

This mounting vulnerability is not inconsistent with the taboo on killing lions. To the contrary, it is the price the lions pay for their status. Every simile raises the question whether the lion can be stopped, if not killed, and the emerging answer is to narrow the margin of survival. "Even though it will kill him," a harried lion may charge. Then, since the lion's death is prospective, the hero is momentarily thrust into a later stage of his life, as Hektor is when compared to a lion about to die (*Il.* 12.42). The premature pessimism is an example of the simile anticipating the story, just as it did when the approaching hunters portended the rescue of Paris. The difference is that the taboo stifles the simile's potential. Hunters draw near and dogs bite

---

33. The one shepherd of the people who herds sheep, Aeneas, reminisces about a Greek raid just a few lines before the epithet is bestowed (*Il.* 20.91-93; 20.110). But Aeneas missed the raid, while the only other shepherd who sees combat, Melanippus, is upbraided by Hektor for cowardice (*Il* 15.545-577). The only other explanation for how the Greeks supply themselves is shipments of wine from Thrace (*Il.* 9.71-72).

but lions do not turn up captured or immobilized. They do, however, in Mycenaean seals (Figs. 1–2).[34]

Figure 1. Vapphio Seals. National Museum, Athens

Figure 2. Rutsi Seals. National Museum, Athens

A third seal treads close to the forbidden moment, which it presents as a man-and-animal duel (Fig. 3).[35] Neither dogs nor prey pollute the scene.

The symmetrical composition of Fig. 3 suggests transference of the lion's qualities to the hero, and such transference is the theme of some

34. Fig. 1, captured: *tholos* tomb at Vaphio n1775, Athens National Museum. Fig. 2, immobilized: *tholos* tomb at Rutsi n8328.

35. Fig. 3: gold flattened cylinder from shaft grave 3, Athens National Museum. For the Near Eastern origin of the motif of men stabbing lions, Helck 1979:191-207 in his summary of Near Eastern influence on Bronze Age Greek art.

interpretations of the similes.[36] But transference requires a fusion of man and animal, here accomplished in visual terms.[37] In the case of a sphinx, a comparable fusion of woman and animal is accomplished in mythic terms. In either case, the fusion is metaphorical, the sphinx herself being a partial metaphor, whereas the image of the seal or ring is an arrested metaphor in which the two terms of the comparison do not quite coincide.

Figure 3. Gold Cylinder Seal. National Museum, Athens

But where lions are concerned, the epic singer avoids fusion and metaphor, and any simile will show why. To use the example of Menelaos, if the hero were fused with the lion he would attack Paris and kill him.[38] Instead of influencing the story, the figure of speech would dominate and, in this instance, destroy it. Also objectionable would be a sphinx, a talking lion

---

36. Snell 1953:Ch. 8. For similar views, see Fränkel 1921:61 and Schnapp-Gourbeillon 1981:1984.

37. Lion and hero also combine in Assyrian palace reliefs such as Figs. 2 & 3, pl. 10 Kolbe 1981. Whether the anthropomorphic figures manipulating the lions are heroic or divine is disputed by Kolbe (92ff). Unlike the tame creatures attending Greek gods or masters of the animals, the lions are rampant.

38. For the view that, in the *Iliad*, metaphor and simile are not significantly different, see Muellner 1990:60n2. There is only one character in the *Iliad* who is a metaphorical lion, but she is Artemis, so called because she brings death to women (*Il.* 21.483). As both lioness and *Potnia Thêrôn*, she embodies fusion of the lion and the hunter but on a divine rather than human plane.

that would blur the distinction between the noisy battlefield and the similes, where the only utterances are the barks and shouts of men and dogs.[39] The interdependence or symbiosis of the battlefield and the similes presumes a fundamental separation, with no lions in the one and few men in the other, and with a narrative gate, usually ὥστε, in between.

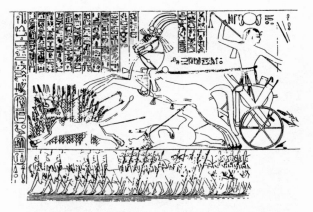

Figure 4. Bas-relief from Medinet Habu.

If Greek epic does not show interpenetration of hunt and battle, a very different but contemporary medium, Egyptian art, does. In Fig. 4, the hunter uses a chariot and the lions oblige him by appearing in what might be a battlefield or even a racetrack.[40] If such complaisance is more than Greeks can expect, it is not unfitting for Ramses III, who is exercising his royal monopoly on hunting lions. The image lacks the tension of the Greek counterparts because the hunter cannot fall. He is the opposite of the epic lion hunter who cannot fully succeed. But no god-king is available to kill the

---

39. There are no Homeric sphinxes if only because there are no lionesses, but Vermeule 1979:69 observes that the sphinx never stalks or kills heroes, even though she is a post mortem escort for them. In the formulation of Hölscher 1972:61, the lions take epic heroes only to the point of death but not beyond.

40. A bas-relief from the temple of Medinet Habu, Fig. 39, Wreszinski 1932:6, 19. This sixteenth century image differs from Old-Kingdom portrayals of the lion-hunter on foot and from Assyrian pictures of more vigorous but doomed lions who defy hunter-kings (5, 25, Figs. 53, 54).

Iliadic lion.[41] With their images of transference, the Mycenaean gems suggest that lion-wrestling Herakles might be equal to the task, but he is one or two generations too soon, while his son and grandsons are minor warriors (*Il.* 2.653, 679). Agamemnon and Diomedes, who imitate Herakles by wearing the lion skin, have done nothing to earn the right and two better men, Hektor and Achilles, do not wear the skin.[42] No wonder that the first combat simile of Achilles goes to the other extreme, an attack by a nameless, demotic mass:

> Πηλεΐδης δ' ἑτέρωθεν ἐναντίον ὦρτο λέων ὥς,
> σίντης, ὅν τε καὶ ἄνδρες ἀποκτάμεναι μεμάασιν
> ἀγρόμενοι πᾶς δῆμος· ὁ δὲ πρῶτον μὲν ἀτίζων
> ἔρχεται, ἀλλ' ὅτε κέν τις ἀρηϊθόων αἰζηῶν
> δουρὶ βάλῃ, ἑάλη τε χανών.
>
> (*Il.* 20.164-168)[43]

> From the other side, the son of Peleus rose against him
> like a ravening lion that the county (πᾶς δῆμος) has
> been straining to kill. At first he pays them no mind and
> goes his way, but when some one of the battlequick
> young men has hit him with a spear, he whirls, gaping.

Like 'farm' in the translation of the simile of Menelaos' failure (*Il.* 17.108), 'county' conveys the political and military idea that the lion is an outlaw. But once the response is troops, the lion simile has virtually ceased to

---

41. Qualities of the lion and qualifications for the task: μένος (*Il.* 5.136, etc.), ἀλκή (*Il.* 5.299, etc.), σθένος (*Il.* 7.256, etc.), χάρμη (*Il.* 16.823), and the leopard's ἄλκιμον ἦτορ (*Il.* 17.109), noted by Hampe 1952.5. But the lion's human foes are fearful (*Il.* 5.140, 17.66); cowardly (*Il.* 15.587); incompetent (*Il.* 15.632) albeit vigorous (θαλεροί *Il.* 3.26).

42. A right Herakles earns by use of his bare hands (Hesiod *Theogony* 332; Sophocles *Trachiniae* 1094; Pausanias 6.5.5) or at most a bow (Apollodorus 2.6.3). The hero even uses the lion's own claws to skin it (Stesichorus *PMG* fr. 229; Euripides *Herakles* 361-363; Pindar *Isthmian* 6.47). The epic heroes are wrongly equipped.

43. Though Körner 1930:10n17 notes that the number of attackers is always inexact, even when small, and the number of lions always exact.

be a simile. It has become a military episode, the same as the battle before or after it. In effect, it is narrative.

As several studies have shown, similes of sacrifice and catastrophe further amplify the lion hero.[44] Against this monster, Paris' game of proportions would be feeble, so Agenor plays Paris' other trick, reversal, and obtains the divine assistance that the example of the Pharaoh suggests is indispensable for dispatching the lion.[45] For Agenor will dispatch him, not kill him, a violation of the taboo, but dispatch him into another narrative plane, where lion men like Diomedes argue with gods to no avail.[46]

In the soliloquy preceding his simile, Agenor assesses his opponent as a lion, but he responds to the earlier similes by assessing Achilles as a perverted lion that will literally sacrifice him. As Agenor puts it, Achilles will 'cut his throat' (δειροτομήσει [*Il.* 21.555]). Used only seven times in the *Iliad* and *Odyssey,* this word appears three times in connection with the human sacrifice in honor of Patroklos, including twice for the human victims (*Il.* 18.336, 23.22).[47] The suppliant Lykaon uses it earlier in Book 21 and Agenor seems to know the results. Another suppliant, Phemios, has better luck with it.[48]

But although these uses establish the basic meaning, they do not exhaust the meaning that will apply to Agenor. He will not be a funerary sacrifice and does not consider being a suppliant. So it is irrelevant to him that the bodies of the youths and the dogs are burned or that neither Lykaon nor Phemios has his throat cut. For him the relevant use of the word is the ordinary or non-funerary, nonsuppliant use found in the *Nekyia,* where Odysseus slits the sheeps' throats and then disposes of their bodies quite differently than

---

44. Whitman 1958:206; Segal 1973:11-16; King 1987:13-28.
45. On divine assistance for archaic lion heroes, see Markoe 1989:88-115.
46. This simile may be compared to a "speech act" in Austin's sense, but the "speech" in this "speech act " is not explicitly Agenor's. Martin (1989:167-170) cites other similes that may be considered speech acts, but all these similes occur in speeches made by heroes.
47. For the contrary view, see Redfield 1975:114.
48. Crotty 1994:84-85 notes that Achilles befriends Lykaon before killing him. But as Achilles will tell Hektor, lions cannot be supplicated (*Il.* 22.262). Human in many emotions, the lion is—or is expected to be—uninvolved in such religious relations as supplication and sacrifice. But the self-consciousness of Achilles' remark to Hektor marks progress toward the new values Crotty finds expressed in Book 24.

Achilles does the bodies in the *Iliad*. Odysseus proceeds to skin the animals (*Od.* 11.35, 45-46). Agenor is afraid of being flayed.

Agenor's fear exposes a paradoxical aspect of the taboo. Somewhere big cats are being killed for their hides, not to mention their bones, used as amulets at Troy, Tiryns, and elsewhere.[49] Yet the *Iliad* makes no mention of royal hunting preserves like those in Egypt or Persia, or of more modest sources like lion hunts.[50] So there is no apparent source for Iliadic royal hides—not until Achilles suggests a new one, human beings. One hero will flay another.

Agenor is all the more vulnerable in the light of an episode mentioned by his father, Antenor, and elucidated by the *Nostoi*. Antenor received a Greek embassy at his house (*Il.* 3.204), and an incident in the *Iliou Persis* shows that he identified himself to the Greeks by a leopard skin. He later hung the skin on his door during the sack of Troy. It was a signal, and when the Greeks saw it they spared his house.[51]

Achilles will have known of the embassy, perhaps of the skin. But whether the threat to flay Agenor is the Greek hero's response to the family emblem or is only Agenor's fearful projection, a link between the threat and the emblem has been made and is not forgotten. This link might develop in two ways: first, as δειροτομήσει implies, Agenor may be associated with the leopard skin as a representation of a dead animal, and be slain. Or Agenor may be associated with the leopard skin as a representation of the powers of self-definition used by Paris. The simile is the vehicle for the latter

---

49. Bronze Age lion bone finds at Thera (Morgan 1988:45), including teeth used as amulets. At Troy VIIa, Blegen (1958:4.1, 5); at Tiryns, Lonsdale (1990:104n3 with referencess).

50. But Menelaos' comment that lions and leopards have less θυμός than boars may reflect the fact that the first two species were tamed in Egypt, the last, wild everywhere (*Il.* 17.20-22). On Egypt's tame lions and leopards, see Ranke 1923:275, 377, 435, 626; Wreszinski 1932:6.

51. Strabo 13.1.53 and the *Argumentum Soph. Antenoridai* in Radt 1964:4.160, which reports that the Greeks saw the skin on the door of the house and spared the inhabitants. The testimonia gathered by Davies (1988) and Bernabé (1988) report no other contact between Antenor and the Greeks.

development. Rather than a passage from life to death, it effects a passage from death to life.[52]

The simile also allows Agenor to use Paris' trick of reversing roles with his foe. In this instance, Agenor will be the cat, Achilles the hunter. Agenor thus claims a whole poem's worth of feline, if not leonine, killing power, while Achilles inherits the failures of hunters and herdsmen. Like Paris' simile, this one marks the hero's response to the surrounding narrative. Before imagining himself as a leopard, he compares himself to wild animals that might be leopards or prey, symbols of the fate he eventually rejects. The first thing Agenor's animal will do is outrun Achilles. Note the direction, away from Troy, the city of the rival dynasty of Priam, and note the specific destination:

> εἰ δ' ἂν ἐγὼ τούτους μὲν ὑποκλονέεσθαι ἐάσω
> Πηλεΐδῃ Ἀχιλῆϊ, ποσὶν δ' ἀπὸ τείχεος ἄλλῃ
> φεύγω πρὸς πεδίον Ἰλήϊον, ὄφρ' ἂν ἵκωμαι
> Ἴδης τε κνημοὺς κατά τε ῥωπήϊα δύω·
>
> *(Il.* 21.556-559)

suppose I leave these men to be overrun by
Achilles, Peleus' son, and run on my feet to some
place else, away from the wall to the plain of Ilium,
until I come to the spurs of Ida and slip into the thickets.

If the distance to Ida is absurdly long, as some editors have reckoned, that only accents the true purpose of this escape plan, which is not to run a race but to enter another milieu.[53] There Agenor will become Achilles' skinnable animal, but, by a characteristic reversal, he will be much harder to catch. His behavior will be animal and human all at once:

---

52. Insofar as the simile expresses Agenor's will to survive, it offers an instance of "focalization" as in de Jong 1985:257-270, but this focalization occurs in a narrative consisting of the whole epic cycle. For a similarly broad context for descriptions of heroes' dress and armor, see Foley 1977:141-143.

53. Twenty miles, according to Leaf 1902 ad. loc. 21.558; Shipp 1972:307. For maps and descriptions of the locale, see Leaf 1914:Ch. 4.

ἑσπέριος δ' ἂν ἔπειτα λοεσσάμενος ποταμοῖο
ἱδρῶ ἀποψυχθεὶς προτὶ Ἴλιον ἀπονεοίμην
(Il 21.560-561)

then in the evening, when I have bathed
in the river and washed off the sweat, I could
venture back to Ilium.

Even when Agenor remembers that Achilles might catch him on the way (Il. 21.563-564), he never concedes that he might have to fight and die on Ida. Yet this is not mere wishful thinking. Instead it draws on family history, just as the simile does. Ida is part of the territory Agenor rules as one of the Antenoridae (Il. 16.738; Strabo 13.1.33). The daydream of escape provides Agenor with his animal comparison and his clan tie, and of course with the background for the action of the simile.

It does not, though, provide the conclusion he will eventually reach. After rejecting the daydream (565), Agenor says Achilles is too strong (566); then changes his mind and says Achilles might not be strong enough to defeat him (568-569). Then, at 570, he complains that Zeus guarantees Achilles' success, so he has changed his mind a second time. Aristarchus must have thought once was enough and athetized the line.[54] That way Agenor would remain committed to resisting Achilles and the next sentence would be translated as follows:

ὣς εἰπὼν Ἀχιλῆα ἀλεὶς μένεν, ἐν δέ οἱ ἦτορ
ἄλκιμον ὁρμᾶτο πτολεμίζειν ἠδὲ μάχεσθαι.
(Il. 21.571-572)

---

54. Or, since Achilles does not win, Aristarchus may have been trying to preserve Zeus' reputation. Relevant is Rahn's comment that for all his power, epic Zeus is not master of the animals (1953:481). Only once does Zeus encourage a hero just before or during a combat featuring a lion simile (Hektor, Il. 16.667). Once he encourages those compared to hunters and dogs and once he puts fear into the Ajax lion, which nevertheless retreats grudgingly. For a different Zeus, cf. Orphic fr.117 ed. Kern 1922.

> So he said. He collected himself and waited for
> Achilles, and his brave heart was eager to fight and to do battle.[55]

But after a speech about running away like an animal, ἀλείς *aleis* means 'cowering' like prey. Since ἀλείς is the word of a man who will not fight, Agenor has changed his mind a third time. Then comes ἄλκιμον ἦτορ 'brave heart', or a fourth change in as many lines.[56]

Athetization will not redeem this confusion, but letting the simile be part of the hero's thinking will.[57] Having imagined himself as an animal, he must reckon with pursuit by Achilles the lion and so with likely death (φεύγω and forms of κλονέω *Il.* 21.574, 576, 578). Since *aleis* is for prey, it represents this threat. Yet it also represents another possibility, that of lying in ambush. It can designate either side, an ambiguity that persists until the simile, when Agenor chooses to be a leopard and leaps at the foe.

Throughout this speech, the Achilles lion is Lord's "hidden habit," felt but not expressed. It never confronts the leopard, just as it never did in Book 3. Instead the two big cats are like two north magnetic poles that approach one another, then bounce apart.

Why this special trait of lion-leopard encounters? To preserve the story from the lion's power to kill some and immortalize others. In Book 3, this power could have halted the song; in Book 21, it could halt the song too soon, by the deaths of Hektor, Agenor, and the mass of the Trojans. Not only would Achilles have failed to evolve, as Crotty and others have shown,[58] but the epic bestiary might be thought to protest: the leopard has an *êthos* too, which is reversal. So in Book 22, Achilles is hawk yet hare, dog yet racehorse, star yet dream (*Il.* 22.139, 308, 189, 22, 318; 23.199). None has anything like leonine killing power, but the range far exceeds that of similes of any other two-man combat. Leopard craft has replaced lion strength as a poetic model.

This model permits lion similes offered by characters but with one exception, a lion in a non-military context. It excludes similes offered by the singer (*Il.* 24.572). He has ended his partnership with the leonine heroes and

---

55. 'Collected himself' is the sense of Lattimore 1951, Fitzgerald 1974, and Chapman 1612.
56. On Agenor's hesitation, see Fränkel 1921:61n3.
57. For a different interpretation, see Lonsdale 1990:37-38.
58. See nn 48, 49.

also with the lions that may no longer hunt or kill. One of the lions of the last books even turns reflective. In Apollo's words, Achilles is a lion because "he knows (or has seen) wild things" (*Il.* 24.41).[59] The lion no longer just acts; he observes.

The unprepossessing lions of the *Odyssey* exhibit the same shift. One lion is a manifestation of Proteus, but this role is also played by the leopard (*Od.* 4.456). Another lion is caught in a net (*Od.* 4.791). A third, sad and wet, eyeballs the prey but doesn't budge (*Od.* 6.130), and a fourth gobbles his meat without killing or hunting it (*Od.* 9.292). Each of these four stands in contrast to Iliadic lions, a breed that does not consort with lesser fry, get netted, starve without a fight, or eat without a kill.[60] But other than a lion meant to encourage Telemachus, no more appear until Odysseus returns home and kills the suitors like a lion that has eaten a cow (*Od.* 14.334, repeated *Od.* 17.125; *Od.* 22.401, repeated *Od.* 23.47).

As that most unwarlike of creatures, an erotic lion, the lion of Book 6 marks an especially sharp change. Because this lion's prey would have to be compared to a young girl, not a warrior, it is inappropriate for him to attack, and so there is no prey mentioned. But there are no hunters or dogs either. In the erotic milieu they, too, are inappropriate. So the lion is stranded, like Odysseus. He cannot interact with his surroundings, just as the hero cannot interact with the girl unless he keeps what might be called his lion under cover.[61] To cite a relevant wordplay from the *Iliad*, Odysseus must be ποικιλομήτης or a disguiser of his μήδεα (*Il.* 11.482).

Except in the later books, Odyssean lions do not designate victors, nor does Agenor's leopard, and the reason is the presence of a similar feminine or domestic element in the scene. Not only is the leopard a female, but the implicit lion, Achilles, is a hunter and thus a potential husband and father. When paired, these two defective felines form a simile that is both complex but negative and balanced but unpredictable. One element, the leopard, is unknown, while the other, the lion, is overdetermined. Too much meaning

---

59. Snell 1953:201 and Lloyd 1960:185-192 take the opposed view that the lion is an iconic constant in Greek literature and art.

60. For the view that Odyssean lions convey psychological detail, see Buchholz 1973:10; bring about a reversal of gender roles, see H. Foley (1978); advance a subgeneric plot, see Magrath 1982.

61. See Watrous (this volume).

collides with too little, and the expected transaction cannot occur. Neither the lion-hunter nor the leopard-prey can kill and neither of them can die.

At first this encounter seems disappointing, especially since the leopard simile mentions "stabbing" the feline for the first time. But the simile's influence over the narrative breaks the deadlock and creates new consequences. When Apollo steps in, a predictable move, he finds he cannot save Agenor in the predictable way, a speech and a soft landing. Apollo is too busy. Agenor's courage has drawn Achilles to the gates of Troy. To prevent a massacre, Apollo must lure Achilles away, a ruse he can only accomplish by becoming Agenor and carrying out the Trojan's daydream of sprinting for Mount Ida.

Several epic gods impersonate the comrades and relatives of a hero or heroine.[62] The leopard simile has contrived a very different situation. Apollo is impersonating a hero, not a comrade, and finds himself participating in the battle with only one of his many advantages, his speed. If he forgets to bring Agenor back, the reason is not just that he is busy, but that he is doing what Agenor would do, running, and making the real Agenor superfluous. The redefinitions and reversals have hit him, too, turning the protector into a human, like the protégé.

Meanwhile the Trojans run into town "like fawns" (*Il.* 22.1). This is the biggest kill of all, and the leopard has spoilt it! So, in a reversion to leonine poetics, the *Iliou Persis* administers condign punishment.[63] The lion's whelp, Neoptolemus, has the honor of killing the lion's prey, Agenor. Agenor's leopard can save his life, but only within the confines of the episode in which it serves as a foil.

But even this riposte does not squelch the variability the leopard has introduced. When Achilles makes the mistake of saying he wishes he were a lion, eating Hektor raw (*Il.* 22.346), Hektor predicts that the original leopard, Paris, will defeat him with the help of Agenor's god, Apollo, at Agenor's spot, the Skaian gate (*Il.* 22.360). A visual record of this scene makes the

---

62. Apollo: *Il.* 17.73, 17.322, 20.81; Aphrodite: *Il.* 3.387; Poseidon: *Il.* 13.45; Athena: *Il.* 2.182, 4.087, 22.227.

63. Davies 1988:T2 61, confirmed by Pausanias 10.27.2. Cf. Pausanias 10.26.2, where Lesches is reported to have sung that Odysseus spared Agenor's brother during the *Doloneia*.

victor ποικιλωτάτη 'most variegated' (Fig. 5).[64] His leopard skin is neither fashion nor armor, but sign: a last military aberration, a last loss for the lion, and a last victory for comparison over comparison, and comparison over narrative.[65]

Figure 5. Paris as Leopard. British Museum, London

Paris is an archer, killing from afar; Agenor would be safer if he were an archer, too. The lion heroes, in contrast, are spearmen fighting among the *promakhoi* 'those fighting in the front ranks'. The leopard-lion struggle may thus be imagined as a debate between spear throwers and bowmen, with the taboo on lion killing as the subject.[66] The spearmen want to maintain the taboo, which gives them courage.[67] But if the *Iliad* grants them their wish, other parts of the cycle may have been different.

---

64. A ladle in the British Museum E808.

65. Lorimer 1950:295 holds that the skin is armor. In the terms used by Eustathius, the leopard is associated with similes achieving διανάπαυσις, the lion with similes achieving αὔξησις. Eustathius observes the effect of similes on subsequent narrative (οἰκονομία) but not of previous narrative on similes (176.20-22, 253.24-25, 1065.29-31).

66. To sharpen the debate, Aristarchus athetized 3.18-20, which equip Paris with spears before his confrontation with Menelaos. For the use of the bow, Lorimer 1950:277-296 and McLeod 1966:Ch.1 on the social and perceived moral differences between archery and spear fighting.

67. For similes as a spur to valor, see Willcock 1964:141-154 cited by Lonsdale 1990.123. For a psychological explanation of the taboo, see Snell 1953:201, observing the many similarities between humans and other large predatory mammals.

Even the *Iliad* provides for essential archers like Paris and Pandarus (*Il.* 11.369-382, 4.104-147).[68] In the first of these passages Paris boasts of negating Diomedes' lion-like quality, and in neither does the archer observe the precaution of the archer's *aristeia* when Teucer hides behind a spearman's shield (*Il.* 7.266-344). Instead the arrow seems to come from nowhere, violating expectations and, in the second instance, also violating a truce. Like the leopard, archery is crucial yet marginal, inferior yet effective.

In a culture like the Pharaoh's, this debate should never arise. Sole lion hunter, he has leopards on a leash and commands corresponding military power.[69] His lion similes are numerous, unambiguous, and brief, with no third term and no implications of single combat. The divine sponsor of Thutmoses III explains the Pharaoh-Lion as a manifestation of heavenly wrath:

> I have come that I cause thee to trample down the Tehenu
> (Libyans); the Utertiu (Southerners) belong to the might of thy
> glory. I cause them to see thy majesty as a fierce lion as thou
> makest them corpses throughout their valleys.[70]

The literature included by Pritchard elsewhere in his standard collection does not suggest any quarrel between those who wear a skin and those who resemble the animal. Yet Agamemnon and Achilles quarrel partly because one is king, meaning that he has the lion skin, and the other is champion, meaning that he has leonine courage. Having stated this difference, Nestor does not know how to resolve it (*Il.* 1.275-281).[71]

If the cultural and military split between lion skin and lion, like that between lion and leopard, is Greek and not Egyptian, it is all the more remarkable that λέων *leôn* is a Near Eastern loan word, perhaps Egyptian,

---

68. Arrows fell three of the five victims reported by Nestor in *Il.* 11.659-663.

69. For a pharaoh with a leopard's head, see Spiegel 1908:s.v. "Löwenkopf." For leopard skin as royal and noble garb in the Old Kingdom, priestly in the New, see Ranke 1923:596.

70. Pritchard 1955:374. For other triumphalist examples, see Stella 1978:375-380, including hymns to Mesopotamian monarchs.

71. Cf. Diomedes *Il.* 9.37-39. Following his lion simile, Sarpedon states the difficulty at greater length (*Il.* 12.310–328). Kings, he says, should be both rich and brave but rich from bravery, not just from being kings.

and that πάρδαλις *pardalis* is another, perhaps Persian.[72] The Greeks were borrowing the panoply of Pharaonic symbolism and, as the *Iliad* shows, making wide and varied use of what they borrowed. But they could not or would not borrow the context, which was absolute monarchy. As a result, they found themselves comparing vulnerable chieftains and the invulnerable king of beasts, mortals and quasi-immortals.[73] One motive for the borrowings might have been to increase the stature of Greek rulers. But borrowing πάρδαλις as well led not only to the poetic development sketched in this essay but also to a parallel duality in visual art. A lion became a feline with a mane; a leopard, the same or much the same feline with spots; a feline without either of these two markings might be a leopard or a lioness.

Lion champion and leopard challenger, lion champion and lion king, creatures of dress and creatures of craft: the singer has a tale to tell and will not linger over irresolvable conflicts. But a sword pommel from the shaft graves has no narrative duties and so it portrays a drawn battle between leopard and lion (Fig. 6).[74] Here the lion is bearing down on the leopard and is sure to bite. But this is only one perspective. Rotate the pommel clockwise by one quarter and the leopard is biting back. Rotate the pommel another quarter, or halfway, and the combatants dissolve in a swirl of limbs. Rotate the pommel the rest of the way and the lion is again on the verge of victory.[75]

Besides giving several meanings to one event, the pommel distributes them among perspectives. The perspective giving the lion the advantage is like the body of the story, where Achilles cannot lose, and the lion simile feeds him victims. The perspective establishing the leopard as an equal is like Agenor's simile. Neither is an interpretation by itself, nor are they an adequate interpretation when taken together. The circular movement must be included, too. During this movement both combatants are running, just as all the parties at the end of Book 22 are running. All is confusion and for a

---

72. λέων as Egyptian, Billigmeier 1975 with references to earlier speculation. For both words as non-Indo-European, see Chantraine *DELG*: s.v., with speculation on a Persian origin for πάρδαλις.

73. According to Masson 1967:113, most Egyptian loan words denote objects introduced by commerce. Masson regards "lion" and its cognates as a Mediterranean isogloss that spread west from Egypt or Syria (85-86).

74. From shaft grave #4 at Mycenae, Athens National Museum. Skeptical about art's applicability to epic are Hölscher 1972:48 and Buchholz 1973:9-10.

75. Matz 1951:1-7.

moment death disappears. Then it reappears, born of the confusion. The leopard marks this passage in and out of confusion, from an old mode of death to a new one.

Figure 6. Sword Pommel. National Museum, Athens

Afterword

"Much Have I Traveled in the Realms of Gold"

The preceding twenty pages expound as many lines of Chapman's Homer Believing that *poikilos* was a human quality, Chapman attributed it to the leopard and called her "freckled," with stress on "her":

> And as a panther, having heard the hounds trail doth
> disclose
> Her freckled forehead, and stares forth from out some
> deep-grown wood
> To try what strength dares her abroad, and when her
> fiery blood
> The hounds have kindled, no quench serves of love to
> live or fear,

Though struck, though wounded, though quite through she
    feels the mortal spear,
But till the man's close strength she tries or strows
    earth with his dart,
She puts her strength out.

                (509–515, Chapman's numbering)

The panther's skin "discloses itself" in contrast to an earlier scene where it did the opposite and covered the hero:

                fair Paris stept before
The Trojan host; athwart his back a panther's hide
    he wore.

Though the Greek is different, Menelaos dresses the same way at the start of the *Doloneia*:

    And first a freckled panther's hide hid his broad
        back athwart.

"Athwart" links this line to Paris and "freckled" links it to the simile, inviting triangulation of the passages. The pun "hide hid" states the poetics of epic animal skin.

    Earlier, Chapman identifies Ida as Agenor's "strength" and describes the lion imagery in Agenor's soliloquy as a "discourse of blood." Unable to make sense of *Il.* 21.570, Aristarchus' athetized line, Chapman adds thoughts that convey the confusion of a man changing his mind four times. The italicized words are not in the Greek:

              He (Achilles) holds special state
in Jove's high bounty; *that's past man, that every way*
    will hold,
And that serves all men every way That made him bold.

Chapman translated the poetics as well as the poetry, bequeathing a text relevant to both.

IV

TEXTUAL HOMER

9

Homêros ekainopoiêse:
Theseus, Aithra, and Variation
in Homeric Myth-Making

Thomas E. Jenkins

There are three explicit mentions of Theseus in Homer; the date and authenticity of all are warmly disputed.[1] To excise these lines from the text does not seem to impair the flow of the narrative or the syntax, however one might feel about the content of the lines. At *Iliad* 1.265 Nestor recounts that in the halcyon days of his youth, he consorted with the mightiest of the Greek heroes including Θησέα τ' Αἰγεΐδην ἐπιείκελον ἀθανάτοισιν 'Theseus, son of Aegeus, similar to the gods'. This bravura verse ends a list of famous warriors including Peirithoos, Kaineus, Exadius, and others. Grammatically the line could be removed, leaving the overall sense of the passage seemingly unscathed.[2] Similarly, Theseus' fleeting appearances in the *Odyssey* could be (and on occasion have been) excised. As Odysseus looks over the crowd of women in the underworld, he notes a striking trio:

> Φαίδρην τε Πρόκριν τε ἴδον καλήν τ' Ἀριάδνην,
> κούρην Μίνωος ὀλοόφρονος, ἥν ποτε Θησεύς

---

1. Sourvinou-Inwood 1970:98n22 offers a catalogue of scholars who explore the possible relationship between the so-called Peisistratean recension and the references to Theseus within Homer (*Il.* 1.265, *Od.* 11.321, 11.631). An additional line, *Il* 3.144, is a special case, as we shall see.

2. Van der Valk 1964:519 notes that a very late scholiast brands the line as νόθος 'bastard', a not uncommon denigration of lines deemed problematic by later commentators. The line was athetized already by Aristarchus (as were all mentions of Theseus).

ἐκ Κρήτης ἐς γουνὸν Ἀθηνάων ἱεράων
ἦγε μέν, οὐδ' ἀπόνητο.

(Od. 11.320-323)

I saw Phaedra and Prokris and beautiful Ariadne,
daughter of Minos the grim-thinking, whom once Theseus
wished to bring from Crete into the land of sacred Athens—
but he had no joy of her.

Phaedra, Prokris, and Ariadne are all women linked intimately to Athens or Theseus, and their stories carry distinctly local overtones.[3] As far as the *structure* of the Homeric catalogue is concerned, however, all three women could be banished without any necessary alteration to the rest of the passage. Finally, Theseus is invoked toward the culmination of the underworld scene, when Odysseus laments that fear of retribution by Persephone prevented him from seeing other warriors in the underworld, such as Θησέα Πειρίθοόν τε, θεῶν ἐρικυδέα τέκνα 'Theseus and Peirithoos, glorious sons of gods' (Od. 11.631). In each of the three verses that mention Theseus expressly, the lines are self-contained, and neatly excisable by those who believe they have grounds for excising.[4]

It is not here my purpose to argue about the authenticity of these particular lines regarding Theseus (though I do believe them genuine Homeric variants). I bring them up as a prelude to reflections on another "Athenian" line, one which, I believe, sheds light on both the process of Homeric myth-making and the play of variations—including variations on the myth of Theseus—within Homer. At first glance, Il. 3.144 seems to have little connection with the other allusions to Theseus, though, as we shall see, it often shares a similar fate at the hands of editors. I quote the passage in full (Il. 3.141-145):

αὐτίκα δ' ἀργεννῇσι καλυψαμένη ὀθόνῃσιν
ὁρμᾶτ' ἐκ θαλάμοιο τέρεν κατὰ δάκρυ χέουσα

---

3. For stories concerning Prokris, see especially Apollodorus 3.15.1; for Ariadne, Catullus 64; for Phaedra, Euripides' and Seneca's *Hippolytus*.
4. See for instance, Kirk, Leaf and Willcock, as discussed later in this essay.

οὐκ οἴη, ἅμα τῇ γε καὶ ἀμφίπολοι δύ' ἕποντο,
<u>Αἴθρη Πιτθῆος θυγάτηρ, Κλυμένη τε βοῶπις</u>
αἶψα δ' ἔπειθ' ἵκανον ὅθι Σκαιαὶ πύλαι ἦσαν.

Immediately she [Helen] veiled her head with shimmering cloth
and rose from the chamber as she wept a tender tear.
She went not alone, but accompanied by two handmaidens,
<u>Aithra, daughter of Pittheus and ox-eyed Klymene.</u>
Straightaway they went to where the Skaian gates were.

Aithra and Klymene accompany Helen as she obeys the summons from Priam and journeys to the main gate of Troy. An innocuous and inoffensive verse, one might argue. But, as we shall see, the Alexandrian editor Aristarchus athetized the verse as patent nonsense, and some modern editors too have argued that the verse is a late Athenian interpolation, an interloper into the text that should be treated differently from the hexameters surrounding it. I argue, by contrast, that the verse should indeed be treated differently, not because it is inauthentic, but because it demonstrates epic's ability to subsume and manipulate a variation in myth, to weave threads of mythic divergences into the very fabric of epic itself. In this manner, epic approaches lyric in its tolerance, perhaps even eagerness, for variant song traditions.

So what is the myth that causes such anxiety to ancient and modern editors alike? I believe that the line is a reference to the early rape of Helen by Theseus, a variation on Helen's woes attested in other tales of the heroine,[5] but appearing only this once in Homer. Plutarch offers the most thorough exposition of the myth in the "Life of Theseus," a passage of particularly great length and complexity.[6] Briefly, the story runs as follows: Theseus and his comrade Peirithoos journeyed to Sparta, where, after seeing Helen

---

5. Herodotus 9.73; Apollodorus 3.107, and the *Epitome* 1.23. Interestingly, it appears that the lyric poet Alcman also composed a version of the tale. A scholiast on *Il.* 3.242 notes that Helen feels shame because of her previous kidnapping (presumably by Theseus): Ἑλένη ἁρπασθεῖσα—παρὰ Ἀλκμᾶνι τῷ λυρικῷ 'Helen had been snatched away, according to the lyric poet Alcman'. The tale was also recited by Euphorion of Chalkis and Alexander of Pleuron.

6. Plutarch, *Life of Theseus*, 31.1-34.2.

dancing in the temple of Artemis Orthia, the two enamored men carried her away. After their success, the kidnappers drew lots to see which hopeful wooer would marry the prize; Theseus won. Attempting to conceal the evidence of his crime, he hid Helen in the town of Aphidna, a city in Attica. There, he placed his mother Aithra in charge of Helen, and entrusted both of them to his friend Aphidnus. Eventually, word of Helen's whereabouts leaked out, and Helen's enraged brothers, the Dioskouroi, stormed the city and rescued her. In so doing, the brothers seized Aithra in retaliation (a victim of very unfortunate circumstances) and kidnapped her to Sparta. I quote the end of Plutarch's telling of the tale in full:

Αἴθραν δὲ τὴν Θησέως μητέρα γενομένην αἰχμάλωτον
ἀπαχθῆναι λέγουσιν εἰς Λακεδαίμονα, κἀκεῖθεν εἰς Τροίαν
μεθ' Ἑλένης, καὶ μαρτυρεῖν Ὅμηρον ἕπεσθαι τῇ Ἑλένῃ
φάμενον

Αἴθρην Πιτθῆος θύγατρα Κλυμένην τε βοῶπιν.

οἱ δὲ καὶ τοῦτο τὸ ἔπος διαβάλλουσι ... ἴδιον δέ τινα
καὶ παρηλλαγμένον ὅλως λόγον ὁ Ἴστρος ἐν τῇ
τρισκαιδεκάτῃ τῶν Ἀττικῶν ἀναφέρει περὶ Αἴθρας, ὡς
ἐνίων λεγόντων, Ἀλέξανδρον μὲν τὸν [ἐν Θεσσαλίᾳ]
Πάριν ὑπ' Ἀχιλλέως καὶ Πατρόκλους μάχῃ κρατηθῆναι
παρὰ τὸν Σπερχειόν, Ἕκτορα δὲ τὴν Τροιζηνίων πόλιν
λαβόντα διαρπάσαι, καὶ τὴν Αἴθραν ἀπάγειν ἐκεῖ
καταληφθεῖσαν. ἀλλὰ τοῦτο μὲν ἔχει πολλὴν ἀλογίαν.[7]

They say that Aithra was made a slave-of-war and carried back
Sparta, after which she went to Troy alongside Helen, and that
Homer testifies to this, speaking of those who follow Helen:

Aithra, daughter of Pittheus, and Klymene with the looks of
the ox.

---

7. Plutarch, *Life of Theseus*, 34.1-2.

Some throw out this verse of Homer: Hister records a peculiar and entirely different story (*logos*) about Aithra in the thirteenth book of his "Attic History." Some say that Alexander (Paris) was overcome in battle by Achilles and Patroklos along the banks of the river Spercheios in Thessaly. Hektor, however, stormed and plundered the city of Troizen, and took Aithra back as a captive. But this is too bizarre (*a-logos*).

Helen's first kidnapping then was not by Paris, but by Theseus, an eerie harbinger of things to come. Plutarch, happy to offer variant causes for Aithra's presence in Troy,[8] notes that another tale claims that Hektor kidnapped the queen in Troizen; Plutarch dismisses that particular variation, however, as *a-logos* presumably because the great coincidences of time and place strain credulity. Illogicality is precisely the charge leveled at the line by Aristarchus (as mediated by Aristonicus in the so-called A Scholia):[9]

Αἴθρη, Πιτθῆος θυγάτηρ εἰ μὲν τὴν Θησέως λέγει μητέρα ἀθετητέον. ἀπίθανον γάρ ἐστιν Ἑλένης ἀμφίπολον ⟨εἶναι⟩ τὴν οὕτως ὑπεραρχαίαν, ἣν οὐκ ἐκποιεῖ ζῆν διὰ τὸ μῆκος τοῦ χρόνου. εἰ δὲ ὁμωνυμία ἐστί, καθάπερ καὶ ἐπὶ πλειόνων, δύναται μένειν.[10]

Aithra, daughter of Pittheus. If he means the mother of Theseus, the line must be athetized, for it is hardly credible that a handmaiden of Helen would be so very old: she could not possibly have lived that long. If, however, the name is simply a homonym (as it is in most cases), then it can stand.

---

8. Clader 1976:61 surmises that there might be cultic significance to the presence of Aithra near Helen, since Aithra's name seems to come from the Greek for something bright or blazing: "In other words, when the Twins brought their sister back from the son of the Sea-god, they brought back the 'Burning Lady' with her." Clader further demonstrates how images of light and illumination tend to cluster around Helen.

9. See Nagy 1997:103-104 for an account of the different classes of Iliadic Scholia.

10. Erbse 1969:384.

Aristarchus rejects the line because to keep it would create, in his view, an impossible chronological quandary. Aithra would be too superannuated to be a handmaiden. The line, therefore, must be banished from any text that represents a 'pure' Homer. Both Plutarch and Aristarchus devalue a variation because of the problems it presents to *external* reason, to *logos*, not because of any *internal* contradiction with the poetics of epic.

Some modern scholars, by contrast, have viewed the line askance not because of concerns over Aithra's age, but because the tale is at odds with the story of Helen usually sung about in Homeric poetry.[11] In the middle of a story about Helen's rape by Paris—and directly before Paris' defense of his wife—there stands this strange verse about Helen's previous rape by Theseus.[12] Willcock tries to dismiss the awkward variation out-of-hand: "What seems most likely is that Homer *or a predecessor* chose at random from the epic stock a name for the handmaid of Helen, and happened to hit upon Aithra, daughter of Pittheus. The explanatory legend then arose through the attempts of mythologists and poets to integrate this awkward detail into the total picture."[13] For Willcock, the line *preceded* the variation of the myth, and whatever mythological import the line contains only came into existence at a much later date; Willcock's formulation neatly exculpates Homer from any participation in variation-making.

Kirk reverses Willcock's argument and maintains that the line entered the Homeric tradition only after the Athenian myth was well established: "In the Odyssean occurrences of *Il.* 3.143 (at 1.331, 18.207) no names are attached to

---

11. See van der Valk 1964:436 for a history of scholars who attack the line or defend it. Van der Valk himself argues for the line's authenticity; he posits that it should remain (a) because of the connection to the Dioskouroi or (b) because a queen of Helen's stature surely has "women of note who accompany her as servants." Sourvinou-Inwood 1970:98n22 offers a broader catalogue of scholars who explore the possible relationship between the so-called Peisistratean recension and all references to Theseus within Homer.

12. However, Aithra's rescue is also found included in Proclus' summary of the now-lost *Iliou Persis*, 'Fall of Troy': Δημοφῶν δὲ καὶ Ἀκάμας Αἴθραν εὑρόντες ἄγουσι μεθ' ἑαυτῶν 'Demophon and Acamas (sons of Theseus) located Aithra and took her back with them' (Dionysius of Halicarnassus 1.68.2ff=Davies fr. 4, Allen frr. 3 and 4). See also Davies 1989:78. Although Aithra has but a cameo appearance in Homer, she does seem to have a supporting, if not starring, role in other versions of the Trojan War.

13. Willcock 1978:218.

the maidservants in a following verse, as here, which adds some support to Aristarchus' (Arn/A) provisional athetesis of the present verse: if this Aithra is Theseus' mother, he maintained, then it should go, but if she is merely an accidental homonym, then it can stay. But the coincidence not only of Aithra but also of Pittheus (who was Theseus' grandfather and king of Troizen) is too much to swallow, and the verse is almost without doubt an Athenian interpolation."[14] On Kirk's view, the line, with a reference to a mythical variation, could be inserted *by itself* into a pre-existing (if somewhat contrary) tradition of epic narrative.

I argue that the line helps to frame the entire *teikhoskopia* 'view from the wall' and that efforts to question (or worse, athetize) the line without considering the *end* of the *teikhoskopia* are ultimately fruitless. Indeed, the line signals a variation of the type that other genres, such as historiography, philosophy, and lyric so heartily embrace. To see how variation is accepted and manipulated in one of these genres, let us examine how the theme of Helen's multiple rapes is handled by an acknowledged master of "theme and variation": Stesichorus. For Stesichorus, the sexual history of Helen was of ever-abounding interest (and according to the story of the Palinode[15] of temporary yet bitter regret). A scholiast on Euripides' *Orestes* (249) records how Stesichorus narrated the aetiology of Helen's troubled sexual past:

Στησίχορός φησιν ὡς θύων τοῖς θεοῖς Τυνδάρεως Ἀφροδίτης
ἐπελάθετο ... ἔχει δὲ ἡ χρῆσις οὕτως οὕνεκά Τυνδάρεος
ῥέζων ποτὲ πᾶσι θεοῖς μόνας λάθετ' ἠπιοδώρου Κύπριδος·
κεῖνα δὲ Τυνδάρεου κόραις χολωσαμένα διγάμους τε καὶ
τριγάμους τίθησι καὶ λιπεσάνορας.[16]

Stesichorus says that Tyndareus neglected Aphrodite when he was sacrificing to the god . . . The exact wording is: "Because when Tyndareus was sacrificing to all the gods he forgot the Cyprian one, of the sweet gifts, the goddess became enraged. She cursed the

---

14. Kirk 1985:282.
15. Plato, *Phaedrus*, 243a.
16. Schwartz 1887:123=Page fr.46. The fragment has variously been assigned to the *Helen*, the *Oresteia*, and the *Fall of Troy* of Stesichorus.

daughters of Tyndareus to be doubly wed and thrice wed and deserters of husbands."

Homer nowhere speaks so baldly of Helen's various marital rearrangements as does Stesichorus in this passage, nor is there any overt reference in Homer to the three marriages. I assume that "twice-married" refers to Tyndareus' daughter Clytemnestra : she married Agamemnon, only to betray him after taking on Aegisthus as lover.[17] The third marriage of Helen (besides to Menelaos and Paris) is to Theseus, for Pausanias records how Stesichorus' genius for this particular mythical variation provided a role-model for later lyric poets (Pausanias 2.22.6):[18]

πλησίον δὲ τῶν 'Ανάκτων Εἰληθυίας ἐστὶν ἱερὸν ἀνάθημα 'Ελένης, ὅτε σὺν Πειρίθῳ Θησέως ἀπελθόντος ἐς Θεσπρωτοὺς ''Αφιδνά τε ὑπὸ Διοσκούρων ἑάλω καὶ ἤγετο ἐς Λακεδαίμονα 'Ελένη. ἔχειν μὲν γὰρ αὐτὴν λέγουσιν ἐν γαστρί, τεκοῦσαν δὲ ἐν ''Αργει καὶ τῆς Εἰληθυίας ἱδρυσαμένην τὸ ἱερὸν τὴν μὲν παῖδα ἣν ἔτεκε Κλυταιμνήστρᾳ δοῦναι—συνοικεῖν γὰρ ἤδη Κλυταιμνήστραν 'Αγαμέμνονι—αὐτὴν δὲ ὕστερον τούτων Μενελάῳ γήμασθαι. καὶ ἐπὶ τῷδε Εὐφορίων Χαλκιδεὺς καὶ Πλευρώνιος 'Αλέξανδρος ἔπη ποιήσαντες, πρότερον δὲ ἔτι Στησίχορος ὁ 'Ιμεραῖος, κατὰ ταὐτά φασιν 'Αργείοις Θησέως εἶναι θυγατέρα 'Ιφιγένειαν.

Near the Lords (*Anaktes*) is a sacred space of Eilethyia, an *anathema* (objects dedicated) by Helen; it dates to the time when Theseus, accompanied by Peirithoos, left for Thesprotia and (the town) Aphidna was captured by the Dioskouroi. Helen was led back to Lacedaemon. They say that Helen was with child, and that she gave birth in Argos, thereafter dedicating a shrine to Eilethyia.

---

17. A story well integrated into the epic corpus. See for example *Od*. 3. 266; *Od*. 11.453.

18. It does not apparently suit Stesichorus' purposes to dwell on the marriage of Helen to Deiphobus after Paris' death, obliquely alluded to at *Od*. 4.274 and *Od*. 8.517, but never expanded upon in our received text of Homer.

> She gave the daughter she bore to Clytemnestra, to live with her—Clytemnestra was already married to Agamemnon and Helen herself would marry Menelaos. Concerning this tale, Euphorion of Chalkis and Alexander of Pleuron composed poems, but <u>first of all Stesichorus from Himera agrees with the Argives that Iphigeneia was the daughter of Theseus.</u>

The genre of lyric itself places a high premium on diversity of tradition and delights in working out inherited tales to their (sometimes surprising) conclusions. Stesichorus not only sings that Theseus raped Helen, but that she became pregnant from the union—a particularly full-bodied variation. Moreover, the daughter proves to be Iphigeneia, immediately transferred to and adopted by Clytemnestra. Stesichorus has taken a localized song tradition (one popularized by the people of Argos) and adopted it for his poetic purposes.

Many ancient authors laud Stesichorus as being a type of Homer incarnate, a poet in whom poetic inspiration runs so vigorously that only Homer may be called upon as a parallel. He was praised by Longinus as being 'very Homeric' ('Ομηρικώτατος);[19] Antipater of Thessalonica avers that Homer made his home a second time in the breast of Stesichorus[20] ἃ πρὶν 'Ομήρου ψυχὰ ἐνὶ στέρνοις δεύτερον ᾠκίσατο. Yet this appellation seems to apply not because both poets told the same stories (indeed, Stesichorus often varies from Homer), but because each proves a powerful poet, influential to later generations. Stesichorus' legacy (and his charm) was his willingness to appropriate and synthesize variant traditions, which in turn provided material for later poets as they recreated their own stories.

A recently found papyrus fragment comments on just this facet of Stesichorus' poetics; a scholar, Chamaeleon, explains how Euripides followed Stesichorus' genealogy for many ancient heroes:

αὐτὸ[ς δ]έ φησ[ιν ὁ] Στησίχορο[ς] τὸ μὲν ε[ἴδωλο]ν ἐλθεῖ[ν
ἐς] Τροίαν τὴν δ' 'Ελένην π[αρὰ] τῶι Πρωτεῖ καταμεῖν[αι·

---

19. Longinus, *On the Sublime*, 13.3. Herodotus is also granted the distinction "very Homeric," though Plato gets the nod for being the most Homeric of them all.
20. *Anthologia Graeca*, Book 7, 75.4.

οὔ]τως δὴ ἐκ[α]ινοποίησε τ[ὰς] ἱστορ[ί]ας [ὥ]στε
Δημοφῶντ[α] μὲν τ[ὸ]ν Θησέως ἐν τ[ῶ]ι νόστωι με[τὰ] τῶν
Θεc[τια]δων [ ] ἀνενεχ[θῆναι λέγ]ειν [ἐ]ς [Αἴ]γυπτον,
[γενέσθα]ι δὲ Θη[σεῖ] Δημοφῶ[ντα μ]ὲν ἐξ Ἰό[πης] τῆς
Ἰφικ[λέους, Ἀ]κάμαν[τα δὲ ἐκ] Φα[ίδρας] ἐκ δὲ τῆς
Ἀμ[αζόνος Ἱππο]λυτη[ς]..λη.[...] περι.[.]υτων[ ] τῆς
['Ε]λένης[ ]ε Ἀγαμέμ[ν]. οντον.[Ἀ]μφίλοχον [ ] ωνουδε²¹

Stesichorus himself says that the phantom [of Helen] went to
Troy, and Helen remained with Proteus. He so innovated his
stories that he says Demophon, son of Theseus, was brought along
with the Thestiadai to Egypt, in his work "The Homecoming." He
also says that Demophon was Theseus' son by Iope (daughter of
Iphikles), that Acamas was his son by Phaedra, and Hippolytus by
the Amazon, that . . . from Helen . . . Agamemnon . . .
Amphilochus.

The commentator dwells on two facets of Stesichorus' telling of myth.
Firstly, Stesichorus helped to propagate the notion that Helen did not actually
go to Troy, but that a phantom, a body double, traveled with Menelaos while
the real Helen waited patiently in Egypt. Secondly, Stesichorus exploits
myths that boast vivid local color, as he explores Theseus' progeny from a
stunning variety of women.²² The commentator's word choice describing
Stesichorus' activities, *ekainopoiēse* 'fashioned newly', is difficult to parse:²³
does it mean that Stesichorus made up these stories from scratch? Or, as I
think must be the case, that he took preexisting stories, but privileged what

---

21. P.Oxy. 2506 (S. 193) ed. Page fr. 26 col. i., lines 12-32. Supplements are by
Lobel and Page.
22. Though the fragment is lacunose, I conjecture that the commentator states that
Iphigeneia is the daughter of Theseus and Helen—the variant recorded by Pausanias
2.22.6, above. I base my conjecture on the style of the catalogue and the fact that
Agamemnon is next mentioned (perhaps with reference to the subsequent adoption of
Iphigeneia by Agamemnon and Clytemnestra).
23. See Bassi 1993:57. "The meaning of ἐκαινοποίησε τὰς ἱστορίας is difficult in
this context. Is the writer saying that Stesichorus made the 'traditional story' about
Helen new? Or that he made a 'new inquiry' (in the sense that he introduced a new
way of interpreting epic mythos)?"

seemed *to later readers* as the odd variant, the surprising turn?[24] Stesichorus' poetics embrace abundant multiplicity—the poet can even tell a story, and in the next breath declare it untrue.

A case in point is the famous Palinode. Plato records that Stesichorus was struck blind for blaspheming against Helen when he sang that she sailed to Troy as Paris' adulterous wife.[25] The contrite (or wily) Stesichorus thereupon composed a palinode, a "retraction," which begins (*PMG* 192.1):

οὐκ ἔστ' ἔτυμος λόγος οὗτος
οὐδ' ἔβας ἐν νηυσὶν ἐϋσέλμοις
οὐδ' ἵκεο πέργαμα Τροίας.

That story is not true [*etumos*].
You did not sail on the well-oared ships.
You did not visit the citadel of Troy.

Changing his song, Stesichorus offers the tale that an *eidolon*, a phantom, went in Helen's place, and that the real Helen remained safely (and chastely) in Egypt throughout the war.[26] For Stesichorus, what is true, *etumos*, matches

---

24. The privileging of certain variants surely reflected the biases of the local communities for whom Stesichorus (and other lyric poets) composed their songs. See Burnett 1988:142-143: "Men of Stesichorus' profession were needed everywhere as colonies multiplied and rites and ceremonies proliferated. The poets no doubt made use of remembered hymns and traditional cult refrains, as well as the gnomes of their great predecessors, but as they trained local choruses they were free to make radical changes, and of course in the case of the cults of heroic founders they were forced to invent fictions, if not forms. They could draw fresh musical themes from the local heritage of secular melody, and they could expand the narrative content of performances by using folktale as well as epic and myth." Stesichorus and other lyric poets were free to rework myths to suit both the audience and the occasion.

25. Plato, *Phaedrus* 243a. Pausanias 3.19.11 records that Helen, the cause of the blindness, sent word to Stesichorus from the Isle of Leuke (i e., after her immortalization) that the poet should recant his slander.

26. No one knows for sure how many palinodes Stesichorus actually produced; the beginning of S 143 (not given here) seems to intimate that there were two, but the testimony is both unique and fragmentary. In any case, even one palinode suggests that Stesichorus was so open to variation that myths could not only vary, but contradict. A contradicting myth, however, can never actually cancel the object of its

what it is expedient: variations are made to be crafted and propagated as the muse (or the audience) beckons.[27] Stesichorus' palinode makes problematic the idea of 'true' in terms of the poetics of myth: in lyric, multiple variations are equally legendary—and equally true.[28]

Back to Homer. If the poetics of lyric allow multiple variations to run rampant, if lyric indeed thrives on telling myths in myriad ways, how then do the poetics of oral epic function? For Stesichorus, there are many myths about Helen, many insinuations about Theseus, and all of them are true (or false) as the moment demands. As we have seen, for Stesichorus, the capture of Aithra during a rape of Helen is true, as far as concerns the poetics of lyric.[29] But is line 3.144 of the *Iliad* 'true' (*etumos*)? If Stesichorus, who grappled with the Theseus/Helen myth, had created the *Iliad,* the answer would be tunefully in the affirmative; but can we say the same of the poetics of oral epic?

Simply put, yes. The line should be kept, since it is the linchpin that helps to fasten together much of what happens in the *teikhoskopia.* The celebrated ending of the *teikhoskopia* refers, I suggest, to the *beginning* of the

---

contradiction; it only spawns a doublet, producing two versions of a tale where there had been just one. See below.

27. Woodbury 1967:175 sums up Plato's distinction between the two poets: "The difference between (Homer and Stesichorus), in Plato's view, was that Stesichorus was truly poetical in a sense in which Homer was not, in his capacity to detect and correct error in mythology." But in a dialogue that concerns the complex interplay of speech and counterspeech—first a *logos,* then a counter-*logos* about the value of love—trying to pin down Plato's thoughts concerning contrariness is a difficult business indeed. Nagy 1990a:421 organizes the true/false dichotomy as a split between local and panhellenic versions of a myth: "In contrast with the complex and diplomatic pattern of subordination that characterizes Homer as the most Panhellenic in outlook, the story affirmed by Stesichorus in his *Helen* song is relatively simplex and uncompromising: Helen did not go to Troy, and that particular story is simply not *etumos* 'genuine' (Stesichorus *PMG* 192.1). In other words the versions of Stesichorus and the Cycle are comparable to each other by virtue of being less complex, less synthetic, than the version of Homer."

28. A point well formulated by Bassi 1993:69: "The result is that *neither* of the two oppositional stories about Helen can be taken as unambiguously true (or false). Indeed, given the weakness of its claims and the resulting ineffectual denial of Homeric truth, the burden of proof is shifted away from the epic narrative and onto the lyric."

29. And the capture of Aithra by Hektor is 'true' as concerns the *logos* of the historian Hister, above.

teikhoskopia, to the much-vexed line featuring the equally vexed Aithra. Helen's ruminations about the Greek army terminate abruptly and obliquely. She offers, for the briefest of moments, a recollection, a glimpse, of the same mythological past sung by Stesichorus:

δοιὼ δ' οὐ δύναμαι ἰδέειν κοσμήτορε λαῶν.
Κάστορά θ' ἱππόδαμον καὶ πὺξ ἀγαθὸν Πολυδεύκεα
αὐτοκασιγνήτω, τώ μοι μία γείνατο μήτηρ.
ἢ οὐχ ἑσπέσθην Λακεδαίμονος ἐξ ἐρατεινῆς,
ἢ δεύρω μὲν ἕποντο νέεσσ' ἔνι ποντοπόροισι,
νῦν αὖτ' οὐκ ἐθέλουσι μάχην καταδύμεναι ἀνδρῶν
αἴσχεα δειδιότες καὶ ὀνείδεα πόλλ' ἅ μοί ἐστιν.
ὣς φάτο, τοὺς δ' ἤδη κάτεχεν φυσίζοος αἶα
ἐν Λακεδαίμονι αὖθι φίλῃ ἐν πατρίδι γαίῃ.

(*Il.* 3.236-244)

I am not able to see two leaders of the people,
Castor, tamer of horses, and Pollux, fine with his fists,
my full brothers, born from my mother.
Either they did not journey from beloved Lacedaemon,
or they never made it here, journeying on the ships that ride
    the waves.
Or perhaps they do not wish to join battle with men,
fearing the shame and reproach that is my lot.
So she spoke. But already the life-nourishing soil held them
    fast
in Sparta, in the earth of their own dear fatherland.

Helen, ending her catalogue of famous Greek leaders, asks about the location of her brothers; she believes they are absent out of 'shame' (*aidôs*). I argue that these lines help not only to generate sympathy for Helen,[30] deepen

---

30. Wilamowitz 1920:283. He argues "Diese ganze Szene paßt also gewiß hierher, keine Dublette, aber wohl ein Komplement zu der Epipolesis; aber ihr Hauptzweck liegt in der Sympathie, die sie für Helene erweckt." The entire scene, as it passes, is not a doublet, but rather a complement to the Epipolesis; however its goal is the sympathy that it stirs up for Helen.] Wilamowitz further argues that the story of

her characterization, but that structurally they refer back to 3.144, which first
intimates that the rape of Helen by Theseus is part of the mythological
underpinnings of the scene. Why should Helen mention her brothers now,
and why should they be the final item in the catalogue? It is because Helen is
hoping for *another* rescue by her brothers, for *another* escape from the
unbearable position she has placed herself in. She is ashamed of her behavior,
and of her circumstances, and longs for her brothers to release her from her
plight—after all, they saved her the "last" time, in Stesichorus, in Pausanias,
in Plutarch, in the realm of variation.

The *Iliad,* unlike Stesichorus, does not allow this particular variation to
flourish, but nips it in the bud. Homer allows the variation to be invoked, its
specter to be summoned, but only as counterpoint to the dominant melody of
Helen's unfortunate circumstances.[31] In the case of the *teikhoskopia*, Helen's
lament over her brothers' absence assumes extra poignancy: she misses them,
naturally, because they are her kinfolk, but even more because she sees in
them an antidote to her shame.[32] It is a beautiful, disquieting, moment in
which the distraught Helen reaches to lyric to save her from the ignominy of
epic. But Homer, in effect, traps her in the *teikhoskopia*, able to see the
consequences of her elopement, but unable to flee them. After Helen, who
has narrated the bulk of the *teikhoskopia*,[33] invokes the specter of variation

Castor and Pollux in Sparta was a localized legend, though he avers it is anyone's
guess how old the tale really was. See Wilamowitz 1920:283n1.

31. Herodotus comes to much the same conclusion when he discusses Homer's
version of the rape of Helen by Paris. The historian adduces two passages in which
Homer seems to refer to the tale of the phantom without bluntly exposing the events
themselves. Herodotus believes this is no accident, but a deliberate maneuver on
Homer's part: δοκέει δέ μοι καὶ Ὅμηρος τὸν λόγον τοῦτον πυθέσθαι ἀλλ' οὐ
γὰρ ὁμοίως ἐς τὴν ἐποποιίην εὐπρεπὴς ἦν τῷ ἑτέρῳ τῷ περ ἐχρήσατο....
(II.116) 'It seems to me that Homer knew this story (of Helen's phantom), but
nevertheless it was more appropriate for epic to utilize the other tale....' For
Herodotus, Homer can know multiple versions of a story, but employ one particular
strain to especial advantage: the version that is *epopoiia*, suited to the singing of the
epic at that moment in time.

32. See Austin 1994:48, who perceptively views the entire *teikhoskopia* (and the
embarrassing absence of Helen's brothers) as the "spectacle of (Helen's) own shame,
or lack of it."

33. Indeed, Helen can be seen as a poetess in her own right, singing her own
catalogue of warriors. She even declares that what she is doing is 'telling the tale of
names' (οὔνομα μυθησαίμην [*Il.* 3.235]). The verb *mutheomai* signals marked

(bodily present throughout the scene in the shape of Aithra), oral epic must stop the song: *this* poem is not a repeat of Helen's previous brush with danger. The "lyric" Helen ceases to speak and the omniscient voice of the epic poet again wrests control:[34] the brothers will not come (as in Stesichorus), they are dead, and the earth covers them over.[35]

One might argue that even without line 3.144, the *teikhoskopia* stands all of a piece, and that in this respect the verse could be lumped together with the other "excisable" verses about Theseus. Leaf is confident that the reference must go: "This line is a clear case of interpolation of a later myth.... Homer is, of course, ignorant of the Theseus myth in all its branches."[36] Kirk, as we have seen, is also dubious about the verse; he explains his reasoning more fully at *Iliad* 1.264, where we see Nestor's reminiscence of Theseus as a brave warrior from youth: "It is probably correct to see [line 1.264] as a post-Homeric embroidery, probably of Athenian origin in the sixth century BCE when Theseus-propaganda was at its height." In the case of Nestor's remark, such reasoning has an undeniable attraction: the verse deftly elevates Theseus to the rank of Homeric hero. Theseus' remarked-upon absence in the underworld (*Od.* 11.631) reinforces his stature as a noble hero, and even his appearance in the catalogue of women can be explained as part of a passage with decidedly Athenian overtones. The Aithra verse, by contrast, does not mention Theseus, though it surely alludes to him. But the main point of the

speech, as in a ritual, or singing a tale; for the space of the *teikhoskopia*, Helen *is* a singer, responding to the audience of Priam. Only near the end does Helen's omniscience fail; up to that point, she is the master of the *mûthos*, knowing all the heroes, and the stories attached to them.

34. A key structural element of the *teikhoskopia*, as outlined by Edwards 1980.103, is the interplay between traditional epic catalogues and the voice of Helen. By placing the *teikhoskopia* in the mouth of the cause of the war, "the poet has conveyed not only some interesting information about the Greek leaders but also the most startling characterization in the *Iliad*, that of the grief-stricken and lonely Helen."

35. An alternate tradition in the *Cypria* explains that Castor and Pollux, caught while rustling cattle, had engaged in battle with Idas and Lynceus, resulting in Castor's death. See Davies 1989:42. Amusingly, Eustathius solemnly records that Alexander did not tell Helen about her brothers' death because he did not wish for her to cry; see van der Valk 1971:645.

36. Leaf 1914:130 notes that the story occurred in the *Iliou Persis* as well as on the Chest of Kypselos in Pausanias V.19. But surely the story did not appear *ex nihilo*, Leaf does not explain why the tale, as attested in later art, must have influenced the Homeric tradition, and not the other way around.

line seems not to be Aithra's connection with Theseus, but with *Helen*, for whom Aithra is the eternal embodiment of the shame of rape. Yes, Theseus is a part of the legend, and an important part, too; but Homer suppresses his name, emphasizing instead the bond between the two women, who are both, in their own ways, captives of war. The line cannot, I think, be convincingly touted as Theseus-propaganda. Though any mention of a local hero brings *kleos* 'glory' to a community, the aim of this verse seems more specific.

Recent research on Indo-European epic also supports the venerability of the line. Stephanie Jamison has convincingly argued that the *teikhoskopia* itself is an ancient trope (with cognates in the Indian epic *Mahâbhârata*). She demonstrates that a *teikhoskopia* is a traditional feature of Indo-European myths; in narrative, a *teikhoskopia* immediately precedes the moment in which a woman who has been illegally snatched may be rescued back: "an illegal abduction is quite different [from a legal one]: there is a legal remedy, which I will call the reabduction or counterabduction. The injured party or parties can assemble a posse and pursue the abductor, with intent to fight and recapture the woman."[37] Homer seems here to be playing with this ancient notion (and presumably custom) of counterabduction. On the one hand, it is Menelaos who is counterabducting Helen, for Paris quite roguishly made off with her in Sparta. Menelaos is prepared to fight Paris for his wife, man to man, directly after the *teikhoskopia*, and the hope is to resolve the conflict by the death of one of the suitors. On the other hand, Homer has conjured up Helen's *previous* counterabduction, one that has distinctly freakish overtones. During the siege of Aphidna, Theseus *did not* fight on Helen's behalf (and it is tempting to think that Helen had her own *teikhoskopia* there, searching for her rescuers), but was conspicuously absent. In fact, Theseus was miles away, in Thesprotia.[38] I suggest that, in the *Iliad*, this truancy of Theseus at Aphidna foreshadows Paris' own disappearance at Troy; in the same way that Theseus' absence from a duel over Helen fails to conform to Indo-European standards of a proper counterabduction, Paris' defense of Helen also goes horribly wrong. Like Theseus, Paris disappears, magically whisked away by Aphrodite in a pocket of air (*Il.* 3.381). From the moment line 3.144 is uttered, the auditor suspects that this counterabduction by Menelaos will not

---

37. Jamison 1994:9.
38. See again Pausanias 2.22.6, as quoted above.

work properly—it seems that counterabductions of Helen never operate as they are "supposed" to do.

I end with a coda of sorts. Considerations of Helen as an object of mythical variation in Homer need not be confined to *Iliad* 3. In a curious moment near the beginning of the *Odyssey*, there is a passage that seems to meditate on how epic itself functions, how it evokes variations, just as Stesichorus plays with multiple true *etumos* versions of a myth. In Book 4, Telemachus, searching for news of his father, arrives at the house of Menelaos, unbeknownst to his host. Helen enters the room and upon seeing Telemachus exclaims:

> ἴδμεν δή, Μενέλαε διοτρεφές, οἵ τινες οἵδε
> ἀνδρῶν εὐχετόωνται ἱκανέμεν ἡμέτερον δῶ;
> <u>ψεύσομαι ἢ ἔτυμον ἐρέω;</u> κέλεται δέ με θυμός.
>
> (*Od.* 4.138-140)

> Zeus-cherished Menelaos, do we know who
> these men are who ask to enter our home?
> Shall I say a false thing [*pseudo-*] or true [*etumos*]?
> My spirit bids me on.

In the first two lines, Helen helps to place the scene, and to size up the situation; she sees the young men in the house, notes that one of them looks like Odysseus[39] and ponders: ψεύσομαι ἢ ἔτυμον ἐρέω 'Shall I lie, or say something true?'. Helen's question is peculiarly phrased, as if she weighs equally the two options, and does not necessarily favor the one over the other. Fitzgerald glosses over the difficulty in his translation, and renders 'Shall I dissemble what I feel?'[40]—which does not quite grasp the tenor of the passage.[41] Like the blinded Stesichorus of the Palinode, Helen here feels

---

39. Clader 1976:30 notes the implicit parallel between this naming scene and the one in the *Iliad*: "[Helen] displays here her uncanny power of recognition, which seems similar to her naming of the heroes in Γ and which appears again in Menelaos' tale of how she imitated the voices of the Achaeans' wives (277-279)."
40. Fitzgerald 1961:69.
41. Butler's rendering, 'Shall I guess right or wrong?' adheres more closely to the syntax of the Greek.

compelled to split the world into true (*etumos*) and false, with no middle turf, and no grace-granting 'variation' to which to appeal.[42] On the face of it, Helen's half-line in the *Odyssey* seems a compression of the poetics of oral epic, a binary schema that separates all utterances, all discourse, all *mûthoi*, into the realm of true/untrue, acceptable or not. An epic based purely on the dichotomy *etumos/pseudês* would be Aristarchus' ideal text: an editor could throw out everything "false."

But as we have seen in the case of Aithra, above, "false" in epic does not mean dissonant but contrapuntal. Even in the scene under consideration, the "binary" Helen then slips into the drinks a *pharmakon* (φάρμακον), a drug, of such potency that a person who lost parents or who had siblings killed by harsh bronze would yet fail to weep.[43] It is a drug that causes 'forgetfulness' (*lêthê*) of all unpleasant things: it is in effect an eraser of history, of the variations of the past. Up to this point in the narrative, the room has been full of tension and angst. Menelaos' near-eulogy over Odysseus reduces the crowd to tears: the room groans, Helen weeps, Telemachus sobs, Menelaos cries, even Nestor's son cannot keep his eyes dry as he reflects on his lost brother Antilochus. The mood of gloom is so oppressive that Menelaos suggests that the guests try to cheer up for dinner, but that all tales, *mûthoi*, should be postponed until morning.[44] Directly after this pronouncement, Helen slips the fateful drug into the drinks, a drug that dissolves sorrow and disquiet, νηπενθές τ' ἄχολον, in all who partake.[45] In this scene, the drug actually undoes history. Before its administration, everyone in the room was grieving; now they are carefree. Before, Peisistratus tried to excuse his torrential weeping on behalf of his brother Antilochus; now, his cheeks will remain free of tears even should he see his own brother slaughtered (*Od*

---

42. The difficulties of separating true from false in myth go back even to Hesiod. At *Theogony* 26, the Muses boast ἴδμεν ψεύδεα πολλὰ λέγειν ἐτύμοισιν ὁμοῖα 'We know how to say many false things (*pseudea*) that are identical to true ones (*etuma*). But if the Muses are a poet's ultimate authority for knowing truth, how can one *ever* separate the true stories from the false? The Muses' declamation makes suspect all attempts to distinguish between true and false tales: the variations emanate from the same unimpeachable authority, and poets can never, therefore, declare one tale to be certifiably *etumos* at the expense of other variations.

43. *Od.* 4.219-232.

44. *Od.* 4.214.

45. *Od* 4.221.

4.223-226). Menelaos commanded no stories, no *mûthoi*, until morning; now, Helen is ready to sing her own *mûthos*.[46] She bids the audience to take pleasure in tales, *mûthoi* (μύθοις τέρπεσθε), and then launches into a story, claiming that she cannot narrate all the exploits of Odysseus, but will sing just one example, μυθήσομαι (*Od.* 4.239-240).[47]

The drug has caused the narrative in this portion of Book 4 to become its polar opposite; what had been a "true" story about a wordless grieving over dinner turns into a "false" story replete with conviviality and a lively set of tales about Odysseus' exploits in Troy. The passage is a paradox: it boasts joyful "lamenters" and "mute" storytellers, a bizarre occasion in which two seemingly contradictory narratives melt into one. Epic could have picked either scene to fill the "slot" needed for the welcoming scene in Book 4. It could have just included a somber welcome for Telemachus and weeping over the lost Odysseus. Or it could have just presented a rousing dinner with an animated pair of stories for conversation. But the genius of this passage (and of Helen)[48] is that epic combines the two variations into one scene. *Neither* scene—of joy, or of sorrow—is the true (*etumos*) scene in the sense that the other is false (*pseudês*).[49] Together, working in counterpoint, the twin variations offer a more complex and satisfying tale than either alone might have done.

---

46. *Od.* 4.240.

47. Helen narrates an example that aptly proves the efficacy of the drug She recounts Odysseus' infiltration of Troy in the guise of a beggar, informing her of all the Greeks were doing. Almost as an afterthought, Helen adds how she lamented running away with Paris in the first place. In this manner, Helen's speech should both antagonize her guests with further reminiscences of Odysseus and her husband with thoughts of her elopement. But the drug is so powerful that Menelaos goes so far as to praise her for the propriety of her tale (*Od* 4 266), and the guests seem largely unperturbed as well. Only Telemachus intimates that the tales are grievous and that sleep would help the travelers (*Od* 4.292-295).

48. Clader 1976:33 views Helen as a type of poet, and the *pharmakon* as a metaphor for the 'drug' of epic singing: "the brew, νηπενθές, anti-πένθος, is the brief symbol for Homer's extended self-conscious expression of the effect of epic poetry " In other words, epic poetry has the power to erase previous singing (in this case, of woe) and replace it with another tune, another variation

49. See Carlisle (this volume) for a greater exploration of the meaning of *pseudo*-words in Homeric verse.

Excising lines or scenes from Homer is a difficult business. Such activity assumes that Homer is a single, monolithic, unalterable text, and that discrepancies within the framework of the narrative are caused by the forces of corruption or self-serving interest on the part of the interpolator. For Aristarchus and like-minded editors, the goal of their research was "the recovery of an original Homer,"[50] a text unsullied by incompatibilities, non-sequiturs, and variants (which are endemic to lyric authors such as Stesichorus). But Gregory Nagy has recently affirmed the desirability of a multitext format of Homer, one that rejects the Aristarchan principles of exclusion and aims instead to incorporate all known "variants." Aristarchan editorial goals focus exclusively on textual issues; they ignore the extent to which a performative tradition necessarily spawns variants From the viewpoint of oral epic performance, there is no such thing as inauthentic Homer: though Homer must change through time, any synchronic "snapshot" of Homer constitutes "real" Homer, for the duration of the singer's song.[51] Homer's attraction to variants is so strong that even "contradictory" songs may be woven into the text as contrapuntal melodies. In this case, the verb *ekainopoiêse* 'to fashion anew' is as true a description of Homer's myth-making as it is of Stesichorus'. Aithra may remain in Homer not because she is a name plucked at random, but because her story, her variation, lends greater poignancy (and greater poetry) to the drama of the *teikhoskopia*.

---

50. Nagy 1996a:149.

51 See Nagy 1996b:153ff. For an account of the interrelation between oral epic and the performance traditions of Homeric rhapsodes.

Bibliography

Ackerman, H. C., and Gisler, J.-R , eds. 1981-1997 *Lexicon Iconographicum Mythoolgiae Classicae* (*LIMC*). Artemis Verlag

Alexiou, M. 1974. *The Ritual Lament in Greek Tradition.* Cambridge, Mass

Allen, T. W. 1920. *Homeri Opera Vols I-II*; 1917, *Vols III-IV* Oxford

———. 1924. *Homer. The Origins and the Transmission.* Oxford

Allen, T. W. and Sikes, E. E., eds. 1963 (2nd ed.) *The Homeric Hymns* Oxford.

Austin, N. 1991. "The Wedding Text in Homer's *Odyssey.*" *Arion* 2·227-243

———. 1994. *Helen of Troy and Her Shameless Phantom.* Ithaca.

Bakhtin, M. 1968. *Rabelais and His World.* Cambridge.

Bassi, K. 1993. "Helen and the Discourse of Denial in Stesichorus' Palinode." *Arethusa* 26:51-71.

Bernabé, A. 1988. *Poetarum Epicorum Graecorum Testimonia et Fragmenta* Leipzig.

Billigmeier, J.-C. 1975. "The Origin of the Greek Word λέων." *Talanta* 6 1-6.

Brelich, A. 1958. *Gli eroi greci Un problema storico-religioso* Rome

Buchholz, H., Johrens, G., and Maull, I. 1973. *Jagd und Fischfang* Archaeologica Homerica J. Göttingen.

Bundy, E. L. 1962. "Studia Pindarica I: The Eleventh Olympian Ode, II The First Isthmian Ode," *University of California Publications in Classical Philology* 18. Both articles reissued as *Studia Pindarica* Berkeley and Los Angeles, 1986.

Burkert, W. 1985. *Greek Religion.* Cambridge, Mass

Burnett, A. 1988. "Jocasta in the West. The Lille Stesichorus " *Classical Antiquity* 7:107-154.

Chantraine, P. 1936. "Homérique Μερόπων 'Ανθρώπων " *Mélanges Franz Cumont. Annuaire de l'Institut de Philologie et d'Histoire Orientales et Slaves 4*: 121-128.

———. 1953, 1958. *Grammaire homérique vol. I*; *vol. II* Paris.

———. 1968, 1970, 1975, 1977. 1980. *Dictionnaire étymologique de la langue grecque* (*DELG*). Paris.

Chapman, G. 1857 (first published 1612). *Homer's Iliad* London.

Clader, L. L. 1976. *Helen. The Evolution from Divine to Heroic in Greek Epic Tradition.* Leiden.

Collins, L. 1988. *Studies in Characterization in the Iliad.* Frankfurt-am-Main.

Crotty, K. 1984. *The Poetics of Supplication: Homer's Iliad and Odyssey* Ithaca.

Cunliffe, R. J. 1988 (first published 1924). *A Lexicon of the Homeric Dialect* Norman and London.

Davies, M. 1988. *Epicorum Graecorum Fragmenta* Göttingen.

————. 1989. *The Epic Cycle* Bristol Classical Press.

————. 1991. *Poetarum Melicorum Graecorum Fragmenta* Oxford

de Jong, I. J. F. 1985. "Focalisation und die Homerischen Gleichnisse " *Mnemosyne* 38:257-270.

Denniston, J. D. 1954. *The Greek Particles.* (2nd ed.) revised by K J Dover Oxford.

Dimock, G. E. 1952. "The Name of Odysseus." *The Hudson Review* 9 56-70

Doherty, L. E. 1991. "The Internal and Implied Audiences of *Odyssey* 11 " *Arethusa* 24:145-176.

Duggan, J., ed. 1975. *Oral Literature Seven Essays.* Edinburgh and New York.

Edwards, M. W. 1980. "Structure of Homeric Catalogues " *Tranactions of the American Philological Association* 110:81-103.

Erbse, H. 1969. *Scholia Graeca in Homeri Iliadem (Scholia vetera).* Berlin and New York.

Erndl, K. 1991. *Many Ramayanas. The Diversity of a Narrative Tradition in South Asia.* Berkeley, Los Angeles, Oxford.

Fitzgerald, R. 1961. *The Odyssey.* New York.

————. 1974. *The Iliad of Homer* Garden City.

Foley, H. 1978. "Reverse Similes and Sex Roles in the *Odyssey* " *Arethusa* 11:14-21.

Foley, J. 1977. *Immanent Art From Structure to Meaning in Traditional Oral Epic.* Bloomington.

Fontenrose, J. 1968. "The Hero as Athlete." *CSCA* 1:73-104

Frame, D. 1978. *The Myth of Return in Early Greek Epic.* New Haven and London.

Fränkel, H. 1921. *Die homerischen Gleichnisse* Göttingen

Fuqua, C. 1991. "Proper Behavior in the *Odyssey* " *Illinois Classical Studies* 16:49-58.

Gaisser, J. H. 1969. "Adaptation of Traditional Material in the Glaucus-Diomedes Episode." *Transactions of the American Philological Association* 100:165-176.

Gantz, T. 1993. *Early Greek Myth. A Guide to Literary and Artistic Sources* Baltimore and London.

Germain, G. 1954. *Essai sur les origines de certains thèmes odysséens et sur la genèse de l'Odyssée.* Paris.

Gernet, L. 1968. "Dolon le loup." *Anthropologie de la Grèce antique* Paris

Gill, C., and Wiseman, T. P. eds. 1993. *Lies and Fiction in the Ancient World.* Austin.

Graver, M. 1995. "Dog-Helen and Homeric Insult." *Classical Antiquity* 14.1:41-61.

Gresseth, G. 1970. "The Homeric Sirens." *Transactions of the American Philological Association* 101:203-218.

Hague, R. 1983. "Ancient Greek Wedding Songs: The Tradition of Praise." *Journal of Folklore Research* 20:131-143.

Hainsworth, J. 1991. *A Commentary on Homer's Odyssey (Books V-VIII).* Oxford.

Hampe, R. 1952. *Die Gleichnisse Homers und die Bildkunst seiner Zeit* Tübingen.

Helck, W. 1979. *Beziehungen Ägyptens und Vorderasiens zur Ägäis bis ins 7 Jh. vor Chr.* Erträge der Forschung 120. Darmstadt.

Herzfeld, M. 1993. "In Defiance of Destiny: The Management of Time and Gender at a Cretan Funeral." *American Ethnologist* 20.2:241-255.

Heubeck, A. and A. Hoekstra. 1989. *A Commentary on Homer's Odyssey, vol. II, Books IX-XVI.* Oxford.

Higbie, C. 1990. *Measure and Music. Enjambement and Sentence Structure in the Iliad.* New York.

———. 1995. *Heroes' Names, Homeric Identities.* New York.

Hölscher, F. 1972. "Die Bedeutung archaischer Tierkampfbilder." *Beiträge zur Archäologie* 5. Würzburg.

Immisch, O. 1911. "ALIBANTES." *Archiv für Religionswissenschaft* 14 449-464.

Irwin, E. 1974. *Color Terms in Greek Poetry.* Toronto.

Jamison, S. 1994. "Draupadi on the Walls of Troy." *Classical Antiquity* 13.5-16.

Jenkins, T. E. 1995. "Stesichorus and Homer." CorHaLi Conference, Lille.

Jones, H. L. 1917-1932. *The Geography of Strabo, vols. 1-8.* New York and London.

Kamptz, H. von. 1982. *Homerische Personennamen:Sprachwissenschaftliche und historische Klassifikation.* Göttingen.

King, K. 1987. *Achilles: Paradigm of the War Hero from Homer to the Middle Ages.* Berkeley, Los Angeles, and London.

Kirk, G. S. 1962. *The Songs of Homer.* Cambridge.

———. 1985. *The Iliad: A Commentary. Vol I Books 1-4.* Cambridge.

———. 1992. *The Iliad: A Commentary. Vol II. Books 5-8* Cambridge.

Koester, H., ed. 1998. *Pergamon: Citadel of the Gods.* Harrisburg.

Kolbe, D. 1981. *Die Reliefprogramme religiös-mythologischen Charakters in neuassyrischen Palästen.* Frankfurt-am-Main.

Körner, O. 1930. *Die homerische Tierwelt* Munich.

Kretschmer, P. 1945. "Penelope." *Anzeiger der Akademie der Wissenschaften in Wien* 82:80-93.

Krischer, T. 1971. "Formale Konventionen der homerischen Epik " *Zetemata* 56. Munich.

Lang, M. 1969. *The Palace of Nestor, II. The Frescoes* Princeton.

———. 1995. "War Story into Wrath Story." *Ages of Homer A Tribute to Emily Townsend Vermeule* (ed. J. B. Carter and S. P. Morris). Austin: 149-162.

Lasserre, F. 1967. *Strabon: Géographie Tome III (Livres V et VI).* Paris.

Lattimore, R. 1951. *The Iliad of Homer.* Chicago.

———. 1969. "Nausikaa's Suitors." *Classical Studies Presented to Ben Edwin Perry.* Urbana: 88-102.

Lawson, J. C. 1926. "Περὶ ἀλιβάντων." *Classical Review* 40:52-58, 116-121.

Leaf, W. 1912. *The Iliad.* New York.

———. 1914. *Troy: A Story in Homeric Geography.* London.

Leutsch, E. L., and Schneidewin, F. G. 1839. *Corpus Paroemiographorum Graecorum (CPG).* Göttingen. Reprint 1958, Hildesheim.

Lévi-Strauss, C. 1976. *Structural Anthropology, vol. II.* Tr. M. Layton. Chicago.

Lexicon Iconographicum Mythologiae Classicae (LIMC) ed. Ackerman, H. C. and Gisler, J.-R. eds. Artemis Verlag. 1981-1997.

Lincoln, B. 1989. *Discourse and the Construction of Society· Comparative Studies of Myth, Ritual, and Classification.* Oxford, New York.

Lloyd, G. 1960. *Polarity and Analogy in Greek Thought* Cambridge.

Lonsdale, S. 1990. *Creatures of Speech: Lion, Herding, and Hunting Similes in the Iliad.* Stuttgart.

Loraux, N. 1998. *Mothers in Mourning.* Tr. C. Pache. Ithaca.

Lord, A. 1960. *The Singer of Tales.* Cambridge, Mass.

———. 1975. "Perspectives on Recent Work on Oral Literature" in Duggan 1975:1-24.

Lorimer, H. 1950. *Homer and the Monuments.* London.

Lowenstam, S. 1993. *The Scepter and the Spear.* Lanham, Md.

Luce, T. J., ed. 1982. *Ancient Writers.* New York.

Magrath, W. 1982. "Progression of the Lion Simile in the *Odyssey.*" *Classical Journal* 77: 205-212.

Marinatos, S. 1968-1974. *Thera I–VI.* Athens.

Martin, R. 1989. *The Language of Heroes: Speech and Performance in the Iliad.* Ithaca.

Masson, E. 1967. *Recherches sur les plus anciens emprunts sémitiques en grec.* Paris.

Matz, F. 1951. *Torsion: eine formenkundliche Untersuchung zur ägäischen Urgeschichte.* Mainz.

Mazon, P. 1967. *Introduction à l'Iliade.* Paris.

McLeod, W. 1966. *The Bow in Ancient Greece with Particular Reference to the Homeric Poems.* Harvard University Dissertation.

Monro, D. B. 1891. *A Grammar of the Homeric Dialect.* (2d ed.) Oxford.

———. 1901. *Homer's Odyssey. Books XIII-XXIV.* Oxforα.

Morgan, L. 1988. *The Miniature Wall Paintings of Thera.* Cambridge.

Morris, I., and Powell, B. eds. 1997. *A New Companion to Homer.* Brill.

Morris, S. 1992. *Daidalos and the Origin of Greek Art.* Princeton.

Most, G. 1989a. "The Stranger's Stratagem: Self-Disclosure and Self-Sufficiency in Greek Culture." *Journal of Hellenic Studies* 109:114-133.

———. 1989b. "The Structure and Function of Odysseus' Apologoi." *Transactions of the American Philological Association* 119:15-30.

Moulton, C. 1977. *Similes in the Homeric Poems. Hypomnemata* 49. Göttingen.

Muellner, L. 1976. *The Meaning of Homeric εὔχομαι Through Its Formulas.* Innsbruck.

———. 1990. "The Simile of the Cranes and Pygmies: A Study of Homeric Metaphor." *Harvard Studies in Classical Philology* 93:59-101.

———. 1996. *The Wrath of Achilles.* Ithaca.

Myres, J. L. 1952. "The Pattern of the *Odyssey.*" *JHS* 72:1-11.

Nagler, M. 1977. "Dread Goddess Endowed with Speech." *Archeological News* 677-685.

Nagy, G. 1973. "On the Death of Actaeon." *Harvard Studies in Classical Philology* 77:179-180.

————. 1979. *The Best of the Achaeans Concepts of the Hero in Archaiac Greek Poetry.* 1999. Second edition with new preface by the author. Baltimore.

————. 1982. "Hesiod" in Luce: 1982: 43-72.

————. 1990a. *Pindar's Homer: The Lyric Possession of an Epic Past.* Baltimore and London.

————. 1990b. *Greek Mythology and Poetics.* Ithaca.

————. 1995. "An Evolutionary Model for the Making of Homeric Poetry: Comparative Perspectives." *The Ages of Homer: A Tribute to Emily Townsend Vermeule* (ed. J. B. Carter and S. P. Morris). Austin: 163-179.

————. 1996a. *Homeric Questions.* Austin.

————. 1996b. *Poetry As Performance: Homer and Beyond.* Cambridge.

————. 1997. "Homeric Scholia." Morris, I., and Powell, B. Leiden: 101-122.

————. 1998. "The Library of Pergamon as a Classical Model." *Pergamon: Citadel of the Gods* (ed. H. Koester). Harrisburg:185-232.

Narayana Rao, V. 1991. "A Ramayana of Their Own: Women's Oral Tradition in Telugu." *Many Ramayanas: The Diversity of a Narrative Tradition in South Asia.* Berkeley, Los Angeles, Oxford:114-136.

Nilsson, M. 1927. *The Minoan-Mycenaean Religion and Its Survival in Greek Religion.* New York.

Page, D. L. 1955. *The Homeric Odyssey.* Oxford.

————. 1962. *Poetae Melici Graeci (PMG).* Oxford.

Papadopoulou-Belmehdi, I. 1994. *Le chant de Pénélope.* Paris.

Parry, M. 1971. *The Making of Homeric Verse* (ed. A. Parry). Oxford.

Pearson, A. C. 1917. *The Fragments of Sophocles.* Cambridge.

Peradotto, J. 1990. *Man in the Middle Voice: Name and Narration in the Odyssey.* Princeton.

Pfeiffer, R. 1949-1953. *Callimachus, vols. I-II.* Oxford.

Podlecki, A. J. 1971. "Some Odyssean Similes." *Greece and Rome* 18:81-90.

Pollard, J. 1977. *Birds in Greek Life and Myth.* Plymouth.

Porzig, W. 1942. "Die Namen fur Satzinhalte im Griechischen un im Indogermanischen." *Untersuchungen zur indogermanischen Sprach- und Kulturwissenschaft* 10. Berlin and Leipzig.

Pratt, L. 1993. *Lying and Poetry from Homer to Pindar: Falsehood and Deception in Archaic Greek Poetics.* Michigan.

————. 1994. "*Odyssey* 19.535-50: On the Interpretation of Dreams and Signs in Homer." *Classical Philology* 89:147-152

Prendergast, G. L. 1875. *A Complete Concordance to the Iliad of Homer.* London. Revised by B. Marzullo, 1971. Hildesheim.

Pritchard, J. 1955. (2nd ed.) *Ancient Near-Eastern Texts Relating to the Old Testament.* Princeton.

Radt, S. 1971. *Tragicorum Graecorum Fragmenta.* Göttingen.

Rahn, H. 1953. "Tier und Mensch in der homerischen Auffassung der Wirklichkeit. Ein Beitrag zur geistwissenschaftlichen Selbstkritik." *Paideuma* 5:277-297, 431-480.

Ranke, H., and Erman, A. 1923. (2nd. ed.) *Ägypten und ägyptisches Leben in Altertum.* Tübingen.

Redfield, J. 1975. *Nature and Culture in the Iliad: The Tragedy of Hektor.* Chicago.

Rohde, E. 1925. *Psyche: The Cult of Souls and Belief in Immortality Among the Greeks.* London.

Roosevelt, T., and Heller, E. 1911. *African Game Animals.* New York.

Roscher, W. 1886-1903. *Ausführliches Lexicon der griechischen und römischen Mythologie.* Leipzig.

Russo, J., Fernandez-Galiano, M., and Heubeck, A. 1992. *A Commentary on Homer's Odyssey. Vol. III, Books XVII-XXIV.* Oxford.

Russo, J. 1991. *A Commentary on Homer's Odyssey, Vol. IV. Books XIX-XX.* Oxford.

Ste. Croix, G. de. 1981. *The Class Struggle in the Ancient Greek World: From the Archaic Age to the Arab Conquest.* Ithaca.

Saussure, de F. 1916 *Cours de linguistique générale.* Critical ed. 1972 by T. de Mauro. Paris.

Schnapp-Gourbeillon, A. 1981. *Lions, héroes, masques. Les représentations de l'animal chez Homère.* Paris.

————. 1982. "Le lion et le loup. Diomédie et Dolonie dans *l'Iliade.*" *Quaderni di Storia* 8:45-77.

Schneidewin, F. 1833. *Ibyci Rhegini Carminum Reliquiae.* Göttingen.

Schwartz, E. 1887. *Scholia in Euripidem, vol. 1.* Berlin.

Schweighauser, J., ed. 1801-1807. *Athenaei Naucratitae Deipnosophistarum.* Strasbourg.

Scott, W. 1974. *The Oral Nature of the Homeric Simile* (*Mnemosyne Supplement* 28). Leiden.

Seaford, R. 1994. *Reciprocity and Ritual: Homer and Tragedy in the Developing City-State.* Oxford.

Segal, C. 1973. *The Theme of the Mutilation of the Corpse* (*Mnemosyne Supplement* 27). Leiden.

———. 1994. *Singers, Heroes, and Gods in the Odyssey.* Ithaca.

Shelmerdine, C. 1995. "Shining and Fragrant Cloth in Homeric Epic." *The Ages of Homer: A Tribute to Emily Townsend Vermeule* (ed. J. B. Carter and S. P. Morris). Austin.

Shipp, G. 1972. *Studies in the Language of Homer.* Cambridge.

Slatkin, L. M. 1991. *The Power of Thetis: Alllusion and Interpretation in the Iliad.* Berkeley, Los Angeles, Oxford.

Snell, B. 1953. *The Discovery of the Mind.* Tr. T. Rosenmeyer. Oxford.

Sourvinou-Inwood, C. 1971. "Theseus Lifting the Rock and a Cup Near the Pithos Painter." *JHS* 91:94-109.

Spiegel, J. 1971. *Das Auferstehungsritual der Unas-Pyramide: Beschreibung und erlauterte Übersetzung.* Wiesbaden.

Stanford, W. B. 1963. *Sophocles' Ajax.* Salem.

Stella, L. 1978. *Tradizione Micenea e la Poesia dell'Iliade* (Filologia e Critica Supp.). Rome.

Suzuki, M. 1989. *Metamorphoses of Helen: Authority, Difference, and the Epic.* Ithaca.

Thalmann, W. G. 1984. *Conventions of Form and Thought in Early Greek Epic Poetry.* Baltimore.

Thompson, D'Arcy W. 1936. *A Glossary of Greek Birds.* London.

Turnbull-Kemp, P. 1967. *The Leopard.* Capetown.

Van der Valk, M. 1953. "Homer's Nationalistic Attitude." *L'Antiquité Classique* 22:5-26.

———. 1964. *Researches on the Text and Scholia of the Iliad.* Leiden.

———. 1971. *Eustathii Commentarii ad Homeri Iliadem Pertinentes. Vol. 1.* Brill.

Vermeule, E. 1979. *Aspects of Death in Early Greek Art.* Berkeley, Los Angeles, and London.

Vodoklys, E. J. 1992. *Blame-Expression in the Epic Tradition.* New York.

von der Muehll, P. 1962. *Homeri Odyssea.* Stuttgart.

Ste. Croix, G. de. 1981. *The Class Struggle in the Ancient Greek World: From the Archaic Age to the Arab Conquest.* Ithaca.

Wace, A. J. B., and Stubbings, F. H. 1962. *A Companion to Homer.* London.

Wackernagel, J. 1916. *Sprachliche Untersuchungen zu Homer.* Göttingen.

Walter, L. 1892. *A Companion to the Iliad.* London.

Watkins, C. 1994. *Selected Writings,* vols. I and II. *Innsbrucker Beiträge zur Sprachwissenschaft* 80. Innsbruck.

————. 1995. *How to Kill a Dragon: Aspects of Indo-European Poetics.* New York and Oxford.

Webster, T.B.L. 1954. *From Mycenae to Homer.* Paris.

West, M. L. 1985. *The Hesiodic Catalogue of Women.* Oxford.

West, S. 1989. "Laertes Revisited." *PCPS* 35:113-143.

Whitman, C. 1958. *Homer and the Homeric Tradition.* Cambridge, Mass.

————. 1920. *Die Ilias und Homer.* (2nd ed.) Berlin.

Wilamowitz-Moellendorff, U. von. 1884. *Homerische Untersuchungen* Berlin.

Willcock, M. 1964. "Mythological *Paradeigmata* in the *Iliad.*" *Classical Quarterly* 14:141-154.

Willcock. M. M. 1978-1984. *The Iliad of Homer.* New York.

Williams, B. 1993. *Shame and Necessity.* Berkeley.

Woodbury, L. 1967. "Helen and the Palinode." *Phoenix* 21:157-176.

Wreszinski, W. 1932. *Das Löwenjagd im alten Ägypten.* Leipzig.

Homeric Passages

Iliad

Il. 2.26-30, 36
Il. 2.81, 56-57, 69
Il. 2.139-141, 36
Il 2.147-150, 37
Il. 2.210, 51
Il. 2.211-224, 37
Il. 2.216-219, 38
Il. 2.225, 35
Il. 2.225-242, 39
Il. 2.243-245, 45
Il 2.245-263, 46
Il. 2.246-264, 35
Il. 2.265-270, 48
Il. 2.271-278, 52
Il. 2.484-760, 30
Il. 2.653, 191
Il. 2.876, 64
Il. 3.21-28, 180
Il 3.33-37, 183
Il. 3.141-145, 208
Il. 3.144-48, xxiii
Il 3.156-160, 13
Il 3.164, 13
Il. 3.173, 11
Il. 3.173-176, 14
Il. 3.180, 12
Il 3.236-244, 219
Il. 3.410-412, 3
Il. 4.374-375, 58
Il 4.399-400, 59
Il. 4.404, 59
Il. 4.412-418, 60
Il 5.554-558, 177
Il. 5.630-631, 63
Il. 5.635-639, 63
Il. 5.648-651, 65
Il. 6.152-153, 61

Il. 6.163-165, 61
Il 6.198-199, 64
Il. 6.344-348, 11
Il 6.407-439, 9
Il 9.115, 70
Il 9.561, 104
Il. 15.158-159, 68
Il. 17.108-111, 186
Il 18.583-587, 187
Il. 20.164-168, 191
Il 23.575-577, 72
Il. 24.219-223, 69
Il 24.260-262, 74
Il. 24.761-775, 6

Odyssey

Od. 3.17-20, 70
Od. 3.96-101, 71
Od. 5.308-311, 145
Od. 6.100-109, 165
Od 6.130-134, 166
Od. 6.135-136, 171
Od 8.246-249, 22
Od. 8.523-531, 141
Od. 11.36-43, 24
Od. 11.223-224, 26
Od. 11.225-234, 25
Od 11.320-323, 208
Od. 11.328-332, 27
Od. 11.362-369, 23
Od. 11.362-374, 83
Od 11.374, 32
Od. 11.385-386, 28
Od. 11.387-389, 29
Od. 11.610, 32
Od. 13.107-108, 134

General Index

Achilles, xviii, 4, 7-9, 16, 19-20, 28, 30, 32-33, 38, 40, 43-44, 49, 51, 53, 56, 66-70, 82, 87, 109-110, 117, 140, 143, 152, 170, 172, 174, 177-180, 182, 184, 187, 191-198, 200-201, 203, 211
Aedon, 102, 104, 111-112, 114-116, 118, 122, 126, 130
Aeschylus, 64, 104, 130, 180
Agamemnon, 14, 28-29, 36-38, 40, 42-43, 46-50, 52-53, 58-60, 62-63, 65, 69-70, 104, 138, 140, 144, 151, 169, 172, 185, 191, 200, 214-216, 222-223, 225
Agenor, 177-186, 192-199, 200, 201
agón, 57-58, 60, 72-73, 89
aidôs, 12, 177
Aithra, vi, 207, 209-213, 218, 221-222, 224, 226
Alcaeus, 98, 105, 129
Alexander, 6, 169, 209, 215, 221
Alkinoos, xviii, 21-24, 28-33, 83, 85, 87, 89, 86-88, 132, 167
Alkyone, 104, 114, 117-118, 120-121, 126-127, 129, 131
Alybas, 148, 153-157
Andromache, 5, 7, 9-10, 142, 172
Antikleia, 24, 26, 158
Antilochus, 72, 224
apatêlia, 79
Aphrodite, 3-4, 10, 16, 19, 31-32, 83, 125, 128-129, 142, 1167-168, 172, 174,181, 184, 213, 222,
Apollo, 66-67, 104, 117-118, 129, 131, 151, 172, 177-178, 191, 187-198, 208-209
Arete, xviii, 21, 27-30, 132-34
Aristophanes, 68, 96, 100, 104-105
Aristotle, 51, 53, 96-97, 102, 105,
Artemis, xiv, 19, 114, 126-127, 131, 132, 165-168, 170, 172-173, 175-176, 189, 210
Athena, 67, 70, 72, 83, 85-86, 87, 89, 99-100 107, 110, 123, 139, 166, 198
Bellerophon, 61, 65, 90, 172
Briseis, 8-9, 44, 70, 142-143, 172
Ceyx, 121-124
Cretan, xiii, 5, 7, 79, 80,
Cyclops, 148, 152
Demodokos, 19, 22, 31-32, 73, 84, 89, 141
Diomedes, 25, 58-62, 65, 169, 170, 177, 184-185, 191-192, 200
Dionysius, 102-103, 106-103, 108, 212
Doloneia, 82, 86, 90, 180-182, 186, 198, 203
Egypt, 80, 179, 190, 193, 200-201, 216-217
Elpenor, 24, 26, 140, 144, 146-148, 153
etumos, 75, 217, 218, 223-225
Eumaios, 35, 67, 77, 77-83, 85, 125, 127, 172
Euripides, 61, 104, 110, 116, 130, 191, 208
Eustathius, 95, 104, 113, 127, 154, 157, 160, 199, 221
Glaukos, 60-62, 64-65
halcyon, 98-106, 108-111, 115-121, 124, 126, 129, 133-135, 207
Hektor, xiv, 5-11, 15-16, 20, 67-68, 83, 86-87, 140, 144, 147, 152, 169, 174, 179, 182, 184-187, 191-192, 195-196, 198, 211, 218
Helen, xviii, 3-20, 75, 104, 167, 209-211, 225, 227-229
Hera, 20, 120, 127
Herakles, 32-33, 62-65, 90, 177, 191

239